Daniel Högger

The Recognition of States

Daniel Högger

The Recognition of States

A Study on the Historical Development in Doctrine and Practice with a Special Focus on the Requirements

LIT

Cover picture: *Leo Hollandicus* by Claes Janszoon Visscher (1648)

Basler Dissertation 2014

Bibliographic information published by the Deutsche Nationalbibliothek
The Deutsche Nationalbibliothek lists this publication in the Deutsche Nationalbibliografie; detailed bibliographic data are available in the Internet at http://dnb.d-nb.de.

ISBN 978-3-643-80196-8
Zugl.: Basel, Univ., Diss., 2014

A catalogue record for this book is available from the British Library

Klosbachstr. 107
CH-8032 Zürich
Tel. +41 (0) 44-251 75 05 Fax +41 (0) 44-251 75 06
E-Mail: zuerich@lit-verlag.ch http://www.lit-verlag.ch
Distribution:
In the UK: Global Book Marketing, e-mail: mo@centralbooks.com
In North America: International Specialized Book Services, e-mail: orders@isbs.com
In Germany: LIT Verlag Fresnostr. 2, D-48159 Münster
Tel. +49 (0) 2 51-620 32 22, Fax +49 (0) 2 51-922 60 99, E-mail: vertrieb@lit-verlag.de
In Austria: Medienlogistik Pichler-ÖBZ, e-mail: mlo@medien-logistik.at
e-books are available at www.litwebshop.de

Acknowledgements

This work was accepted as a doctoral dissertation at the Faculty of Law at the University of Basel, Switzerland in spring 2014. Apart from a few updates, revisions, and minor amendments the text was submitted in the form present. I would like to acknowledge the many people who have contributed to the completion of this volume and made the years of completion so inspiring, challenging, and enjoyable.

I would like to express my genuine gratitude to my supervisor Prof. Dr. Anne Peters for giving me the opportunity to conduct my doctoral research at her Chair and for her guidance, encouragement, and support as well as her trust by involving me in her work. My gratitude also goes to Prof. Dr. Stephan Breitenmoser for his willingness to preside over my doctoral colloquium, and to Dr. Tilmann Altwicker for acting as member of the colloquium committee as well as for the friendly and encouraging discussions. I also want to thank Prof. Dr. Markus Schefer for supporting and accommodating me and my work.

I wish to thank the *Swiss National Science Foundation* as well as the *Forschungsfonds of the University of Basel* and the *Stiftung zur Förderung der rechtlichen und wirtschaftlichen Forschung an der Universität Basel* for enabling my research with their financial generosity.

The manuscript has been written with the LaTeX document preparation system. For all their advice, help, and time in this regard I am thankful to Dr. Andres Gartmann, Dr. Nicolas Weidmann, and Paul Stanley, QC. I also want to acknowledge for their patience, help, and support concerning all my computer-related panic attacks, Jörg Frauenhoffer, head of the IT service centre at the Faculty of Law, and his team. I am grateful to Giovanna Delbrück together with the entire staff of the Faculty of Law library for their amazing help in acquiring all sources and literature needed. For her support in the publication process I am grateful to Isabel Opatz of LIT-Verlag. Moreover I am obliged to all friends, colleagues, and co-workers in and outside the Faculty. Very many thanks. In particular I want to acknowledge and thank my godfather, Edy Grüninger, for his constant encouragement.

And finally I want to thank my sister, Madeleine Engesser, for her continuous support. I am, furthermore, deeply indebted to my parents, Denise F. Hoegger-Grüninger and Dr. Georges P. Högger, for their permanent love and support going far beyond the time of my dissertation, as well as to my partner Dr. Alissa Palumbo for always supporting me and being there. This work is dedicated to the four of them.

Basel, in February 2015 Daniel Högger

Contents

List of Abbreviations

AC	Law Reports, Appeal Cases
AdG	Archiv der Gegenwart
AJIL	American Journal of International Law
All ER	All-England Law Reports
AmPolSciRev	American Political Science Review
AmUILRev	American University International Law Review
AnnDig	Annual Digest of Public International Law Cases
arrêt	*Arrêt du Tribunal fédéral* (Decision of the Swiss Federal Court)
ASILPROC	Proceedings of the American Society of International Law
AVR	Archiv des Völkerrechts
AöR	Archiv für öffentliches Recht
BayOLGZ	*Entscheidung des Bayrischen Obersten Landesgerichts in Zivilsachen* (Decision of the Higher Regional Court of Bavaria for Civil Matters)
BerGesVR	Berichte der Deutschen Gesellschaft für Völkerrecht
Bevans	Treaties and Other International Agreements of the USA 1776-1949
BFSP	British and Foreign State Papers
BGE	*Bundesgerichtsentscheid* (Decision of the Swiss Federal Court)
BJPIR	The British Journal of Politics & International Relations
BostonUIntlLJ	Boston University International Law Journal
BYIL	British Yearbook of International Law

CEH	Central European History
cf	*confer* (compare)
ch	chapter
CLP	Current Legal Problems
CSPU	Communist Party of the Soviet Union
CTS	Consolidated Treaty Series
CUP	Cambridge University Press
de Clercq	M Jules de Clercq, *Recueil des traités de la France* (A Pedone 1880-1907)
dpa	Deutsche Presse-Agentur (German Press Agency)
ed/eds	editor/editors
edn	edition
eg	*exempli gratia* (for example)
EJIL	European Journal of International Law
EmoryIntlLRev	Emory International Law Review
ER	English Reports
estm	estimated
EWHC	England & Wales High Court (Administrative Court)
ff	following pages
FLR	Family Law Reports
FRG	Federal Republic of Germany
FRUS	Foreign Relations of the United States
GB	Great Britain
GDR	German Democratic Republic
GG	*Grundgesetz für die Bundesrepublik Deutschland vom 23 Mai 1949 (BGBl, 1)* (Basic Law for the Federal Republic of Germany)
GlobGov	Global Governance
HAHR	Hispanic American Historical Review
HarvIntlLJ	Harvard International Law Journal
Hertslet	Edward Herslet, *The Map of Europe by Treaty* (Butterworth 1875-1891)
HPTh	History of Political Thought

ICCLP Review	International Center for Comparative Law and Politics Review
ICJ Rep	International Court of Justice Reports
ICLQ	The International and Comparative Law Quarterly
ICLR	International Community Law Review
IDI	Institut de Droit International
ie	*id est* (that is)
ILM	International Legal Materials
ILR	International Law Reports
Intl Conciliation	International Conciliation
INTSer	Indian Treaty Series
IO	International Organization
IPRG	*Bundesgesetz vom 18 Dezember 1987 (Stand am 1. Mai 2013) über das Internationale Privatrecht, SR 291* (Swiss Federal Code on Private International Law)
IPRG	*Bundesgesetz vom 18 Dezember 1987 über das Internationale Privatrecht, SR 291* (Switzerland's Federal Code on Private International Law)
IPRspr	*Die deutsche Rechtssprechung auf dem Gebiete des internationalen Privatrechts*
IR	International Relations
IS	International Security
ISR	International Studies Review
JHistIntLaw	Journal of the History of International Law
KB	King's Bench Reports
LJIL	Leiden Journal of International Law
LNOJ	League of Nations Official Journal
LNTS	League of Nations Treaty Series
Millenium - JIntSt	Millennium - Journal of International Studies
MLR	Modern Law Review
MN	margin number
MPTMH	Major Peace Treaties of Modern History
NationsNatl	Nations and Nationalism

NATO	North Atlantic Treaty Organization
NILR	Netherlands International Law Review
NRG2	Georg Friedrich von Martens *et al*, *Nouveau Recueil général de traités*, 2me série
NZZ	Neue Zürcher Zeitung
ÖZöRV	Österreichische Zeitschrift für öffentliches Recht und Völkerrecht
OUP	Oxford University Press
PAPhS	Proceedings of the American Philosophical Society
PPA	Philosophy & Public Affairs
QB	Queen's Bench
RdC	Recueil des Cours de l'Académie de Droit International de la Haye
RDILC	Revue de droit international et de législation comparée
RevIntlStud	Review of International Studies
RIAA	Reports of International Arbitral Awards
s	section
SBAG	Schweizer Beiträge zur allgemeinen Geschichte
SM	Schweizer Monatshefte
Spec Supp	Special Supplement
SSR	Socialist Soviet Republic
STAAT	Der Staat
sub-s	subsection
Supp	Supplement
tr	translator
UN	United Nations
UNGA	United Nations General Assembly
UNSC	United Nations Security Council
UNTS	United Nations Treaty Series
UNYB	United Nations Year Book
US/USA	United States of America
USSR	Union of Socialist Soviet Republics

VCLT	Vienna Convention on the Law of Treaties
WLR	Weekly Law Reports
YaleLJ	Yale Law Journal
ZaöRV	Zeitschrift für ausländisches öffentliches Recht und Völkerrecht
ZPO	*Zivilprozessordnung* (German Code of Civil Procedure)
ZSG	Zeitschrift für Schweizerische Geschichte
ZöR	Zeitschrift für öffentliches Recht

Table of Treaties and Other Material

Table of Cases

I Introduction

1 Introduction

In the second half of the year 2014 international politics and media were dominated by the conflict in the Eastern Ukraine, the Scottish referendum on independence, the annexation of the Crimean Peninsula, the Catalan endeavours for secession from Spain, and the advancement of the IS ('Islamic State') in Iraq and Syria. At first sight these situations appear completely different from one another. However, upon a closer look it becomes apparent that they share a common core: They are ultimately about the realization of an independent State.

Closely related to this is the question how the other already recognized States will react and whether they will recognize the entity as one of their own kind. This recognition as an independent State by the other States, however, presupposes the fulfilment of certain requirements. The questions of what exactly these requirements encompass as well as the entire issue of State recognition have long been disputed in doctrine and practice. In 1941 Hans Kelsen stated that

> [t]he problem of recognition of states and governments has neither in theory nor in practice been solved satisfactorily. Hardly any other question is more controversial or leads in the practice of states to such paradoxical situations.[1]

This still holds true today, revealing a lack of consensus on this topic, further evidenced by the most recent cases of recognition in the last 20 years. Whereas some entities were recognized as independent States without much ado, such as Slovakia and the Czech Republic, others were granted recognition only after extensive negotiations and the fulfilment of further requirements, like Serbia and Georgia. Again others were only recognized by some States but not by others, eg Kosovo. Furthermore, there are entities that would not be recognized, at least by the majority of States, as independent States despite of their de facto existence, like Abkhazia.

Due to its complexity, State recognition has been examined with different

[1] Hans Kelsen, 'Recognition in International Law: Theoretical Observations' (1941) 35(4) AJIL 605, 605.

approaches. This proliferation of many approaches led to an abundance of research. While not intended to be an exhaustive bibliography, the following works are among the most distinguished and often cited on the subject. Among the works exploring generally the legal doctrine of recognition are the ones by Kelsen,[2] Lauterpacht,[3] Chen,[4] Grant,[5] Crawford,[6] and Raic.[7] Fabry approached the topic from a politological viewpoint by focusing on the relation between self-determination and State recognition in the last 200 years.[8] And Hillgruber,[9] then, studied recognition historically. Recognition as part of the general history of international law is also touched upon in the works by Grewe[10] and Ziegler.[11] And Buchanan used yet another perspective by choosing a moral-theoretical approach on contemporary recognition.[12]

The following study examines the historical development of State recognition focusing on the recognition requirement by employing an interdisciplinary approach. The time-frame investigated here spans from the mid-17th century, the time of the Peace of Westphalia, until the end of the 20th century. The aim of this study is not, however, to find and propose a revision

---

[2] Kelsen (n 1).

[3] Hersch Lauterpacht, 'Recognition of States in International Law' (1944) 53 YaleLJ 385; Hersch Lauterpacht, *Recognition in International Law* (CUP 1947).

[4] Ti-Chiang Chen, *The International Law of Recognition: With Special Reference to Practice in Great Britain and the United States* (Praeger 1951).

[5] Thomas D Grant, *The Recognition of States: Law and Practice in Debate and Evolution* (Praeger 1999).

[6] James Crawford, *The Creation of New States in International Law* (2nd edn, OUP 2006).

[7] David Raič, *Statehood and the Law of Self-determination* (Kluwer Law International 2002).

[8] Mikulas Fabry, *Recognizing States: International Society and the Establishment of New States Since 1776* (OUP 2010).

[9] Christian Hillgruber, *Die Aufnahme neuer Staaten in die Völkerrechtsgemeinschaft: Das völkerrechtliche Institut der Anerkennung von Neustaaten in der Praxis des 19. und 20. Jahrhunderts* (Peter Lang 1998).

[10] Wilhelm G Grewe, *The Epochs of International Law* (Walter de Gruyter 2000).

[11] Karl Heinz Ziegler, *Völkerrechtsgeschichte: Ein Studienbuch* (2nd edn, CH Beck 2007).

[12] Allen Buchanan, *Justice, Legitimacy, and Self-Determination: Moral Foundations for International Law* (OUP 2004); Allen Buchanan and Robert Keohane, 'The Legitimacy of Global Governance Institutions' in *Legitimacy in International Law* (Springer 2008).

of State recognition in a normative sense. Rather, it should be analyzed and understood, how recognition of States has developed in doctrine and practice over time. It is assumed – and will be demonstrated – that State practice differs considerably from doctrine. In order to examine State practice, an explanatory model, the 'recognitional fitness' is conceptualized. This model, which is based on the theoretical approaches of constructivism and the English school of international relations theory, is composed of three required elements. It is these three elements which the recognizing States have to see fulfilled by the entity prior to recognizing it as a State: Effectiveness, legality, and legitimacy. Nevertheless, this model is not meant to be a normative framework for future recognition, but rather a tool to study the historic development of State recognition.[13]

The study is structured as follows. It begins with an examination of the contemporary doctrine on the recognition of States. Besides the requirements for recognition, it will also discuss the modes and consequences together with premature recognition, withdrawal of recognition, and non-recognition. By examining cases of State recognition after the end of the Cold War, a discrepancy between doctrine and State practice regarding State recognition will be pointed out and the resulting research problem formulated. Based on the assumption that recognition includes both legal as well as political elements,[14] the following part will elaborate the theoretical foundations from which the explanatory model, the 'recognitional fitness', will be drawn. The fourth part will, with the aid of this explanatory model, inquire the development of State recognition concentrating particularly on its requirements. However, given the vast number of cases of State recognition within the last 400 years, the samples examined cannot claim to be exhaustive. Rather this study will be carried out with a focus on certain cases that are illustrative for the development and continuous change of recognition. Besides State practice, the doctrine for the given era will

[13]For an normative approach to this question, see Buchanan (n 12) 262-77.

[14]Also Lauterpacht was of the opinion that 'there is probably no other subject in the field of international relations in which law and politics appear to be more closely interwoven.'(Lauterpacht, *States* [n 3] v).

also be analyzed. In the final part the results will summarized and possible conclusions for future State recognition will be considered.

II The Recognition of States in International Law

2 The concept of recognition and the principle of effectiveness

In international relations, recognition is a crucial and frequently applied concept. It can be defined as the determination 'of the existence of a certain set of facts, with a parallel commitment to apply to this factual situation the relevant legal consequences envisaged by international law.'[15] This definition points to the relation between facts and international law on which the traditional concept of recognition rests. According to the Latin phrase *ex factis jus oritur*,[16] only factual, that is, effective situations can become lawful situations. This notion of the 'normative Kraft des Faktischen'[17] is known as the 'principle of effectiveness'.

The significance of this principle – and eventually of recognition – originates from the structure of the international society.[18] It is characterized by the absence of a superior power with legislative and judicial competences able to guarantee legal security and stability by legitimizing new situations. As a result, the individual States are entrusted with these tasks. So far, though, the international community of States has not been able to promulgate generally accepted rules to legalize certain new situations.[19] This is why the existence or non-existence of factual situations seemed to have become the decisive basis of valuation regarding their legality.[20] In these situations, 'the creation of rights presupposes... the factual situation, in which these rights are actually exercised.'[21] An example for such a situation is a blockade, which together with an official notification requires effectiveness

---

[15] Boleslaw A Boczek, *International Law: A Dictionary* (The Scarecrow Press 2005) 98.

[16] Latin for 'from facts arises law'.

[17] 'Normative power of the factual' (my translation). See also Georg Jellinek, *Allgemeine Staatslehre* (3rd edn, O Häring 1914) 331 et passim.

[18] Jochen A Frowein, 'Recognition' in Ruediger Wolfrum (ed), *The Max Planck Encyclopedia of Public International Law* (OUP 2012) vol VIII, 656; Lauterpacht, 'Recognition of States' (n 3) 385.

[19] Antonio Cassese, *International Law* (2nd edn, OUP 2005) 13.

[20] ibid, 13.

[21] Hiroshi Taki, 'Effectiveness' in Ruediger Wolfrum (ed), *Max Planck Encyclopedia of Public International Law* (OUP 2012) vol III, 350; also Karl Doehring, 'Effectiveness'

in order to be legal.[22] The basic idea of the principle of effectiveness is, however, not to enforce the right of the strongest, but rather to work towards greater legal security and stability in international relations.[23]
For a long time, in addition to its significance, effectiveness was considered not only necessary, but also sufficient for a situation to be recognized as legal. As long as international law did not prohibit the use of force, occupation was considered an appropriate instrument for territorial acquisition. Hence, still in 1920, the opinion existed that for its legality, it was irrelevant whether the territory was populated, provided that the occupation was effective. This had to be demonstrated by effective seizure on behalf of the occupying power, and by the performance of certain symbolic acts such as planting the flag.[24] Since then, and particularly since the creation of *ius cogens* norms, eg the prohibition of force, this view changed.[25] According to the principle *ex injuria ius non oritur*,[26] a new, yet effective, situation brought about with means unlawful under international law cannot become legal.[27] Also, effectiveness is not perceived as substitute for the illegality of the manner a situation was induced. In this case, the principle of *ex injuria jus non oritur* overrides the principle *ex factis jus oritur*. Moreover, if a situation is effective, but was established by illegal means, it is not permitted for others to recognize it as legal. In consequence, 'plain' effectiveness no longer suffices for the recognizability of a new situation, when brought about in an illegal way.[28] Nevertheless and despite the constraint

---

in Rudolf Bernhardt (ed), *Encyclopedia of Public International Law* (North-Holland 1984) vol 7, 70-71.

[22] Other situations listed which require effectiveness are annexation, occupation, acquisitive prescription but also diplomatic protection in case of dual citizenship. See Taki (n 21) 351.

[23] Doehring (n 21) 70; Taki (n 21) 350.

[24] Kurt Perels, 'Okkupation' in Heinrich Schnee (ed), *Deutsches Koloniallexikon* (Verlag von Quelle & Meyer 1920) vol II, 673-74.

[25] Cassese, *International Law* (n 19) 13; Taki (n 21) 352.

[26] Latin for 'from injustice law does not arise'.

[27] This notion with regard to illegal occupation is known as 'Stimson Doctrine', named after Henry L Stimson, former United States Secretary of State. On this see sub-s 2.4.3. ('Non-recognition').

[28] Doehring (n 21) 74.

of the necessity of legality, effectiveness remains prima facie necessary for the recognition of new situations.

The concept of recognition applies to various situations. While it is most relevant regarding entities claiming to be States or governments, it also comes into play with regard to belligerencies,[29] insurgencies,[30] international organizations,[31] as well as further issues such as frontiers,[32] and the status of neutrality.[33] Recognition of the existence of a certain set of facts comes with the duty to bear the relevant legal consequences arising from it. Hence, failure to observe these legal consequences by acting contrary to them bears the risk of violating the estoppel principle.[34] Recognition, thus, has a *Klarstellungsfunktion*,[35] contributing to legal security in international relations. Despite its wide use and crucial role in international law, recognition is a complex concept. This complexity originates from the uniqueness of the concept as an 'amalgam of political and legal elements in a degree

---

[29] Valentina Azarov and Ido Blum, 'Bellingerency' in Ruediger Wolfrum (ed), *The Max Planck Encyclopedia of Public International Law* (OUP 2012) vol I.

[30] Emily Crawford, 'Insurgency' in Ruediger Wolfrum (ed), *The Max Planck Encyclopedia of Public International Law* (OUP 2012) vol V, 225-26. On the difference between the concepts 'belligerency' and 'insurgency', see Christopher Quaye, *Liberation Struggles in International Law* (Temple University Press 1991) 29f, and Robert R Wilson, 'Recogni-tion of Insurgency and Belligerency' (1937) 31 ASILPROC 136.

[31] Kirsten Schmalenbach, 'International Organizations or Institutions, General Aspects' in Ruediger Wolfrum (ed), *The Max Planck Encyclopedia of Public International Law* (OUP 2012) vol V, 1132-33.

[32] Victor Prescott and Gillian Doreen Triggs, *International Frontiers and Boundaries: Law, Politics and Geography* (Martinus Nijhoff 2008) ch 5.

[33] Michael Bothe, 'The Law of Neutrality' in Dieter Fleck (ed), *The Handbook of Humanitarian Law in Armed Conflicts* (2nd edn, OUP 2008).

[34] 'the essence of estoppel is that a party who takes a position that the other party relies and acts upon should not be permitted to take a contrary position in litigation to the detriment of the other party who acted in good-faith reliance on the earlier position.' 28 AmJur 2d Estoppel and Waiver §2.

[35] Ingo Münch, *Völkerrecht: Ohne Internationale Organisationen und Kriegsvölkerrecht* (de Gruyter 1971) 113.

which is unusual even for international law.'[36] Whereas the consequences of recognizing a certain set of facts are defined by international law, it is the States deciding individually, decentralized and at their own political discretion whether these requirements for recognition are actually met.

[36] Alwyn V Freeman, 'The First Meeting of the Inter-American Council of Jurists' (1950) 44 AJIL 374, 378; similarly Kelsen (n 1) 605; Jean Georges Sauveplanne, 'Recognition and Acts of State in the Conflict of Laws' (1960) 7 NILR 17, 17.

3 The recognition of States

States are subjects of international law, ie they are able to enjoy international rights and have international obligations. In order for an entity to be a State and, hence, a subject of international law, it has to meet certain requirements. As there is no superior authority in the international realm competent to conclusively establish such requirements or to assess their fulfilment, it is up to the States themselves to decide upon the recognition of an entity's statehood. In doing so, a State ascertains the fulfilment of the requirements and, thus, the legal subjectivity of the entity whose status was previously undetermined. In this way, recognition allows for 'the normalization of relations between the recognizing state and the newly recognized state.'[37]

3.1 Requirements for recognition

In international legal doctrine, it is generally assumed that recognition presupposes the fulfilment of three requirements of statehood, also known as Georg Jellinek's 'three elements':[38] (i) a permanent population, (ii) a defined territory, and (iii) an effective government.[39]
Also the Montevideo-Convention lists in its Article 1 a 'permanent population' among the elements of a State.[40] Yet, it gives no further explanation on the characteristics of such 'a population'. The Administrative Court of Cologne shed some light on defining it in its judgement of the *Sealand*-case (1978) stating that

---

[37] Merrie Faye Witkin, 'Transkei: An Analysis of the Practice of Recognition – Political or Legal?' (1977) 18 HarvIntlLJ 605, 606.

[38] Georg Jellinek, *Allgemeine Staatslehre* (2nd edn, O Häring 1905) 281-340.

[39] Also referred to in *Deutsche Continental Gas-Gesellschaft v Polish State* (1929) 5 AnnDig 11, 13.

[40] The Montevideo-Convention extends Jellinek's three requirements by the additional element 'capacity to enter into relations with other States' (Convention on the Rights and Duties of States ['Montevideo-Convention'] [signed 26 December 1933, entered into force 26 December 1934] 165 LNTS 19). Yet, this fourth, additional requirement is rather a consequence than a prerequisite for statehood (Crawford, *Creation* [n 6] 61).

> [a State] as an amalgamation of many individuals...has the duty to promote community life. This duty does not merely consist of the promotion of a loose association aimed at the furtherance of common hobbies and interests. Rather it must be aimed at the maintenance of an essentially permanent form of communal life in the sense of sharing a common destiny.[41]

The size of the population is irrelevant for statehood, and no minimum size is specified. This becomes evident when one compares the number of people living in the Vatican State (842; estm July 2014) or Tuvalu (10782; estm July 2014) with the size of the population of India (1,236,344,631; estm July 2014) and China (1,355,692,576; estm July 2014).[42] The population does not have to be settled, and can move around within the territory. Furthermore, the population is not required to be one nation, but can be composed of different groups, thus ethnic, linguistic or religious uniformity is not essential.[43]

A defined territory is the second requirement for statehood. The territory of a State is a geographic area comprised not only of the land but also of territorial sea, internal waters and the airspace above.[44] The size of the territory, however, is irrelevant as States come in all different sizes.[45] The territory of a State can be divided in several, non-connected parts, such as islands separated by seawater, as in the case of Indonesia. Furthermore, parts of a State's territory can be entirely separated from the main territory by other States' territory, so-called enclaves. Examples for such enclaves are Alaska and Hawaii as part of the US or Campione d'Italia as part of Italy surrounded by Swiss territory. It is crucial that only 'a part of the surface of the earth' and only those parts which have 'come into existence in a

---

[41] *In re Duchy of Sealand* (Administrative Court of Cologne) (1978) 5 ILR 683, 687.

[42] Central Intelligence Agency (CIA), 'The World Factbook' ⟨https://www.cia.gov/library/publications/the-world-factbook/rankorder/2119rank.html⟩ accessed 31 January 2015.

[43] *Western Sahara* (Advisory Opinion) [1975] ICJ Rep 12.

[44] Boczek (n 15) 120; Kay Hailbronner and Marcel Kau, 'Der Staat und der Einzelne als Völkerrechtssubjekte' in Wolfgang Graf Vitzthum (ed), *Völkerrecht* (de Gruyter 2010) 176.

[45] For example Monaco: $2km^2$ and China $9,596,961km^2$ (Central Intelligence Agency (CIA) [n 42]).

natural way' can be recognized as State territory.[46] Although at the time of recognition, the size and shape of a territory in question have to be roughly determined, its exact borders can (still) be matter of dispute.[47]

The third requirement for statehood is the existence of a government exercising control over population and territory. This control must be exclusive. This exclusivity of the control is based on two closely connected elements: internal and external sovereignty.[48] Internally, the government must be able to establish and enforce a legal order exclusively as the highest authority in the State. Externally, sovereignty means the capability to act free from any exterior inference, thus, independent from any other authority, within the system of international law.[49] The mere existence of a government, though, is not sufficient. Rather, the government has to be 'effective'. The meaning of 'effectiveness' regarding governments is indicated by the International Committee of Jurists in its report on the Aaland question. Therein, the view is submitted that Finland did not become an independent state 'until a stable political organisation had been created, and until the public authorities had become strong enough to assert themselves throughout the territories of the State without the assistance of foreign troops.'[50]

3.2 Modes of recognition

3.2.1 Individual and collective recognition

Recognition can take place either by an individual State or collectively by a group of States on the occasion of an international conference such as

[46] *In re Duchy of Sealand* (n 41) 685.

[47] *North Sea Continental Shelf* (*Federal Republic of Germany v Denmark; Federal Republic of Germany v Netherlands*) (Judgement) [1969] ICJ Rep 4, para 46; also *Deutsche Continental Gas-Gesellschaft* (n 39) 15.

[48] Bardo Fassbender and Albert Bleckmann, 'Article 2(1)' in Bruno Simma (ed), *The Charter of the United Nations: A Commentary* (CH Beck 2002) vol 1, MN 4.

[49] *Island of Palmas Case* (*Netherlands v United States of America*) (1928) 2 RIAA 831, 838.

[50] *Report of the International Committee of Jurists Entrusted by the Council of the League of Nations with the Task of Giving an Advisory Opinion upon the Legal Aspects of the Aaland Islands Question* (*Aaland Island Case*) (1920) 3 LNOJ Spec Supp 3, 9.

the signing of a multilateral peace treaty.[51] In addition to individual States, the UN, among other international organizations, deals with the question of recognition. According to its Charter, the members of the organization are the States that participated in the United Nations Conference on International Organization in San Francisco on 1 January 1942 or had signed the Declaration by United Nations of 1 January 1942.[52] Additionally, the membership is open to all other 'peace-loving' States.[53] Admission depends on the approval by the General Assembly based on the recommendation of the Security Council.[54] The approval and the associated collective recognition as a State by the General Assembly, however, do not replace the recognition by the individual States. The limitation of the effect of recognition by the UN has been expressed thusly:

> The fact remains, however, that the States have refused to accept any such rule [ie the replacement of individual recognition by collective recognition] and the United Nations does not possess any authority to recognize either a new State or a new government of an existing State. To establish the rule of collective recognition by the United Nations would require either an amendment of the Charter or a treaty to which all Members would adhere.[55]

Nevertheless, several entities were admitted to the UN by votes of members, which had not recognized the entity in question in their bilateral relations.[56] Although the voting behaviour of a UN member State might allow

[51] For example General Treaty for the Re-establishment of Peace ['Peace of Paris (1856)'] (signed 30 March 1856, entered into force 27 April 1856) 114 CTS 409, . See on this in more detail s 7.4 ('The Ottoman Empire').

[52] Charter of the United Nations (adopted 26 June 1945, entered into force 24 October 1945) 59 Stat 1031, art 3.

[53] ibid, art 4 para 1.

[54] ibid, art 4 para 2.

[55] Memorandum on the Legal Aspects of the Problem of Representation in the United Nations, Transmitted to the President of the Security Council by the Secretary-General (Lie), 8 March 1950 (1950) 4 IO 356, 357-58.

[56] ibid, 358. Examples for such entities listed are Nepal and Transjordan (Jordan).

conclusions to be drawn about the respective attitude towards the entity's status in general, it would be wrong to equate a state's approval for the membership of an entity into the UN with recognition in the bilateral relations between the State and the entity.[57] Furthermore, admission into the UN, and thus the collective recognition by a majority of the General Assembly, does not automatically imply the recognition by all individual members, as the admission of Israel has shown.[58] Nevertheless, the admission to the UN and therefore the recognition of an entity as a State is binding for all UN members with regard to the observance of rights and duties of the UN Charter.[59] Despite this fact, recognition of States is basically still the act of individual States, even if it occurs simultaneously with a collective procedure.

---

[57] A special occurrence was the adoption of the resolution concerning the status of Palestine in the United Nations (Status of Palestine in the United Nations, UNGA Res 67/19 [4 December 2012] UN Doc A/RES/67/19). This vote was not on the full UN membership of Palestine, but rather on its status as a non-member observer *State*. But, similarly, to vote in favour of new UN members and the recognition of their status as States, the approving States are not automatically willing to recognize the entity in their bilateral relations. Thus, and despite the given support for this resolution, the Ambassador of Switzerland to the UN Paul R Seger emphasized that this approval does not mean that Switzerland commits itself to recognize Palestine as a State bilaterally ('Nahost: Schweiz stimmt für Palästina als UNO-Beobachterstaat' *Swiss Press Agency (SDA) Dispatch* [Zürich, 30 November 2012]).

[58] The admission of Israel to the UN has been denied by 12 members (Afghanistan, Burma, Egypt, Ethiopia, India, Iran, Iraq, Lebanon, Pakistan, Saudi Arabia, and Yemen). Until recently, some of these and other UN members repeated their refusal to recognize Israel as a State. Saudi Arabia, for instance, added the following reservation to the Vienna Convention on Diplomatic Relations upon its accession on 10 February 1981: 'Accession to this Convention shall not constitute a recognition of Israel or lead to any kind of intercourse with it or the establishment of any relations with Israel under the Convention.' (Multilateral Treaties Deposited with the Secretary-General, Status as at 1 April 2009 [2009] UN Doc ST/LEG/SER.E/26, 105). Similarly, Kuwait's reservation to the Vienna Convention on the Law of Treaties as of 24 February 1998 (Mark E Villiger, *Commentary on the 1969 Vienna Convention on the Law of Treaties* (Martinus Nijhoff 2009) 1012).

[59] UN Charter (n 52) art 2.

3.2.2 Implicit and explicit recognition

Recognition can be awarded either implicitly or explicitly.[60] Explicit recognition results from an official declaration or a formal notification. Implicit recognition, on the other hand, occurs by certain conclusive conduct of a State towards an entity. Whether certain conduct is implicating recognition, however, depends primarily on the intention of the acting State.[61] In any case, the intention to recognize or not to recognize an entity has to be clearly demonstrated.[62] Examples for affirmative conduct are the conclusion of a bilateral treaty and the establishment of diplomatic relations.[63] Yet, caution is advised not to assume implied recognition from acts which were not intended to do so.[64] In order to ensure that certain conduct is not misinterpreted as recognition, States have the option to add reservations explicitly excluding recognition in multilateral treaties.[65] Albeit the approval for admission to the UN might indicate a certain general attitude towards a State, it does not necessarily imply that the approving State is willing to recognize the entity in their bilateral relations.

3.2.3 Conditional and unconditional recognition

Normally, the term 'recognition' refers to the simple acknowledgement that an entity possesses all distinguishing features of a State. Distinct from this is the notion of 'conditional recognition'. It stands for recognition which is awarded on account of the fulfilment of requirements additional to the regular ones. This concept is of some complexity. On one hand, State recognition is generally assumed to be based on effectiveness and does

[60] Montevideo-Convention (n 40) art 7.

[61] Rudolf L Bindschedler, 'Die Anerkennung im Völkerrecht' in *Verhandlungen der 7. Tagung der Deutschen Gesellschaft für Völkerrecht in Frankfurt/Main am 13. und 14. April 1961* (CF Müller 1961) vol 4, 6.

[62] Boczek (n 15) 103.

[63] Malcolm N Shaw, *International Law* (6th edn, CUP 2008) 463; Boczek (n 15) 103; however Frowein ('Recognition' [n 18] 658) regards only the establishment of full diplomatic relations as 'unequivocal act from which recognition can always be deduced'.

[64] Frowein, 'Recognition' (n 18) 658.

[65] Shaw (n 63) 462; Boczek (n 15) 103.

not need the fulfilment of any further requirement. Hence, according to the Montevideo-Convention, '[r]ecognition is unconditional and irrevocable'.[66] On the other hand, recognition has at times been granted 'conditionally'. Even more, 'conditional recognition' appears to be a regular act in State practice, reflecting the predominantly political character of recognition. Recent examples for such additional 'conditions' were the protection of religious minorities, or commitments regarding disarmament.[67] Yet, 'conditional recognition' can be granted in different ways, whereas the 'condition' can assume the form of a *condicio* or of a *modus*.[68] Nevertheless, to draw the distinction between *condicio* and *modus* in international public law cannot be done with the same clear-cut precision as in private law.[69]

A *condicio* (condition) makes the effectiveness of a legal arrangement dependent on the occurrence or the non-occurrence of an uncertain,[70] future event.[71] An arrangement subject to a suspensive condition (*condicio suspensiva*) means that the arrangement was not effective as long as the event that it depended on had not yet occurred.[72] The condition has a suspensive effect, ie the arrangement is in a pending state (*condicio pendet*) until the discharge of the condition.[73] Thus if the event does not come to be, then the arrangement does not become effective. By contrast, there is the

[66]Montevideo-Convention (n 40) art 6.

[67]Declaration on Yugoslavia (1992) 31 ILM 1485; Declaration on the 'Guidelines on the Recognition of New States in Eastern Europe and in the Soviet Union' (1992) 31 ILM 1486.

[68]cf 'Modus saepe appellatur conditio, non contra.' ('Modus is often called condition but not the other way round.' (my translation)) Detlef Liebs, *Lateinische Rechtsregeln und Rechtssprichwörter* (CH Beck 2007) 137.

[69]Already noted by Alphonse Rivier, *Principes du droit des gens* (Rousseau 1896) 60.

[70]The *dies*, as a time limitation, on the contrary, made this effectiveness dependent on the occurrence or non-occurrence of a future but *certain* event.

[71]Reinhard Zimmermann, *The Law of Obligations: Roman Foundations of the Civilian Tradition* (Juta & Co / CH Beck 1992) 717; also Max Kaser, *Römisches Privatrecht: Ein Studienbuch* (20th edn, CH Beck 2014) 75, MN 1-2.

[72]On the suspensive condition, see Zimmermann (n 71) 718; Kaser (n 71) 75 and 77, MN 2 and 9.

[73]Zimmermann (n 71) 718; Kaser (n 71) 66 and 67, MN 2 and 9.

resolutive condition (*condicio resolutiva*).[74] Here, the arrangement comes into effect immediately with the transaction, but only for the duration of the non-occurrence of the future, uncertain event. The arrangement ceases to be effective upon fulfilment of the condition. Still today, in contemporary legal systems the categories of suspensive and resolutive conditions are used.[75]These categories correspond to concepts, which in some jurisdictions are called 'condition precedent' and 'condition subsequent'.[76]

Yet, assuming that a State's existence is based on Jellinek's three classic elements, to apply the concept 'condition' – in this case suspensive condition[77] – to the recognition of States has been criticized for being incoherent.[78] A State would either effectively exist or it would not. So, if it does exist by possessing a territory, a population, and an effective government, and provided it would have not occurred by illegal means,[79] then, the options for other States are either to acknowledge or not to acknowledge this. But awarding recognition to a State accompanied with a suspensive condition (*condicio suspensiva*) would, in consequence, mean that a certain condition had to be fulfilled before the recognition came into effect. This again could have two results.[80] Either the existence of the three State features – and

[74]It has been repeatedly pointed to doubts, though, whether Roman law actually knew and used the concept of resolutive condition. See Kaser (n 71) 77, MN 11; Heinrich Honsell, *Römisches Recht* (7th edn, Springer 2010) 28, Fn 1; Zimmermann (n 71) 731.

[75]For example in Switzerland OR arts 151, 154 and in Germany BGB §§158 both with regard to contracts. Furthermore, Schürmann pointing to this distinction regarding art 482 of the Law of Succession in the Swiss Civil Code. (Georg Schürmann, 'Art 482' in *Praxiskommentar Erbrecht* (Helbing 2011) N10-14).

[76]For condition precedent and condition subsequent in US contract law, see Joseph M Perillo, *Calamari and Perillo on Contracts* (6th edn, Thomson/West 2009) 361ff; for the distinction in English contract law, see Guenter H Treitel, 'The Agreement' in *Chitty on Contracts* (31st edn, Sweet & Maxwell 2012) vol 1, para 2-152.

[77]In theory, recognition of a State could also be awarded with resolutive conditions. Yet, this would mean that the fulfilment of such a condition would not lead to recognition but, to the contrary, to the withdrawal of recognition. But then the withdrawal of recognition takes place usually and solely in the event of the disappearance of one of the three basic State requirements.

[78]Thomas Baty, 'So-called "De-Facto" Recognition' (1921-1922) 31 YaleLJ 469, 470.

[79]See sub-s 2.4.3 ('Non-recognition').

[80]Chen (n 4) 268.

therefore the State – would be acknowledged, but the acknowledging State is not yet willing to grant official recognition and to set up diplomatic relations until certain additional conditions are met. Or the recognizing State would indicate that an entity might exist as a State in the future upon the fulfilment of certain conditions that have not yet been met for the time being. Either way, not to recognize a State until the attainment of certain conditions would correspond simply to the denial of recognition.[81] Nonetheless, in practice, recognition of States has been granted with suspensive conditions.[82]

Another possibility to grant 'conditional recognition' is illustrated by the example of the recognition of the former republics of the USSR and the SFRY.[83] In this case, the 'conditions' were rather prerequisites than real conditions in the strict technical term, in that the recognition was not effective until the attainment of a certain additional requirement. So, demands were made prior to recognition, while recognition had been held out as a prospect. In case of non-fulfilment of the demands, recognition would not be granted at all.[84]

Again, another way to grant 'conditional recognition' is as recognition *sub modo*.[85] The concept of *modus*, translating into 'instruction',[86] 'duty',[87]

---

[81] ibid, 268.

[82] For example the Act of the Congress of Berlin (signed 13 July 1878) 153 CTS 172, regarding the recognition of Montenegro (art 27), Serbia (art 34) and Romania (art 44). Although in arts 34 and 43 these requirements were called conditions, it is disputed whether they were not rather technically speaking modi. See on this s 2.2.3 ('Conditional and unconditional recognition').

[83] See on this ch 3 ('Cases of State recognition since the end of the Cold War').

[84] Chen (n 4) 257; Rivier, *Principes du droit des gens* (n 69) 60.

[85] Chen (n 4) 265.

[86] Gottfried Schiemann, 'Modus' in *Brill's New Pauly* (Brill Online 2014) ⟨http://www.paulyonline.brill.nl/entries/brill-s-new-pauly/modus-e808050⟩ accessed 31 January 2015.

[87] William A Hunter, *A Systematic and Historical Exposition of Roman Law in the Order of a Code* (4th edn, Sweet & Maxwell 1903) 934.

‘direction’,[88] ‘obligations’,[89] or ‘purpose’,[90] is used most often, but not exclusively, in the context of a gift or a testamentary benefit.[91] Unlike the *condicio*, the fulfilment or non-fulfilment of a *modus* does not affect the effectiveness of an arrangement. Instead, the arrangement comes into effect immediately, while any non-fulfilment of a particular modus might be answered with coercive measures.[92] Savigny explained the difference between modus and condicio with the following mnemonic: ‘Die Bedingung nämlich suspendiert, zwingt aber nicht, der Modus zwingt, suspendiert aber nicht.’[93] Moreover, the concept of modus is divided into the *modus simplex* and the *modus qualificatus*.[94] The former stands for a duty in the interest of the recipient of a gift, the latter describes a duty in the interest of the donor or a third party. The important distinction is with regard to its fulfilment. Whereas the modus simplex is not supposed to be enforced, the *modus qualificatus* obligates the recipient to fulfil the condition.[95] Regarding the recognition of States, examples for such obligations were perpetual neutrality,[96] or commercial advantages like most favoured-nation treatment.[97] Hence, such imposed obligations are often in the interest of the recognizing State or in the interest of a third party, ie in the interest of the other States, rather than in the interest and to the advantage of the entity recognized.

---

[88] Lauterpacht, *States* (n 3) 262.

[89] Chen (n 4) 265.

[90] David Johnston, *Roman Law in Context* (CUP 1999) 47.

[91] Schiemann (n 86).

[92] Peter Apathy, Georg Klingenberg, and Herwig Stiegler, *Einführung in das römische Recht* (Böhlau Verlag 1994) 184; Kaser (n 71) 79-80, MN 19-21.

[93] ‘The condition suspends but does not enforce; the modus enforces but does not suspend.’ (my translation) (Friedrich Carl von Savigny, *System des heutigen römischen Rechts* (Veit 1840-1863) 213).

[94] See on this Ludwig Mitteis, *Römisches Privatrecht bis auf die Zeit Diokletians: Grundbegriffe und Lehre von den juristischen Personen* (Verlag von Duncker und Humblot 1908) 200.

[95] Nedim Peter Vogt, ‘Art. 246’ in Heinrich Honsell, Nedim Peter Vogt, and Wolfgang Wiegand (eds), *Basler Kommentar: Obligationenrecht I* (5th edn, Helbing 2012) MN 1.

[96] Treaty of London (signed 19 April 1839) 88 CTS 412, art 7, regarding the recognition of Belgium.

[97] See Exchange of Notes at Tirana (22 and 25 June 1922) 5 Bevans 9, on the recognition of Albania by the US.

Therefore, in order to be more precise these kinds of obligation should be described as *modi qualificati* in contrast to the *modi simplices*. However, the failure to fulfil these *modi* does not lead to the withdrawal of recognition.[98] In fact the non-fulfilment is more like a breach of an agreement on which the recognizing State might react with the imposition of sanctions.[99] Using 'conditional recognition' as recognition *sub modo* is therefore consistent with the principle of the Montevideo-Convention that recognition is irrevocable. A similar view is held by the Institut De Droit International stating that '[i]n the case of an obligation assumed by a State at the time of its recognition, failure to fulfil this obligation does not have the effect of annulling recognition or of authorizing its revocation, but involves the consequences of the violation of an international obligation.'[100]

Taken together there are various ways of granting recognition. Regardless of this, attaching further conditions to State recognition has been criticized for turning recognition into an instrument of power for the purpose of enforcing individual or common interests of the recognizant States.[101]

3.2.4 De facto and de jure recognition

The differentiation between *de facto* and *de jure* recognition is a concept usually applied to the recognition of governments rather than States.[102]

---

[98] See on this also Oppenheim: 'The meaning of such conditional recognition is not that recognition can be withdrawn in case the condition is not complied with. The nature of the thing makes recognition, if once given, incapable of withdrawal. But conditional recognition, if accepted by the new State, imposes the internationally legal duty upon such State to comply with the condition, failing which a right of intervention is given to the other party for the purpose of making the recognised State comply with the imposed condition.' (Lassa Francis Lawrence Oppenheim, *International Law: A Treatise* (Longman, Green 1905) 111-12).

[99] Lauterpacht, *States* (n 3) 364; Chen (n 4) 266.

[100] Institut de Droit International (IDI), Resolution Concerning the Recognition of New States and Governments (1936) 30 AJIL Supp 185, art 6.

[101] cf Julius Goebel, *The Recognition Policy of the United States* (Longman, Green 1915) 65; Chen (n 4) 269; Lauterpacht, *States* (n 3) 364.

[102] James Crawford, *Brownlie's Principles of Public International Law* (8th edn, OUP 2012) 152; John O'Brien, *International Law* (Cavendish 2001) 179.

Nevertheless rare cases of *de facto* recognition of States are found in state practice.[103] A reason for these exceptions seems to be that, particularly with regard to the recognition of governments of new States, often no clear distinction is made between the institutions of government and State.[104]

De jure recognition stands for recognition which is definite, absolute, and irrevocable. Compared to this, *de facto* recognition means that recognition is only awarded provisionally and with reservations.[105] It stands for the hesitation of a State to recognize a situation – such as the coming into existence of a new State or government – that seems not to have consolidated yet. *De facto* recognition allows the hesitant State to indicate acknowledgement while waiting and seeing how the new situation might evolve before conclusively giving *de jure* recognition after doubts have been sufficiently removed.[106] By granting *de facto* recognition, a State prevents itself from granting premature recognition.[107] Consequently, *de facto* recognition can precede *de jure* recognition.

The *de facto - de jure* distinction, however, has been criticized for bringing about 'confusion of thought in modern literature and practice of international law.'[108] This confusion might have been caused by the occasional argument that the terms *de facto* and *de jure* actually describe the situation recognized instead of the act of recognition. Be that as it may, it has been

---

[103] On the example of the *de facto* recognition of Latvia by Switzerland or the de facto recognition of the Republic of Indonesia by Great Britain, see Stefan Talmon, *Recognition of Governments in International Law: With Particular Reference to Governments in Exile* (Clarendon Press 1998) 48-49.

[104] ibid, 48-49.

[105] IDI (n 100) arts 3-5.

[106] Shaw (n 63) 460; Frowein, 'Recognition' (n 18) 658.

[107] Rebecca Wallace and Olga Martin-Ortega, *International Law* (Sweet & Maxwell 2009) 80.

[108] Emilio S Binavince, 'Canadian Practice in Matters of Recognition' in R St J MacDonald, Greald L Morris, and Douglas M Johnston (eds), *Canadian Perspectives on International Law and Organization* (University of Toronto Press 1974) 173; similarly Boczek (n 15) 102; Ian Brownlie, 'Recognition in Theory and Practice' in Ronald St John MacDonald and Douglas Millar Johnston (eds), *The Structure and Process of International Law: Essays in Legal Philosophy, Doctrine and Theory* (Martinus Nijhoff 1983) 636; O'Brien (n 102) 178.

also indicated that this differentiation lost its significance in contemporary State practice of recognition.[109]

3.3 Consequences of recognition

The question of the consequences of State recognition has long been disputed and remains the subject of controversy today. The so-called 'great debate'[110] on the necessity of recognition for an entity to reach statehood is dominated by two competing approaches – the constitutive and the declaratory theory. The constitutive approach submits that recognition is an indispensable requirement for statehood.[111] Only after other States have confirmed that all requirements are met, does a State eventually come into existence. Consequently, the entity seeking treatment as a State by other existing States is dependent upon the willingness of the other existing States to recognize it.

This approach is subject to various points of criticism. First, an entity not recognized by other States remains to them legally non-existent. As a result, according to the constitutive view, such a non-recognized entity would be no man's land without any rights or obligations, and ultimately sub-

---

[109] Peter Malanczuk, *Akehurst's Modern Introduction to International Law* (7th edn, Routledge 1997) 88; Wallace and Martin-Ortega (n 107) 79.

[110] Crawford, *Creation* (n 6) 19.

[111] Among the adherents of the constitutive theory are Dionisio Anzilotti, *Corso di diritto internazionale* (3rd edn, Athenaeum 1928) vol 1, 147-48, 158 et passim; Paul Fauchille, *Traité de droit international public* (8th edn, Paris, 1921-1926) vol I.1, 306; Paul Guggenheim, *Traité de Droit international public: Avec mention de la pratique internationale et suisse* (Georg 1953) 190-91; William Edward Hall, *A Treatise of International Law* (2nd edn, Clarendon Press 1884) 103; Kelsen (n 1) 608-9 et passim; Thomas Joseph Lawrence, *The Principles of International Law* (6th edn, DC Heath & Co, Publishers 1895) 83-84; René Le Normand, *La reconnaissance internationale et ses diverses applications: États, governments, belligerants, principes du droit international* (Camis 1899) 268; Oppenheim, *International Law: A Treatise* (n 98) vol 1, 109-10 (with reservations); Franz von Liszt, *Das Völkerrecht systematisch dargestellt* (Haering 1898) 45; Henry Wheaton, *Elements of International Law* (6th edn, Little Brown & Co 1855) 30-31.

ject to foreign occupation.[112] Another point of criticism is the 'relativity of the "State" as subject of international law'.[113] The constitutive approach creates a 'split international personality.'[114] To the recognizing States, the entity is a State and a legal subject, whereas for the non-recognizing States it is not.[115]

The declaratory approach, in contrast, conceives statehood as independent of recognition. Once an entity meets all the requirements for statehood, it is automatically a State regardless of the recognition by other States.[116] Put another way, recognition is simply the acknowledgement by other States that the entity in question has fulfilled all necessary requirements to reach statehood. Thus, recognition, according to the declaratory approach, is retroactive, in the sense that recognition reaches as far back in time to the point when the entity in question fulfilled all the requirements necessary for statehood.[117] In the reverse case, 'recognition would still be determinative for the moment of birth of the State' and as a result 'would lead to the acceptance of the constitutive theory.'[118] The declaratory approach has been endorsed by the Montevideo-Convention, which states: 'The political existence of the state is independent of recognition by the other states.'[119] This statement is also found in Article 13 of the Charter of the Organization of the American States[120] and adapted in the expert opinions No 1[121] and 10[122] of the Arbitration Commission of the Peace Conference on

[112] Georg Dahm, *Völkerrecht* (2nd edn, Walter de Gruyter 1989) 190; Ignaz Seidl-Hohenveldern, *Völkerrecht* (Carl Heymanns Verlag 2000) 139.

[113] Stefan Talmon, 'The Constitutive versus the Declaratory Theory of Recognition: *Tertium Non Datur?*' (2004) 75 BYIL 101, 102.

[114] Boczek (n 15) 101.

[115] Situation in Namibia Resulting from the Illegal Occupation of the Territory by South Africa, UNGA Res 43/26A (17 November 1988) UN Doc A/RES/43/26A.

[116] Boczek (n 15) 101.

[117] Chen (n 4) 177; Raič (n 7) 32.

[118] Raič (n 7) 32.

[119] Montevideo-Convention (n 40) art 3.

[120] Charter of the Organization of the American States (signed 30 April 1948, entered into force 13 December 1951) 119 UNTS 3, amended version (1994) 133 ILM 981.

[121] Badinter Commission, Opinion No 1, 29 November 1991 (1992) 31 ILM 1494.

[122] Badinter Commission, Opinion No 10, 4 July 1992 (1992) 31 ILM 1525.

Yugoslavia (Badinter Commission). Moreover, international,[123] as well as national,[124] jurisprudence refer to the declaratory approach. International legal doctrine seems to favour the declaratory approach, too.[125] However, even among those favouring the declaratory approach, there are some admitting that recognition can have constitutive effects in certain cases for 'it is capable of pushing things further in favour of a particular outcome towards which the existing criteria are pointing but which itself is not reached by considering them alone.'[126]

Some authors have attempted in various ways to combine these two theories into a single coherent construct. Oppenheim, for example, submitted that recognition being 'declaratory of an existing fact, is constitutive in nature.'[127] Rather than a combination of these theories, however, this seems to be a reinforcement of the constitutive viewpoint. He stated furthermore that recognition had a duality function to the extent that it was the recognizing States' performance of a 'quasi-legal duty' – in place of a superior competent organ able to do so – together with the pursuance of 'their own political interests'.[128] Kelsen argued similarly by submitting his view of recognition as 'comprised of two quite distinct acts: a political act and a legal act.'[129] The political act of recognition was, according to Kelsen, declaratory be-

[123] eg *Deutsche Continental Gas-Gesellschaft* (n 39).

[124] For example, in Switzerland: arrêt 5A_329/2009, E2.4; in the US: *New York Chinese TV Programs, Inc v UE Enterprises, Inc* 954 F2d 847, 847 (CA 2 NY).

[125] Among others IDI (n 100) 185; James Leslie Brierly, *The Law of Nations: An Introduction to the International Law of Peace* (6th edn, Clarendon Press 1963) 139; Chen (n 4); Charles Rousseau, *Droit international public* (Sirey 1953) 294; Georges Scelle, *Précis de droit des gens: Principes et systématique* (Sirey 1932-1934) vol 1, 98. More recent are David Harris, *Cases and Materials on International Law* (7th edn, Sweet & Maxwell 2010) 131; Frowein, 'Recognition' (n 18) 658; Matthias Herdegen, *Völkerrecht* (13th edn, CH Beck 2014) 77; Anne Peters, *Völkerrecht: Allgemeiner Teil* (3rd edn, Schulthess 2012) 36 and 39.

[126] Ralph Wilde, 'Recognition in International Law' in Ralph Wilde, Andrew Cannon, and Elizabeth Wilmshurst (eds), *Recognition of States: The Consequences of Recognition or Non-Recognition in UK and International Law* (Chatham House 2010) 7.

[127] Lassa Francis Lawrence Oppenheim, *International Law: A Treatise* (Hersch Lauterpacht ed, 7th edn, Longman, Green 1948) vol 1, 124.

[128] ibid, vol 1, 123.

[129] Kelsen (n 1) 605.

cause it would not have legal consequences.[130] The legal act of recognition, on the other hand, was perceived as something completely different. It would be the conclusion (*la constatation*) by a competent agency – ie the States – that an entity had fulfilled all necessary requirements to be a State. The legal act of recognition therefore was constitutive.[131] Lauterpacht adopted the basic notion of the duality concept of recognition. He argued that recognition is both declaratory and constitutive. While recognition is 'declaratory of an existing fact' it is at the same time 'constitutive, as between the recognizing State and the new community, of international rights and duties associated with full statehood.'[132] From this he concluded that the other States had a duty to grant recognition upon the moment from which an entity meets all requirements for statehood.[133] This declaratory view of a possible duty of recognition, however, has been opposed for not being confirmed in State practice.[134] Verdross, in a similar fashion, aimed to bring the two views together by distinguishing two parts of State recognition.[135] First, the acknowledgement of the recognizing State that an entity had been established by fulfilling all necessary requirements; second, the establishment of diplomatic relations with the newly established State. According to Verdross, the first part, the acknowledgement, is declarative, whereas the second part, the establishment of official relations, is constitutive. However, for the reason that these two acts are regularly performed simultaneously, they would often be seen as a unit.[136] Frowein, too, pointed to this conception of the twofold character of State recognition.[137] For him,

[130]Kelsen (n 1) 606.

[131]ibid, 607.

[132]Lauterpacht, 'Recognition of States' (n 3) 385; Lauterpacht, *States* (n 3) 6.

[133]Lauterpacht, 'Recognition of States' (n 3) 385; Lauterpacht, *States* (n 3) 6. A duty for recognition saw also; Guggenheim (n 111) vol 1, 191, Fn 1; Johann Caspar Bluntschli, *Das moderne Völkerrecht der civilisirten Staten: als Rechtsbuch dargestellt* (Beck'sche Buchhandlung 1868) 71.

[134]Crawford, *Brownlie's Principles of Public International Law* (n 102) 148; Talmon, 'Tertium' (n 113) 103; Bindschedler (n 61) 15 and 25.

[135]Alfred Verdross, *Völkerrecht* (4th edn, Springer 1959) 184.

[136]ibid, 184.

[137]Jochen A Frowein, 'Anerkennung' in Ignaz Seidl-Hohenveldern (ed), *Lexikon des Rechts: Völkerrecht* (Luchterhand 2001) 10.

recognition was declaratory in that it would be an acknowledgement of the fact that by fulfilling the requirements for a State an entity had been established. At the same time, recognition would be constitutive through the establishment of formal relations, between the recognizing and the recognized State. Grant, also engaging with these two theories, pointed to a notable aspect of the dichotomy specifically with regard to additional criteria of recognition.[138] From a constitutive view, recognition was the *sine qua non* for statehood and could not be substituted by another additional criterion. That way, any additional criterion to the traditional ones make recognition more deferrable and hence would expose it to political manipulation. In contrast, the declaratory approach was equating criteria for statehood with criteria for recognition.[139] If recognition occurred automatically whenever all criteria for statehood were met, then, in consequence, any (additional) feature causing recognition must be part of the definition of statehood. Thus, declaratorists may call the additional criteria state features. But for the reason that 'the correspondence between statehood and recognition... is at the heart of the declaratory doctrine', these additional criteria would be turned into criteria for recognition.[140] The declaratory approach, therefore, 'does no more than rearrange the geography of discretion, moving discretion from the timing of recognition to the definition of statehood.'[141]

Yet the dispute between the supporters of the constitutive and the declaratory approach remains altogether largely insignificant in the State practice of recognition.[142] Nevertheless, it is important 'to distinguish between the effects of recognition on the legal status of a "State", and its effects on the State's relationship with other States.'[143] While recognition does not ensure that the recognized entity actually fulfils all requirements of being a State according to international law, the recognizing State has to treat the recog-

---

[138] Grant, *Recognition* (n 5) 83-84.

[139] ibid, 84.

[140] ibid, 83.

[141] ibid, 84.

[142] Frowein, 'Anerkennung' (n 137) 10; Talmon, 'Tertium' (n 113) 101.

[143] Talmon, 'Tertium' (n 113) 101.

nized State as a subject of international law from the moment of recognition in any case.[144] This implies that the recognizing State must not act against the previously granted recognition. In their bilateral relations, the recognizing State as well as the recognized State must respect their respective territorial integrity and political independence.
Recognition not only has repercussions at the international level, but also has a legal effect on the municipal level. Granting recognition to States and governments is generally reserved to the executive of a State whereas the judiciary refers to this decision.[145] Once an entity has been recognized as State, it might access the domestic courts of the recognizing State and claim immunity. Additionally, when appropriate, the acts of the legislative and executive will be given effects in these courts.[146]

3.4 Premature recognition, withdrawal of recognition and non-recognition

3.4.1 Premature recognition

The term 'premature recognition' refers to recognition of a new State prior to fulfilment of all requirements. Premature recognition is problematic particularly with regard to secession.[147] Examples that have been discussed as cases of premature recognition are the recognition of the US by France in

---

[144] Stephan Hobe, *Einführung in das Völkerrecht* (9th edn, A Francke Verlag 2008) 72.

[145] *Government of the Republic of Spain v SS 'Arantzazu Mendi'* [1939] AC 256 , 264. For exceptions to this principle, see sub-s 2.4.3 ('Non-recognition').

[146] Boczek (n 15) 104; Andrew Cannon, 'Consequences of Nonrecognition in UK Law' in Ralph Wilde, Andrew Cannon, and Elizabeth Wilmshurst (eds), *Recognition of States: The Consequences of Recognition or Non-Recognition in UK and International Law* (Chatham House 2010) 12.

[147] Stefan Oeter, 'Selbstbestimmungsrecht im Wandel: Überlegungen zur Debatte um Selbstbestimmung, Sezessionsrecht und "vorzeitige" Anerkennung' (1992) 52 ZaöRV 741, 766. On the concept of secession, see also Marcelo G Kohen (ed), *Secession: International Law Perspectives* (CUP 2006); Daniel Thürer and Thomas Burri, 'Secession' in Ruediger Wolfrum (ed), *Max Planck Encyclopedia of Public International Law* (OUP 2012) vol IX.

1778,[148] the recognition of the Latin-American States by the UK and the US in the 1820s,[149] the recognition of Biafra between 1967 and 1970,[150] and the recognition of Croatia in 1991/92.[151] Regarding secession, premature recognition is problematic not only for the nascent State but also the parent State. Recognition has to be withheld until the new entity achieved permanent consolidation of the State requirements, but especially its independence from the parent State.[152] Otherwise recognition is considered premature, and hence constitutes an intervention in the internal affairs of the parent State.[153] Even more, it might be regarded as intervention in the domestic affairs of the sovereign (parent) State by a third State, and therefore a violation of international law.[154] However, in the event of secession, the concepts of the right of self-determination of the people on one side, and of territorial integrity of States and of the resultant prohibition of intervention on the other side collide. Yet, the decisions on whether all requirements for statehood are fulfilled, whether the process of secession is irreversible, and whose interests – the secessionists' or the parent State's – are more important do not lie with a supranational organ, but rather with the individual recognizing State.[155] Therefore, the conclusion, too, whether the moment of recognition was premature and consequently illegal is subject to

[148] See on this s 6.5 ('The United States of America'). Also Jochen A Frowein, 'Die Entwicklung der Anerkennung von Staaten und Regierungen im Völkerrecht' (1972) 11 STAAT 145, 150-53.

[149] Lauterpacht, *States* (n 3) 8, 10, 14-16, 18.

[150] Biafra was recognized by five States only (Gabon, Ivory Coast, Haiti, Tanzania, and Zambia). Crawford, *Creation* (n 6) 406; David A Ijalaye, 'Was "Biafra" at Any Time a State in International Law?' (1971) 65 AJIL 551, 559.

[151] eg Peter Hipold, 'Die Anerkennung der Neustaaten auf dem Balkan' (1993) 31 AVR 487, 405; Dietrich Rauschning, 'Gedanken zur Anerkennungserklärung' in Volkmar Götz, Peter Selmer, and Ruediger Wolfrum (eds), *Liber amicorum Günther Jaenicke: Zum 85. Geburtstag* (Springer 1998) 389-92.

[152] Oeter (n 147) 767.

[153] John P Grant and J Craig Barker, *Parry & Grant Encyclopaedic Dictionary of International Law* (3rd edn, OUP 2009) 509; Knut Ipsen, *Völkerrecht* (6th edn, CH Beck 2014) 137.

[154] Dahm (n 112) 200; Grant and Barker (n 153) 509.

[155] Rauschning (n 151) 390.

perception of the respecting recognizing State and thus cannot definitely be drawn.[156] Albeit, according to the declaratory view, not directly resulting in the formation of a new State, premature recognition does have a political effect on the international level by strengthening the position of the entity aiming to be recognized as a new State.[157] Moreover, recognition by third States might serve as regulator of the competing claims for territorial sovereignty.[158]

3.4.2 Withdrawal of recognition

As a general rule, recognition cannot be withdrawn.[159] Once accorded, the recognizing State has to behave in correspondence with its unilateral act. A withdrawal, though, would run contrary to the previously accorded recognition and, therefore, violate the estoppel principle.[160] This, again, contributes to a lack of legal certainty in international relations. Consequently, for the purpose of ensuring legal certainty, based on the *pacta sunt servanda*-principle,[161] the rule *acta sunt servanda*[162] applies for recognition too.[163] However, acts to express discontent, such as the recall of an ambassador or the temporary suspension of bilateral diplomatic relations, are not to be regarded as the withdrawal of recognition.[164]

---

[156] Anne Peters, 'Die Anerkennung Kosovos als Ermessensfrage' *NZZ* (Zürich, 1 February 2008) 7.

[157] Rauschning (n 151) 388.

[158] Oeter (n 147) 770.

[159] Montevideo-Convention (n 40) art 6.

[160] See on the estoppel principle, n 34.

[161] Latin for 'agreements have to be kept'. See Vienna Convention on Diplomatic Relations (VCDR) (signed 18 April 1961, entered into force 24 April 1980) 500 UNTS 95, art 26.

[162] Latin for 'acts have to be kept' in the sense of art 26 of the Vienna Convention on the Law of Treaties that the act of recognition is binding and the recognizing state has to act according in good faith.

[163] International Law Commission, 'Introduction by the Special Rapporteur of his Sixth Report' in Report of the International Law Commission on the Work of its 55th Session (5 May-6 June and 7 July-8 August 2003) UN Doc A/45/10, para 268.

[164] cf the cooling of the Israel-Turkish relations over the Gaza flotilla incident in 2010 or the Egyptian decision to cut diplomatic relations to Syria in 2013.

Nonetheless, exceptions to the rule of the prohibition of withdrawal of recognition are conceivable. An exception which might allow for the withdrawal of recognition is the change of circumstances according to the rule *clausula rebus sic stantibus*.[165] Such changes in circumstances regarding States include the loss of the State's people, territory, or both together. In the event of loss of territory and/or people, the withdrawal of recognition might be actually superfluous as the entity would cease to exist as a State.[166] Extinction can occur either through dismemberment,[167] incorporation,[168] or merger respectively.[169] In contrast to this, annexation does not cause the extinction of a State.[170] Annexation as the 'forcible acquisition of territory by one State at the expense of another State' is a breach of the prohibition of the use of force under current international law.[171] Consequently, according to the rule *ex injuria jus non oritur*, this breach will not create a new legal situation. Ergo, the prohibition of annexation works as 'a rule barring extinction of a State.'[172] Other States are banned from recognizing this new situation as legal, since the annexed State continues to exist. In contrast, the (forced) change of government or even discontinuation of a governmental structure is insufficient to result in the extinction of the State.[173]

Another exception that might concede withdrawal is *de facto* recognition which is only provisional and temporary.[174] More problematic is the with-

[165] Latin for 'the clause of things thus standing', meaning that treaties have to be kept and unilateral acts must not be modified, suspended or revoked except in the event of a fundamental change of circumstances. See 'Introduction' (n 63) para 270.

[166] Boczek (n 15) 109.

[167] eg Czechoslovakia which separated into the Czech Republic and the Slovak Republic in 1993.

[168] eg the incorporation of GDR into the FRG in 1990.

[169] eg the unification of South Yemen (People's Democratic Republic of Yemen) and North Yemen (Yemen Arab Republic) to the Republic of Yemen in 1990.

[170] eg Kuwait's annexation by Iraq during the Iraq invasion in 1990.

[171] Rainer Hofmann, 'Annexation' in Ruediger Wolfrum (ed), *The Max Planck Encyclopedia of Public International Law* (OUP 2012) vol I, 408-9.

[172] Ineta Ziemele, 'Extinction of States' in Ruediger Wolfrum (ed), *The Max Planck Encyclopedia of Public International Law* (OUP 2012) vol IX, 560.

[173] Crawford, *Creation* (n 6) 34.

[174] See sub-s 2.2.4 ('De facto and de jure recognition').

drawal of *de jure* recognition, which is regarded as permanent and definite. Yet the distinction of *de jure* and *de facto* recognition not only is rather applied to governments than States. Additionally, this differentiation is barely used in contemporary international law.[175]

3.4.3 Non-recognition

In principle, to be effective seems to be *the* decisive factor for a situation in order to be recognized. Nevertheless, certain situations were not recognized despite their effectiveness resulting from reservations regarding the legality and morality of the means by which the new situation was brought about.[176] The reason for this is the close relation of non-recognition to the notion of *ex injuria jus non oritur* – that new situations cannot become legal if caused by illegal means.[177] Hence, a situation established by illegal means must not be recognized as legal either.[178] The same holds true for the recognition of States. Reasons not to recognize an entity despite its actual effectiveness are invasion and occupation, illegal use of force, apartheid, the lack of independence, and the denial of self-determination. In such cases, even a duty[179] or an obligation[180] for non-recognition has been posited.
A significant incident with regard to the non-recognition of an illegal situation had been the invasion and occupation of the Chinese region Manchuria by Japan in 1931, which was succeeded by the proclamation of the Japanese 'puppet State' Manchukuo. In two identical notes, the US Secretary of State Henry M Stimson notified China and Japan on 7 January 1932 that the US government 'does not intend to recognize any situation, treaty, or agree-

[175] ibid.

[176] See generally on this, for example O'Brien (n 102) 184-86; Joseph Gabriel Starke, *Introduction to International Law* (Butterworths 1989) 153-56; Shaw (n 63) 468-70.

[177] See ch 1 ('The concept of recognition and the principle of effectiveness').

[178] For a recent expression of this view, see Territorial Integrity of Ukraine, UNGA Res 68/262 (27 March 2014) UN Doc A/RES/68/262, with regard to the events in the Ukraine.

[179] Roland Hall Sharp, 'Duties of Non-Recognition in Practice: 1775-1934' (1934) 5 Geneva Special Studies 1; Roland Hall Sharp, *Nonrecognition as a Legal Duty* (Thone 1934).

[180] Jochen A Frowein, 'Non-Recognition' in Ruediger Wolfrum (ed), *The Max Planck Encyclopedia of Public International Law* (OUP 2012) vol VII, 739-40.

ment which may be brought about by means contrary to the covenants and obligations of the Pact of Paris of August 27, 1928, to which China, Japan and the United States, are all parties.'[181] As a result, the notion of non-recognition of situations brought about by illegal means became known as the Stimson Doctrine.[182] On 11 March 1932, the League of Nations adopted a resolution declaring that

> les Membres de la Société des Nations sont tenus de ne reconnaître aucune situation, aucun Traité et aucun accord qui pourraient être obtenus par des moyens contraires au Pacte de la Société des Nations ou au Pacte de Paris.[183]

The Pact of Paris, also known as the Kellogg-Briand Pact, obligated all parties to the treaty to 'condemn recourse to war' and 'renounce it as an instrument of national policy in their relations with one another.'[184] In addition, the Covenant of the League of Nations imposed on the High Contracting Parties 'obligations not to resort to war'.[185] As a reaction, specifically to the situation in China, the League of Nations recommended that its members do not recognize the regime in Manchuria because 'cette reconnaissance n'étant pas compatibles avec les principes fondamentaux des obligations internationales existantes...'[186] After World War II, the prohi-

[181]The Stimson Note, 7 January 1932 (1932) 26 AJIL 342, 342.

[182]For example Thomas D Grant, 'Doctrines (Monroe, Hallstein, Brezhnev, Stimson)' in Ruediger Wolfrum (ed), *The Max Planck Encyclopedia of Public International Law* (OUP 2012) vol III, 183-84; Jerald A Combs, *The History of American Foreign Policy from 1895* (4th edn, ME Sharpe, Inc 2012) 135-36.

[183]'The members of the League of Nations are required not to recognize any situation, any treaty, and any agreement which had been attained by means running contrary to the Covenant of the League of Nations or to the Pact of Paris.' (my translation) Quatrième séance plénière de l'assemblée [1932] SdN JO Supp Spec 101 87, para 1.

[184]Treaty for the Renunciation of War as an Instrument of National Policy ['Briand-Kellogg Pact'] (signed 27 August 1928, entered into force 24 July 1929) 94 LNTS 57, art 1.

[185]Covenant of the League of Nations (signed 28 April 1919, entered into force 10 January 1920) 13 AJIL Supp 128, Preamble.

[186]This recognition is not compatible with the fundamental principles of existing international obligations... (my translation). Exposé des solutions [1933] SdN JO Supp Spec 112 73, 76.

bition of the use of force, ie aggression,[187] in international relations was resumed in the Charter of the newly founded United Nations Organisation in 1945.[188] This principle has been reaffirmed multiple times,[189] often combined with the demand not to recognize such situations that were brought about by the use of such illegal means. However several cases of violations of this prohibition occurred since the end of World War II. Yet, they were all internationally condemned and remained largely unrecognized. Among the cases of such violations often combined with the annexation and/or occupation of the territory are the occupation of East Jerusalem[190] and the Golan Heights by Israel since 1967,[191] the Turkish acquisition of Northern Cyprus in 1974,[192] the enduring occupation of Namibia by South Africa until 1988,[193] and the invasion and annexation of Kuwait by Iraq in

[187] The definition of aggression is found congruently in Definition of Aggression, UNGA Res 3314 (XXIX) (14 December 1974) UN Doc A/RES/3314(XXIX), Annex, art 5, para 3, and in The Crime of Aggression, ICC Res RC/Res 6 [2010], Annex I, art 8bis, para 2.

[188] UN Charter (n 52) art 2 para 4.

[189] Examples are Declaration on Principles of International Law Concerning Friendly Relations and Co-operation among States in Accordance with the Charter of the United Nations ['Friendly Relations Declaration'], UNGA Res 2625 (XXV) (24 October 1970) UN Doc A/RES/2625(XXV), Principle 11; Charter of the Organization of the American States (signed 30 April 1948, entered into force 13 December 1951) 119 UNTS 3, amended version (1994) 133 ILM 981, art 17; Responsibility of States for Internationally Wrongful Acts, UNGA Res 56/83 (12 December 2001) UN Doc A/Res/56/83, Annex, art 41 para 2. See also Vienna Convention on the Law of Treaties (VCLT) (signed 23 May 1969, entered into force 27 January 1980) 1155 UNTS 331, art 52 with regard to treaties; examples of court decisions confirming this, are *Arbitral Tribunal for Dispute over Inter-Entity Boundary in Brcko Area* (1997) 36 ILM 399, para 77; UNGA Res 43/26A (n 115) para 133.

[190] eg The Status of Jerusalem, UNGA Res 37/123C (16 December 1982) UN Doc A/RES/37/123C; UNSC Res 478 (20 August 1980) UN Doc S/RES/478, para 5.

[191] eg The Situation in the Middle East, UNGA Res 37/123A (16 December 1982) UN Doc A/RES/37/123A, paras 2-5.

[192] eg UNSC Res 541 (18 November 1983) UN Doc S/RES/541, para 7.

[193] UNSC Res 566 (19 June 1983) UN Doc S/RES/566, paras 1-4; UNGA Res 43/26A (n 115) para 18.

1990.[194] Also the recent events in the Ukraine drew international condemnation along with an appeal not to recognize this new situation.[195]
An exception to the rule of the denial of recognition due to illegal use of force, however, appears to be the invasion and annexation of Goa by India in 1961. The conflict between India and Portugal in December 1961 began with India launching an attack on Goa, a Portuguese colony on the West coast of the Indian sub-continent. In several letters between the Indian Prime Minister, the Portuguese Prime Minister, the UN Security Council, and the Secretary-General of the UN, both parties of the conflict explained their respective position.[196] Portugal accused India of having 'committed a premeditated and unprovoked aggression against Portugal in Goa.'[197] India, on the other hand, declared that '[t]he problem of Goa was simply a question of colonialism' and therefore 'India had taken certain measures only to protect the large Indian population in Goa which was in revolt against Portugal.'[198] As a consequence two resolutions considering the situation in Goa were submitted in the Security Council. Brought forward by Ceylon, Liberia, and the United Arab Republic, the first draft resolution took the Indian position and demanded Portugal surrender 'its colonial possessions' in India. Taking Portugal's side, the second draft resolution, which was submitted by France, Turkey, the United Kingdom, and the United States, called upon India to withdraw from Goa and to develop together with Portugal a peaceful solution to the conflict. However, neither of the resolutions was adopted. The first was rejected by a majority of seven to four, the latter although receiving seven votes in favour was not adopted either as one of the negative votes was by the USSR, a permanent member of the UN

[194] eg UNSC Res 662 (9 August 1990) UN Doc S/RES/662, paras 1-2. On all these examples see among many others also Thomas D Grant, 'East Timor, the U.N. System, and Enforcing Non-Recognition in International Law' (2000) 33 Vanderbilt Journal of Transnational Law 273, 280-96; Johan D van der Vyver, 'Statehood in International Law' (1991) 5 EmoryIntlLRev 9, 64-65.
[195] Res 68/262 (n 178).
[196] Questions concerning Goa, Damao and Diu [1961] UNYB 129 129ff.
[197] ibid, 129.
[198] ibid, 130.

Security Council.[199] As a result of the rejection of both resolutions, India continued to integrate Goa into Indian territory. Furthermore, due to the absence of an official reaction by the UN Security Council, the other members of the UN acquiesced or recognized the Indian annexation of Goa. In 1974 Portugal also officially recognized India's sovereignty over Goa and other former Portuguese colonies.[200]
Besides the illegal use of force, apartheid also might cause non-recognition.[201] This was the case with the South African homeland States[202] and Southern Rhodesia.[203] Additional reasons for non-recognition are the lack of independence,[204] like in the case of Manchukuo, and the denial of self-determination,[205] which often comes along with foreign occupation, as was the case with the Turkish Republic of Northern Cyprus.[206] But, as the example of Goa has shown, the UN has occasionally recognized such situations despite the prohibition of recognition of situations brought about by illegal means.[207] This might be the result of a kind of opportunism; where the recognition of a new, yet illegal situation, appeared to be beneficial in some way.[208]

---

[199] Questions concerning Goa, Damao and Diu (n 196) 131.

[200] Treaty between the Government of India and the Government of the Republic of Portugal on Recognition of India's Sovereignty over Goa, Daman, Diu, Dadra and Nagar Haveli and Related Matters (signed 31 December 1974) INTSer 53, art 1.

[201] International Convention on the Suppression and Punishment of the Crime of Apartheid, UNGA Res 3068 (XXVIII) (30 November 1973) UN Doc A/RES/3068; on apartheid as a reason for non-recognition, see also Grant, 'East Timor' (n 194) 280-89; Vyver (n 194) 65.

[202] The so-called Independent Transkei and Other Bantustans, UNGA Res 31/6A (26 October 1976) UN Doc A/RES/31/6A, para 3.

[203] UNSC Res 216 (12 November 1965) UN Doc S/RES/216; UNSC Res 217 (20 November 1965) UN Doc S/RES/217; UNSC Res 277 (18 March 1970) UN Doc S/RES/277; UNSC Res 288 (17 November 1970) UN Doc S/RES/288.

[204] Frowein, 'Non-Recognition' (n 180) 739.

[205] cf also Vyver (n 194) 65.

[206] UNSC Res 541 (n 192) para 7.

[207] Quincy Wright, 'The Goa Incident' (1962) 56 AJIL 617, 631-32. Another example is the recognition of certain occupied territories by Israel beyond that assigned in UN resolutions of 1947.

[208] ibid, 631-32.

The existence of a State is, in principle, independent of recognition by other States provided the legality of its creation. Hence, regardless of its non-recognition, such an entity for which the term 'de facto regime'[209] has been proposed can assume at least some basic rights including 'to defend its integrity and independence, to provide for its conservation and prosperity, and consequently to organize itself as it sees fit, to legislate upon its interests, administer its services, and to define the jurisdiction and competence of its courts.'[210] In addition, an unrecognized State is bound to fulfil some basic duties, in particular, to refrain from the threat and use of force.[211] The notion that the rule of abstention from aggression applies equally to non-recognized States is expressed in the Definition of Aggression by the UN stating that the term 'State' refers 'without prejudice to questions of recognition or to whether a State is a member of the United Nations'.[212]
Nevertheless, non-recognition of statehood has consequences on both the international and the domestic level. On the international level, a non-recognized State experiences a certain degree of isolation. Generally, it struggles to claim its rights while other States have difficulty to prompt it to perform its international duties, irrespective of the existence of these rights and duties.[213] Furthermore, the entity is not able to access international organizations such as the UN[214] or to appear as plaintiff or defendant before the International Court of Justice,[215] both of which are restricted to (recognized) States. Also, only agreements between two or more (recognized) States fall within the scope of the Vienna Convention of the Law of

[209] Jochen A Frowein, *Das de facto-Regime im Völkerrecht: Eine Untersuchung zur Rechtsstellung 'nichtanerkannter Staaten' und ähnlicher Gebilde* (Carl Heymanns Verlag 1968); Jochen A Frowein, 'De Facto Regime' in Ruediger Wolfrum (ed), *The Max Planck Encyclopedia of Public International Law* (Oxford 2012) vol II.

[210] Montevideo-Convention (n 40) art 3.

[211] Friendly Relations Declaration (n 189); see also Frowein, 'De Facto Regime' (n 209) 1053.

[212] Definition of Aggression (n 187) art 1; Frowein, 'De Facto Regime' (n 209) 1053.

[213] Shaw (n 63) 471.

[214] UN Charter (n 52) art 4 para 1.

[215] Statute of the International Court of Justice (signed 26 June 1945, entered into force 24 October 1945) 33 UNTS 993, art 34 para 1.

Treaties.[216] Although not creating or preventing the existence of a State or having an effect on the entity's basic rights and duties in international law, recognition and non-recognition are decisive with regard to the bilateral relations of an entity to one or more States. A State, which does not recognize an entity as a State, does not usually maintain official relations with it either. Nevertheless, States that have signed a multilateral treaty are entitled to assume that entities, which they have not recognized but that have also signed the agreement are bound by it just the same.[217]

Consequences of non-recognition also appear on the domestic level. The executive has principal responsibility over foreign affairs including the decision to recognize a State or a government. The domestic courts, then, are bound to follow the executive's decision.[218] If the executive has not recognized a certain situation, the courts are obliged to treat the situation in question correspondingly,[219] that is, to treat the non-recognized entity and its acts as a legal nullity.[220] Considering non-recognized entities as non-existent has been referred to as the 'no recognition, no existence'-principle.[221] It is assumed that this principle applies equally to both non-recognized governments and non-recognized States.[222] As stated by the Draft Articles of State Responsibility, an act of a State organ – the executive, the legislative or the judiciary – is considered an act of the respective State.[223] Hence, the act of an organ of a non-recognized State might accordingly be regarded as act of this State, and therefore null and void. As a rule, States have no obligation to give effect to any extra-territorial con-

[216] VCLT (n 189) arts 1 and 3.

[217] Shaw (n 63) 471.

[218] Shaw (n 63) 471; Sauveplanne (n 36) 18.

[219] Shaw (n 63) 471; Sauveplanne (n 36) 18.

[220] Lauterpacht, *States* (n 3) 147.

[221] See Cannon (n 146) 13.

[222] See ibid, 12.

[223] International Law Commission, 'Draft Articles on Responsibility of States for Internationally Wrongful Acts' in Report of the International Law Commission on the Work of its 53rd Session (10 August 2001) UN Doc A/56/10, art 4 para 1.

sequences of acts by other States.[224] An entity not being recognized is in far less of a position to demand immunity before domestic courts, to get recognition of executive and judicial acts for purposes of conflict of laws, or to appear as claimant before court.[225] In this respect, recognition appears to have a constitutive quality because the act of recognition creates legal effects within a domestic jurisdiction.[226] Once the executive recognizes the entity the courts are required to act in accordance.[227]

In the UK, the decision whether an entity shall be recognized or not depends upon the Foreign Office.[228] The courts are traditionally obliged to follow and to give effect to the decision of the UK Government, and if necessary treat non-recognized entities as non-existent.[229] The reason for this is that the 'State cannot speak with two voices'[230] (*one voice-maxim*)[231] and 'the recognition of a foreign state or government is a matter of foreign policy on which the executive is in a markedly superior position to form a judgment.'[232] The consequence of the strict application of 'no recognition no existence'-principle, however, might result in 'much hardship and inconvenience at a private level.'[233] In *Adams v Adams* (1970) owing to the non-recognition of the Smith government, the English High Court refused to recognize a divorce decree issued by the High Court of unrecognized Southern Rhodesia. As a result of this refusal one of the parties was un-

---

[224]Gerhard Erasmus, 'The Non-recognition of South Africa's Homelands: The Effect of National Policies' in *Festschrift für Wolfgang Zeidler* (de Gruyter 1987) vol 2, 1922.

[225]Ian Brownlie, *Principles of Public International Law* (7th edn, Clarendon Press 2008) 95-96.

[226]Shaw (n 63) 471; Brownlie, however, stresses not to generalize and use these municipal cases as evidence of the constitutivist position. See Brownlie, *Principles of Public International Law* (n 225) 96.

[227]Sauveplanne (n 36) 18.

[228]O'Brien (n 102) 188-89.

[229]*City of Berne v Bank of England* (1804) 32 ER 636 ; *AM Luther Co v James Sagor & Co* (1921) 1 KB 456 ; also Shaw (n 63) 472.

[230]*Government of the Republic of Spain v SS 'Arantzazu Mendi'* (n 145) 264; later also repeated in *Gur Corporation v Trust Bank of Africa Ltd* [1987] QB 599 , 604.

[231]Cannon (n 146) 13 and 16.

[232]*Gur Corporation v Trust Bank of Africa Ltd* (n 230) 604.

[233]Cannon (n 146) 13.

able to remarry.[234] Beginning in the 1960s a rethinking in this matter occurred and two exceptions evolved. In 1966, a first kind of exception, the 'delegated authorities exception',[235] was expressed in *Carl Zeiss Stiftung v Keeler Ltd (No. 2)*.[236] The Court reached the decision that acts of the GDR, which was not recognized by the UK, could be given effect because the authority to perform them was lawfully delegated by the USSR, the *de jure* authority over East Germany. A similar conclusion was reached in *Gur Corporation v Trust Bank of Africa* (1986) with regard to the delegation of legislative powers by South Africa to the Republic of Ciskei.[237] The other kind of exception has been described as the 'private acts exception'.[238] Also in *Carl Zeiss Stiftung v Keeler Ltd (No. 2)*, Lord Wilberforce submitted in his obiter dictum

> that where private rights, or acts of everyday occurrence, or perfunctory acts of administration are concerned (the scope of these exceptions has never been precisely defined) the courts may, in the interests of justice and common sense, where no consideration of public policy to the contrary has to prevail, give recognition to the actual facts or realities found to exist in the territory in question.[239]

Likewise in *Hesperides Hotels Ltd and another v Aegean Turkish Holidays Ltd and another* (1977) the English Court of Appeal held that in spite of non-recognition of certain entities, their acts and laws should be recognized if they concern 'the day to day affairs of the people, such as their marriages, their divorces, their leases, their occupations and so forth'.[240] In addition,

---

[234] *Adams v Adams* [1971] P 188 .

[235] Cannon (n 146) 16.

[236] *Carl Zeiss Stiftung vs Keeler Ltd (No 2)* [1967] AC 853 ; see on this also Brownlie, *Principles of Public International Law* (n 225) 99; Shaw (n 63) 477.

[237] *Gur Corporation v Trust Bank of Africa Ltd* (n 230); also Brownlie, *Principles of Public International Law* (n 225) 100-1; Shaw (n 63) 480.

[238] Cannon (n 146) 16.

[239] *Carl Zeiss Stiftung vs Keeler Ltd (No 2)* (n 236) 954; also cited in Cannon (n 146) 12.

[240] *Hesperides Hotels Ltd and another v Aegean Turkish Holidays Ltd and another* (1978) 1 All ER 277 , 286.

a similar view was expressed in the advisory opinion of the ICJ concerning the continued illegal presence of South Africa in Namibia that 'while official acts performed by the Government of South Africa on behalf of or concerning Namibia after the termination of the Mandate are illegal and invalid, this invalidity cannot be extended to those acts, such as, for instance, the registration of births, deaths and marriages, the effects of which can be ignored only to the detriment of the inhabitants of the Territory.'[241] The 1991 Foreign Corporations Act implemented that issues regarding foreign corporations registered in the territory of an unrecognized entity should be treated 'as if that territory were a recognised State'.[242] With regard to divorce decrees by courts of a non-recognized State, the UK judiciary in *Emin v Yeldag* (2001) abandoned the traditional view[243] and accepted a divorce obtained by a court of the TRNC, despite the non-recognition of the TRNC by the UK.[244] For all that, the general submission of the UK judiciary to the executive and legislative regarding decisions of recognition and non-recognition and hence, the fact that the above described cases are exceptions to the 'no recognition no existence'-principle has been confirmed repeatedly.[245]

In the US, the situation with respect to the separation of powers between the executive and the judiciary regarding recognition is similar to the UK. The decision lies within the competence of the executive and is binding for the judiciary.[246] As a general rule, non-recognized entities are denied access to courts,[247] and their decrees are not examined.[248] There are never-

[241] *Legal Consequences for States of the Continued Presence of South Africa in Namibia (South West Africa) notwithstanding Security Council Resolution 276 (1970)* (Advisory Opinion) [1971] ICJ Rep 16, para 125.

[242] Foreign Corporations Act 1991, s 1.

[243] As expressed in *Adams v Adams* (n 234).

[244] *Emin v Yeldag* (2002) 1 FLR 956 ; also Cannon (n 146) 15; Shaw (n 63) 479.

[245] For example *R (on the application of Kibris Turk Hava Yollari) v Secretary of State for Transport* [2009] EWHC 1918 (Admin) para 244.

[246] For example *Republic of Vietnam v Pfizer, Inc* 556 F2d 892 (CAMinn 1977).

[247] Restatement (Third) The Foreign Relations Law of the United States §205 ; *Republic of Vietnam v Pfizer, Inc* (n 246); *Federal Republic of Germany v Elicofon* 358 FSupp 747 (DCNY 1972); *National Oil Corp v Libyan Sun Oil Co* 733 FSupp 800 (DDel 1990).

[248] *Latvian State Cargo & Passenger SS Line v McGrath* 188 F2d 1000 (CACD 1951).

theless exceptions to the strict application of this denial. If non-recognized entity's access to a court appears to be in the US' national interest, then the entity might be admitted despite the non-recognition upon the suggestion of the executive.[249] The law and acts of unrecognized entities will usually be given effect only as far as they relate to 'private, local and domestic affairs',[250] such as birth, death, or land transfers.[251] For a long time, the matter of access of non-recognized entities to court was affected by the refusal of the US to recognize the USSR from 1922-1933.[252] But already then the courts chose a pragmatic approach by examining questions relating to non-recognition matters on a case-by-case basis and being 'indulgent if a favourable decision was not at variance with the executive certificate, the interests of justice or the fundamental principles of the constitution.'[253] Still, in the event that the US government indicates that the admission of the non-recognized entity conflicts with US national interests, the courts comply.[254] But even recognition of an entity does not necessarily result in the US courts giving effect to its acts. Giving extraterritorial effect to for-

[249] *Transportes Aereos de Angola v Ronair, Inc* 544 FSupp 858 (DCDel 1982); *National Petrochemical Co of Iran v The M/T Stolt Sheaf* 860 F2d 551 (CA2 (NY) 1988); *Ministry of Defense of the Islamic Republic of Iran v Gould, Inc No CV 87-03673-RG* 82 AJIL 591 (CD Cal 1988); in general Interests of United States in Pending Suits 28 USC §517.

[250] *Carl Zeiss Stiftung v V E B Carl Zeiss, Jena* 293 F Supp 892, 900 (DCNY 1968); Restatement (Third) The Foreign Relations Law of the United States §205 (n 247) reporter's notes 3; also on this Crawford, *Brownlie's Principles of Public International Law* (n 102) 162.

[251] *Carl Zeiss Stiftung v V E B Carl Zeiss, Jena* (n 250) 900; cf *Hesperides Hotels Ltd and another v Aegean Turkish Holidays Ltd and another* (n 240); *Legal Consequences for States of the Continued Presence of South Africa in Namibia (South West Africa) notwithstanding Security Council Resolution 276 (1970)* (n 241) para 125.

[252] Crawford, *Brownlie's Principles of Public International Law* (n 102) 160.

[253] eg *Sokoloff v National City Bank of NY* 239 NY 158, 166 (NY 1924); see also O'Brien (n 102) 198.

[254] *The Maret* 145 F2d 431 (CA3 1944); *Latvian State Cargo & Passenger SS Line v McGrath* (n 248); *Estonian State Cargo & Passenger SS Line v US* 116 FSupp 447 (CtCl 1953); see also O'Brien (n 102) 198.

eign acts and laws is a part of the comity among States.[255] Yet, the principle upon which US courts decide whether to give or deny effect to foreign acts is public policy.[256] In the event of a conflict between comity and public policy, the latter has to prevail.[257] It follows that provided a foreign act of a recognized State contrasts with US public policy, the courts refuse to give effect to this act.[258] Another important aspect the courts consider is the importance of the issue of non-recognition regarding the matter at hand. Thus, where non-recognition is 'incidental or simply raised as a doubtful defence', for example in order 'to avoid a normal commercial obligation', the courts might admit the unrecognized entity anyway.[259] In contrast, US courts do not accept a new entity created by an unrecognized State for the sole purpose of overcoming the procedural obstacle. Doing so would undermine the authority of the executive in matters of foreign policy.[260]

In civil law countries, such as Switzerland and Germany, the admission of acts and decrees of non-recognized entities is handled more leniently. In Switzerland, it is also the executive that decides upon recognition and non-recognition.[261] With regard to the application of foreign acts and law, how-

[255] Defined as 'reciprocal courtesy which one member of the family of nations owes to the others.' *Russian Socialist Federated Soviet Republic v Cibrario* 235 NY 255, 669 (NY 1923); see also *Huntington v Attrill* 146 US 657, 669 (US 1923).

[256] *Russian Reinsurance Co v Stoddard* 240 NY 149 (NY 1925); *Russian Socialist Federated Soviet Republic v Cibrario* (n 255).

[257] *Russian Socialist Federated Soviet Republic v Cibrario* (n 255) 263.

[258] *Russian Socialist Federated Soviet Republic v Cibrario* (n 255) 263; *Vladikavkazsky Railway Co v New York Trust Co* 263 NY 369 (NY 1934).

[259] O'Brien (n 102) 198-99.

[260] *Federal Republic of Germany v Elicofon* (n 247); also O'Brien (n 102) 199; Shaw (n 63) 484.

[261] The federal constitution of 1848 assigned in art 74 para 4 the right of recognition of States to the Swiss parliament ('Federal Assembly'). In the revision of 1874, this right was transferred to the executive, the Federal Council. This is concluded from the disappearance of this right from art 85 corresponding to the previous art 74. (Joerg Paul Müller and Luzius Wildhaber, *Praxis des Völkerrechts* (2nd edn, Stämpfli 1982) 157). Also in the latest version of the constitution (1999), the right to recognize entities as States is no longer expressly stated in the part listing the parliamentary powers (arts 163-173). Still, art 166 para 1 requires the parliament after all to 'participate in shaping foreign policy and supervise the maintenance of foreign relations.'

ever, the effectiveness of this law is most relevant, whereas it is subsidiary whether the foreign entity is recognized by Switzerland.[262] The recognition of a foreign act is, however, restricted if manifestly incompatible with Swiss public order.[263] Also in Germany, the executive is responsible together with the legislative for the foreign policy and therewith for the recognition of States.[264] The judiciary does not get involved with recognition.[265] The application by the German judiciary of acts and decrees of non-recognized States and governments is, however, independent of their recognition or the legitimacy of their creation; decisive is merely the effectiveness of the law in the respective territory.[266] Thus, besides judicial decision practice and customary law, also religious law and tribal law might be applicable.[267] This is even true for the law of an occupying power in an occupied territory. In case the occupying territory legislated in an illegal manner, partic-

---

[262] Rulings: BGE 50 II 507, 512; BGE 91 II 117, 126ff; BGE 93 I 265, 269; Doctrine: Ivo Schwander, *Einführung in das internationale Privatrecht – Erster Band: Allgemeiner Teil* (Dike 2000) 189, MN 401; Anton K Schnyder and Manuel Liatowitsch, *Internationales Privat- und Zivilverfahrensrecht* (Schulthess 2011) 87, MN 242.

[263] IPRG, art 27 para 1.

[264] According to art 59 para 1 of the Basic Law (*Grundgesetz, GG*), the Federal President is in charge of recognition of States. He may delegate this task to another State organ, as in the case of the recognition of Malta. The practice, however, shows the opposite. There are several cases of State recognition by Germany that have been awarded by members of the executive other than the president. Examples are the recognition of Madagascar in 1960 by the chancellor and the recognition of Federal Republic of Yugoslavia (today Serbia and Montenegro) in 1996 by the German Cabinet (Michael Schweitzer, *Staatsrecht, Völkerrecht, Europarecht* (10th edn, CF Müller 2010) 111-12, MN 303-4).

[265] IPRspr 1956-1957, no 202.

[266] Rulings: RGst 55, 81, 81-82; IPRspr 1932, no 21; IPRspr 1956-1957, no 202 (n 265); BayOblGZ 1961, 305, 313; IPRspr 1966-1967, no 14, 51. Doctrine: Gerhard Kegel and Klaus Schurig, *Internationales Privatrecht: Ein Studienbuch* (9th edn, CH Beck 2004) 20-21; Hans Juergen Sonnenberger, 'Einführungsgesetz zum Bürgerlichen Gesetzbuche (Art. 1-46), Internationales Privatrecht' in *Münchener Kommentar zum Bürgerlichen Gesetzbuch* (4th edn, CH Beck 2006) vol 10, 62, MN 118; Fritz Sturm and Gudrun Sturm, 'J. von Staudingers Kommentar zum Bürgerlichen Gesetzbuch: Mit Einführungsgesetz und Nebengesetzen' in Julius von Staudinger (ed) (Sellier-de Gruyter 2003) 187, MN 436-37.

[267] Sonnenberger (n 266) 62, MN 118.

ularly beyond the set boundaries of Article 43 of the Hague regulations,[268] the German judiciary has to decide whether to apply illegal but effective law of the occupying power or legal but ineffective law of the occupied State.[269] Above all, the judiciary ought to consider the interest of the people living in the occupied territory and have to accommodate their private matters according to the illegally established law.[270] Like in Switzerland, the application of foreign acts and decrees is generally ruled out in case it is adverse to the German public order, in particular if it is not compatible with fundamental rights.[271]

---

[268] Convention (IV) Respecting the Laws and Customs of War on Land and its Annex: Regulation concerning the Laws and Customs of War on Land (signed 18 October 1907, entered into force 26 January 1910) 187 CTS 227.

[269] Christian von Bar and Peter Mankowski, *Internationales Privatrecht* (CH Beck 2003) vol 2, 128-29, MN 31.

[270] Bar and Mankowski (n 269) vol 2, 128-29, MN 31; Jan Kropholler, *Internationales Privatrecht: Einschliesslich der Grundbegriffe des internationalen Zivilverfahrensrecht* (6th edn, Mohr Siebeck 2006) 55.

[271] ZPO §328 I para 4; BayOblGZ (n 266) 313.

4 Cases of State Recognition since the End of the Cold War

After having considered the contemporary doctrine, the following chapter addresses the State practice by examining some prominent examples of State recognition that took place in the first two decades of the post-Cold War era. It is furthermore the aim to assess the extent to which State practice and doctrine correspond. At this, a particular focus is laid on the requirements for recognition.

4.1 The former republics of the USSR and the Baltics

In the course of the dissolution of the USSR in the early 1990s, the Baltic States were the first to claim independence. Because Lithuania, Latvia, and Estonia were occupied and incorporated by the USSR in World War II, they never actually perceived themselves as Soviet republics.[272]

Lithuania had been the first of the three to make an attempt towards independence. The pursuit of independence intensified after the victory of the candidates of the Sajudis movement, gaining a majority for the Lithuanian Supreme Soviet on 24 February 1990.[273] Upon this development, the Lithuanian Supreme Soviet proclaimed its independence on 11 March 1991, referring to Article 72 of the constitution of the Soviet Union of 1977 giving the right to all its republics to secede from the union.[274] The USSR government not only refused Lithuanian's independence, even more, it threatened to invade Lithuania in order to protect the interests of the USSR in the Baltic republic.[275] Regardless of numerous threats, economic sanctions, and even military manoeuvres within Lithuania by the USSR, the Lithuanian Supreme Soviet adhered to its position and demanded negotiations.It emphasized that Lithuania was not and had never been a part of

[272] AdG, vol 10, 4580, 4584 and 4632.
[273] AdG, vol 60, 34319.
[274] AdG, vol 60, 34320.
[275] AdG, vol 60, 34320-21 and 344404-6.

the USSR, and thus that the proclamation of independence was fully valid and would not be revoked.[276]

Whilst the US and the EC member States expressed their concerns and repeatedly called for peaceful negotiations between Moscow and Vilnius, no State at this point was willing to side with Lithuania.[277] This cautious approach had two reasons. First, the USSR, even if weakened, was still a powerful actor in international relations with a huge arsenal of weaponry; of particular concern was its nuclear weaponry. Thus, any action that could be interpreted as a provocation leading to disintegration of the Union was to be prevented. Second, the western States were overall content with Gorbachev's initiated reform processes. Whereas these reforms were already under severe attack from hardliners within the Communist Party of the Soviet Union (CSPU), the western States did not want to add extra external pressure on the Soviet leader.[278]

The tensions between the USSR and the Baltic republics increased after their decision not to take part in the new union treaty.[279] Its purpose was to preserve the Soviet Union by converting it from a union in to a slightly looser federation of States.[280] Subsequently, the Baltics, together with Armenia, Georgia, and Moldova, boycotted a referendum on the new union treaty, held on the 17 March 1991.[281] Still, of the approximately 186 million voters[282] almost 77 per cent approved of the new union.[283] The three Baltic States for their part decided instead to hold referenda on their respective independence on the 9 February (Lithuania) and 3 March 1991

[276] AdG, vol 60, 34406.

[277] AdG, vol 60, 34407; James Baker, 'Imperatives of Economic Reform: Changes in Soviet and East European Economies, 18 April 1990' (1990) 1(1) US Department of State Dispatch; George Bush, 'The President's News Conference, 22 March 1990' The American Presidency Project (Gerhard Peters and John T Woolley eds ⟨http://www.presidency.ucsb.edu/ws/?pid=18284⟩ accessed 2 February 2014.

[278] Fabry (n 8) 182.

[279] AdG, vol 60, 34894.

[280] AdG, vol 61, 35198.

[281] AdG, vol 61, 35444.

[282] In the RSFSR, Ukrainian SSR, Belorussian SSR, Uzbek SSR, Kazak SSR, Azerbaijan SSR, Kirgiz SSR, Tajik SSR and Turkmen SSR.

[283] AdG, vol 61, 35444.

(Latvia and Estonia).[284] The EC welcomed this decision to hold referenda on Baltic independence.[285] Initially, though, the EC and its member States were reluctant to get involved in the issue of self-determination of the Baltic States, except from calling on the USSR to refrain from violence and to enter into negotiations with the Baltic peoples in order to solve the conflict peacefully.[286] Nevertheless, the EC, as well as the US,[287] emphasized that ten out of twelve member States had never recognized the incorporation of the Baltics into the Soviet Union.[288]In all three referenda, over 80 per cent of eligible citizens voted, and of the voters between 73 and 90 per cent were in favour of independence.[289]

The crucial event for Baltic independence was the attempted coup d'état in the USSR in August 1991. On 19 August 1991, one day before the scheduled signing of the new union treaty, a group of CPSU-members attempted to take over and to disempower President Gorbachev.[290] After Lithuania already declared the restoration of independence on 11 March 1991, Estonia and Latvia, too, took the opportunity and announced their independence from the USSR.[291] Shortly after, several individual States, such as

[284]Prior to the Lithuanian referendum, Gorbachev declared these referenda illegal and their result void (AdG, vol 61, 35324).

[285]'Statement concerning the Baltic States, Doc No 91/044, Luxembourg' (1991) 7 EPC Bull 101.

[286]'Statement concerning in the Baltic Republics Doc No 91/008, Luxembourg' (1991) 7 EPC Bull 54; 'Statement by an Extraordinary EPC Ministerial Meeting concerning the Baltic States Doc No 91/010, Luxembourg' (1991) 7 EPC Bull 55.

[287]Baker (n 277); Bush (n 277).

[288]Statement concerning the situation in the Baltic States, Doc No. 91/020, Luxembourg, 21 January 1991, in 7 EPC Bulletin, 62, 63. When establishing diplomatic relations with the USSR, the Netherlands in 1942 and Spain in 1977 recognized the occupation at least implicitly by not adding reservations regarding the annexation.(Lauri Mälksoo, *Illegal Annexation and State Continuity – The Case of the Incorporation of the Baltic States by the UDSSR: A Study of the Tension between Normativity and Power in International Law* (Martinus Nijhoff 2003) 53, Fn 27).

[289]AdG, vol 61, 35325 and 35445. The first country to recognize Lithuania's independence was Island on 12 February 1991. As a result, the USSR recalled its ambassador from Reykjavik accusing Island to interfere in USSR internal affairs. (AdG, vol 61, 35325).

[290]AdG, vol 61, 35959-66.

[291]AdG, vol 61, 36010-12.

Hungary, Denmark, Bulgaria, and Malta as well as the RSFSR, recognized the re-established independence of the Baltics.[292] And only a few days later, the EC and its member States issued a statement that they 'warmly welcome the restoration of the sovereignty and independence of the Baltic States which they lost in 1940... Therefore the Community and its Member States confirm their decision to establish diplomatic relations with the Baltic States without delay.'[293] In a similar fashion, the US declared its preparedness 'immediately to establish diplomatic relations', after having always supported the Baltic independence.[294] Eventually, on 6 September 1991, the USSR, too, recognized the Baltic independence despite its earlier refusal. On 17 September 1991, Estonia, Latvia, and Lithuania became members of the UN.[295]

It has to be noted that the (renewed) recognition of the independence of the Baltic States by a majority of third States took place without much delay after the respective declaration. The emphasis is striking which was laid on the point that the other States never recognized the annexation by the USSR – this refusal being in accordance with the *non oritur* principle, and thus within the meaning of the Stimson doctrine – and thus never perceived the Baltic States as Soviet republics. Rather, these announcements were reassurances of recognition of Baltic sovereignty and independence and re-establishments of diplomatic relations instead of actual declarations of recognition. In this way, the Baltic States are special cases of former Soviet republics, insofar as their continual and unyielding objection to being treated as if they were part of the USSR.

Following the attempted coup d'état in August 1991, most other Soviet republics seized the moment and declared themselves independent from

---

[292] AdG, vol 61, 36010-12

[293] 'Statement by an Extraordinary EPC Ministerial Meeting concerning the Baltic States, The Hague' (1991) 7 EPC Bull 388.

[294] 'US to Establish Diplomatic Relations With Baltic States, 2 September 1991' (1991) 2(35) US Department of State Dispatch.

[295] UNGA Res 46/4 (17 September 1991) UN Doc A/RES/46/4; UNGA Res 46/5 (17 September 1991) UN Doc A/RES/46/5; UNGA Res 46/6 (17 September 1991) UN Doc A/RES/46/6.

the USSR,[296] some of these declarations were later confirmed in public referenda.[297] Georgia and the Ukraine, however, had expressed their demand for independence even earlier. Georgia proclaimed the restoration of its independence on 9 April 1991, following a referendum with over 98 per cent affirmative turnout.[298] The Ukrainian Soviet Socialist Republic (SSR) also announced its independence on 16 July 1990.[299] Together with a name change to 'Ukraine', this was brought into being on 24 August 1991, but was pending approval in a referendum on 1 December 1991.[300] The EC member States and the US promptly welcomed the outcome of the referendum.[301] Additionally, the US emphasized its expectations for Ukrainian adherence to democratic values and human rights, including minority rights, as well as respect for international obligations, the respect of borders and the adherence to the norms of the Helsinki Final Act, the Charter of Paris, and other CSCE documents. Additionally, the US demanded that the Ukraine commit itself to the goal of achieving 'non-nuclear status' and 'to ensure responsible security policies' including 'responsible, and reliable control of nuclear weapons; to prevent proliferation of dangerous military-related technology; and to support implementation of relevant international agreements, including START (Strategic Arms Reduction Treaty) the Conventional Armed Forces in Europe Treaty, the Non-Proliferation Treaty, and the Biological Weapons Convention. Besides, the Ukraine had to commit itself to economic policies aiming to facilitate free markets and free trade and to assume a share of the Soviet

[296] Azerbaijan (30 August 1991), Armenia (30 August 1991), Belarus (25 August 1991), Moldova (27 August 1991), Kirgizstan (31 August 1991), Kazakhstan (30 August 1991), Turkmenistan (26 October 1991), Tajikistan (9 September 1991), Uzbekistan (31 August 1991).

[297] eg in Armenia, Turkmenistan, and Uzbekistan (AdG, vol 61, 36355-57).

[298] AdG, vol 61, 36355.

[299] AdG, vol 61, 34893.

[300] AdG, vol 61, 35357.

[301] 'Statement by an EPC Ministerial Meeting concerning Ukraine, Doc No 91/427, Brussels/The Hague' (1991) 7 EPC Bull 719; 'Ukrainians Vote for Independence, 2 December 1991' (1991) 2(49) US Department of State Dispatch .

Union's debt.[302] The intent to respect the independence and sovereignty of the Ukraine was later reaffirmed by the US, Russia and the UK in the Budapest-Memorandum signed at the 1994 Budapest Summit.[303] In exchange for this, the Ukraine had to commit to abandon its nuclear arsenal and to become party of the Non-Proliferation Treaty.[304]
In response to these developments, the US defined five principles to base on its policy 'toward the Soviet future'.[305] These principles included (a) self-determination – for the people of the USSR to determine their future in a democratic and peaceful manner consistent with principles of the Helsinki Act while threats, intimidation, coercion, or violence were to be excluded; (b) respect of internal and external borders; (c) democracy, particularly elections, and the rule of law; (d) human rights based on the protection of the individual and including the rights of minorities and (e) respect for international law and obligations with a special emphasis on the Helsinki Final Act and the Charter of Paris.[306] With regard to the Baltics, the US underlined that the US perceives them as special cases because the US never recognized their annexation by the USSR and, therefore, were never seen as Soviet Republics.[307] However, these principles were not explicit recognition criteria, as the republics had not 'declared yet with finality constitutional independence from the Soviet Union'.[308] Neither did Baker use the term 'recognition' in this context. These criteria could nonetheless be seen

[302] Ukrainians Vote for Independence (n 301).

[303] Memorandum on Security Assurances in Connection with Ukraine's Accession to the Treaty on the Non-proliferation of Nuclear Weapons ['Budapest Memorandum'] (19 December 1994) UN Doc A/49/765-S/1994/1399 Annex I.

[304] During the 2014 Ukrainian crisis, however, allegations were raised that recent Russian actions undermined the Budapest Memorandum. See, for example, Ban Ki-moon, 'Secretary-General's Remarks at the Opening Session of the Nuclear Security Summit (The Hague, The Netherlands, 24 March 2014)' (24 March 2014) ⟨www.un.org/sg/statements/index.asp?nid=7540⟩ accessed 1 February 2015.

[305] 'US Approach to Changes in the Soviet Union, 4 September 1991' (1991) 2(36) US Department of State Dispatch .

[306] ibid.

[307] ibid.

[308] Fabry (n 8) 184.

as 'indication of American preferences' which only became prerequisites for recognition once the republic was dissolved.[309]
Confronted with the gradual dissolution of the USSR, as well as with the independence efforts of Slovenia and Croatia,[310] EC members took action and agreed on a common position by adopting the Declaration on the Guidelines on the Recognition of New States in Eastern Europe and in the Soviet Union.[311] Unlike the US at an earlier stage, the EC and its member States addressed explicitly the issue of recognition. By underlining their own attachment to the Helsinki Final Act and the Charter of Paris, and particularly the principle of self-determination, they demanded the former USSR republics to commit themselves to the following points in order to be recognized as States: respect for the provisions of the Charter of the United Nations and the commitments subscribed to in the Final Act of Helsinki and in the Charter of Paris, especially with regard to the rule of law, democracy and human rights; guarantees for the rights of ethnic and national groups and minorities in accordance with the commitments subscribed to in the framework of the CSCE; respect for the inviolability of all frontiers, which can only be changed by peaceful means and common agreement; acceptance of all relevant commitments regarding disarmament and nuclear non-proliferation as well as security and regional stability; and commitment to settle by agreement, including where appropriate by recourse to arbitration, all questions concerning State succession and regional disputes.[312] Furthermore, it was emphasized that no entity resulting from aggression would be recognized.[313] On the same day, the US stated that 'the West should stick to fundamentals and support those who put into practice our principles and values.'[314]

[309] ibid, 184-85.
[310] See s 3.2 ('The former republics of the Socialist Federal Republic of Yugoslavia').
[311] Guidelines on Recognition (n 67).
[312] ibid 1487.
[313] ibid, 1487.
[314] 'America and the Collapse of the Soviet Empire: What has to Be Done, 12 December 1991' (1991) 2(50) US Department of State Dispatch.

On 21 December, the representatives of 11 former USSR republics[315] met in Alma Ata, Kazakhstan, to found the Commonwealth of Independent States (CIS) and to officially dissolve the USSR. The Baltic States, having never considered themselves part of the USSR, did not participate. Georgia did not take part officially, but instead sent an observer.[316] The EC and its member States welcomed the formation of the CIS. In addition, they recognized Russia as the legal successor of the former USSR and expressed their readiness to recognize the other republics of the CIS upon reception of assurances of their readiness to fulfil the requirements contained in the Guidelines.[317] Special emphasis was placed on the ratification and complete implementation of the Conventional Forces in Europe Treaty (CFE) and the assurance of single control over nuclear weapons and their non-proliferation. It was only a few days later, that the EC received assurances from the majority of the former USSR republics, with the only exceptions being Kyrgyzstan and Tajikistan. The EC also reiterated its willingness to recognize the other republics once similar assurances have been received.[318] Eventually, on 23 March 1991, the EC agreed to recognize Georgia upon the fulfilment of all requirements, noting that now all the republics have assured their commitment to the Guidelines.[319] The majority of newly recognized States, ie Armenia,[320] Azerbaijan,[321] Kaza-

[315] Azerbaijan, Armenia, Belarus, Kazakhstan, Kirgizstan, Moldavia, RSFSR, Tajikistan, Turkmenistan, Ukraine, and Uzbekistan.

[316] AdG, vol 61, 36353.

[317] 'Statement concerning the Future Status of Russia and Other Former Soviet Republics, Doc No 91/469, Brussels/The Hague' (1991) 7 EPC Bull 772.

[318] 'Statement concerning the Recognition of Former Soviet Republics, Doc No 91 /472, Brussels/ The Hague' (1991) 7 EPC Bull 773.

[319] 'Statement on the Recognition of the Republic of Georgia, Doc No 92/109, Brussels/ Lisbon' (1992) 8 EPC Bull 164.

[320] Admission of the Republic of Armenia to Membership in the United Nations, UNGA Res 46/227 (2 March 1992) UN Doc A/RES/46/227.

[321] Admission of the Azerbaijan Republic to Membership in the United Nations, UNGA Res 46/230 (2 March 1992) UN Doc A/RES/46/230.

khstan,[322] Kyrgyzstan,[323] Moldova,[324] Tajikistan,[325] Turkmenistan,[326] and Uzbekistan[327] were admitted to the UN on 2 March 1992, followed by Georgia on 31 July 1992.[328] Being among the 51 founding members, the Byelorussian Soviet Socialist Republic and the Ukrainian Soviet Socialist Republic, were part of the UN since 1945.[329] The Byelorussian Soviet Socialist Republic, furthermore, decided to change its name to Belarus and informed the UN of this change on 19 September 1991.[330]
In the course of the breakup of the Soviet Union, several of the so-called autonomous oblasts and regions sought independence in addition to the former republics and the Baltic States. These autonomous oblasts and regions included Abkhazia and South Ossetia in Georgia, Trans-Dniester in Moldova, Chechnya in Russia, and Nagorno-Karabakh in Azerbaijan. But despite their declarations of independence,[331] a number of adopted refer-

---

[322] Admission of the Republic of Kazakhstan to Membership in the United Nations, UNGA Res 46/224 (2 March 1992) UN Doc A/RES/46/224.

[323] Admission of the Republic of Kyrgyzstan to Membership in the United Nations, UNGA Res 46/225 (2 March 1992) UN Doc A/RES/46/225.

[324] Admission of the Republic of Moldova to Membership in the United Nations, UNGA Res 46/223 (2 March 1992) UN Doc A/RES/46/223.

[325] Admission of the Republic of Tajikistan to Membership in the United Nations, UNGA Res 46/228 (2 March 1992) UN Doc A/RES/46/228.

[326] Admission of Turkmenistan to Membership in the United Nations, UNGA Res 46/229 (2 March 1992) UN Doc A/RES/46/229.

[327] Admission of the Republic of Uzbekistan to Membership in the United Nations, UNGA Res 46/226 (2 March 1992) UN Doc A/RES/46/226.

[328] Admission of the Republic of Georgia to Membership in the United Nations, UNGA Res 46/241 (31 July 1992) UN Doc A/RES/46/241.

[329] At the Conference of Yalta (Crimea), the US, the UK and the USSR decided to admit Byelorussian Soviet Socialist Republic together with the Ukrainian Soviet Socialist Republic as original member to the UN (Protocol of the Proceedings of the Crimea Conference [1945] 3 Bevans 1013).

[330] See Growth in United Nations Membership, 1945-present ⟨http://www.un.org/en/members/growth.shtml⟩ accessed 5 February 2014.

[331] Abkhazia on 25 August 1990 (AdG, vol 60, 34894); Chechnya on 8 November 1991 (AdG, vol 61, 36247); South Ossetia on 28 November 1991 (AdG, vol 61, 36355); Nagorno-Karabakh on 2 September 1991) (AdG, vol 61, 36356); Trans-Dniester on 3 September 1991 (AdG, vol 61, 36356).

enda,[332] and in some cases violent and enduring conflicts over the independence of the respective regions, the international society continues to refuse to recognize these regions' claims for independence or reunion with another region or State. Only in a few very exceptional cases have certain States had their independence claims answered with recognition. For example, whereas the EU[333] and the US[334] always denied recognition for Chechnya, several Islamic[335] and two Baltic States[336] recognized its independence – at least temporarily. Another rare example is the Russian recognition of the Abkhazian and South Ossetian independence in 2008.[337] Russia based the recognition on the right for self-determination of peoples.[338] Nonetheless, while repeatedly condemning the violent conflicts and calling for the observation of human rights, several individual States[339] as well as the UN,[340]

---

[332] Adopted referenda on independence in South Ossetia on 19 January 1991 (AdG, vol 62, 36567), in Trans-Dniester on 18 September 2006 (AdG, vol 62, 37028).

[333] Declaration by the Presidency on Behalf of the European Union Concerning Chechnya (17 January 1995) 4215/95 (Presse 011).

[334] 'Supporting Democracy and Economic Reform in the New Independent States, 9 February 1995' (1995) 6(8) US Department of State Dispatch.

[335] Afghanistan (Thomas D Grant, 'Current Developments: Afghanistan Recognizes Chechnya' [2000] 15 AmUILRev 869); Azerbaijan, Kuwait, Saudi Arabia, Turkey and Iran (Grant, *Recognition* [n 5] 118, Fn 8).

[336] Lithuania and Estonia (ibid, 118, Fn 8).

[337] Markus Ackeret, 'Moskau verschärft die Konfrontation: Medwedew anerkennt Unabhängigkeit Südossetiens und Abchasiens' *NZZ* (Zürich, 27 August 2008) 1.

[338] Statement by the Ministry of Foreign Affairs of the Russian Federation (26 August 2008) ⟨http://www.mid.ru/brp_4.nsf/e78a48070f128a7b43256999005bcbb3%20/ff61e0682d1506e1c3257523003f9dd6?OpenDocument⟩ accessed 1 February 2015.

[339] eg regarding the situation in Abkhazia, China, Germany, Italy, Turkey, France, Japan and Panama advocated explicitly for the sovereignty and territorial integrity of Georgia, see UNGA 97th Plenary Meeting, Official Records (15 May 2008) UN Doc A/62/PV.97.

[340] eg the UN Security Council reaffirmed the territorial integrity of Georgia in numerous resolutions. Amongst them are UNSC Res 876 (19 October 1993) UN Doc S/RES/876; UNSC Res 971 (12 January 1995) UN Doc S/RES/971; UNSC Res 993 (12 May 1995) UN Doc S/RES/993; UNSC Res 1666 (31 March 2006) UN Doc S/RES/1666; UNSC Res 1716 (13 October 2006) UN Doc S/RES/1716; UNSC Res 1808 (15 April 2008) UN Doc S/RES/1808.

the EC[341]/EU,[342] and the CSCE[343]/OSCE[344] upheld the concept of inviolability of borders of the former USSR republics since the break-up of the Soviet Union.

4.2 The former republics of the Socialist Federal Republic of Yugoslavia

On 25 June 1991 the former Yugoslav republics Croatia and Slovenia proclaimed their independence from the Socialist Federal Republic of Yugoslavia (SFRY). Slovenia based its claim on the right for self-determination guaranteed in the Constitution of Slovenia and the SFRY as well as on the majority vote of the plebiscite held on 23 December 1990.[345] In a similar fashion, Croatia referred in its decision to the nation's right to self-determination confirmed in its own Constitution, and to the will of the people for independence expressed in a referendum on 19 May 1991.[346] This

[341] In 1993, the EC changed its name to European Union (EU).

[342] eg 'Statement on Nagorno-Karabagh, Doc No 92/230, Brussels/Lisbon' (1992) 8 EPC Bull 330; 'Statement on Nagorno-Karabagh, Doc No 93/353, Brussels' (1993) 9 EPC Bull 405; regarding Abchazia Declaration by the Presidency on behalf of the EU on Georgia (5 May 2008) ⟨http://eeas.europa.eu/delegations/georgia/press_corner/all_news/news/2008/20080418_01_en.htm⟩ accessed 1 February 2015; Declaration by the Presidency on behalf of the EU on the Escalation of Tension between Georgia and Russia (2 May 2008) ⟨http://eeas.europa.eu/delegations/georgia/press_corner/all_news/news/2008/20080502_01_en.htm⟩ accessed 1 February 2015; on South Ossetia Declaration by the Presidency on Behalf of the European Union on Russian President Medvedev's Visit to the Georgian Region of South Ossetia, Brussels (16 July 2009) 12169/09 (Presse 218).

[343] On the Budapest Summit in 1994, the Conference for Security and Co-operation in Europe (CSCE) became the Organization for Security and Co-operation in Europe (OSCE) as from 1 January 1995.

[344] CSCE, 'Budapest Summit Declaration: Towards a Genuine Partnership in a New Era', 5-6 December 1994 [Corrected version dated 21 December 1994], DOC.RC/1/95; OSCE, 'Lisbon Summit Declaration', 3 December 1996, DOC.S/1/96; OSCE, 'Istanbul Summit Declaration', 19 November 1999, SUM.DOC/2/99.

[345] Albert P Blaustein and Gisbert H Flanz (eds), Republic of Slovenia Assembly Declaration of Independence, 25 June 1991 (Oceana Publications 1992) 55, Preamble.

[346] Constitutional Decision on the Sovereignty and Independence of the Republic of Croatia, 25 June 1991 (Oceana Publications 1992) 123, Preamble.

led to tensions between the Serbian minority and the Croatian authorities and evolved into a widespread conflict within Croatia. After several attempts to restore peace and maintain the old status quo of the SFRY, the EC members decided on 27 August 1991 to convene a peace conference and establish an arbitration procedure.[347] The relevant authorities were asked to submit their differences to a commission of five arbitrators chosen by the presidents of the constitutional courts of the EC member States.[348] Robert Badinter, a French lawyer, politician, and former Minister of Justice presided over this commission, which became known as the Badinter commission.

The commission issued its first opinion on 29 November 1991 stating 'that the Socialist Federal Republic of Yugoslavia is in the process of dissolution.'[349] At an extraordinary Ministerial Meeting of the European Political Cooperation (EPC) the EC members discussed the further proceeding regarding the former USSR republics and adopted the Guidelines on the Recognition of New States in Eastern Europe and in the Soviet Union.[350] Furthermore, they issued the Declaration on Yugoslavia in which they scheduled the decision on the recognition of the republics as States for 15 January 1992.[351] According to this declaration, the republics of the SFRY had to confirm their fulfilment of the various prerequisites by 23 December 1991 in order to be recognized as independent States. Besides expressing the wish to be recognized, they had to accept the commitments found in the Guidelines as well as several commitments particularly regarding human rights, contained in the Treaty Provisions for Convention of the Peace Conference on Yugoslavia. Additionally, they had to continue to support the international efforts as well as the continuation of the Yugoslavia conference.[352] The republics that wished to be considered would submit their ap-

[347] 'Statement by an Extraordinary EPC Ministerial Meeting concerning Yugoslavia, Doc 91/252, Brussels' (1991) 7 EPC Bull 389.

[348] ibid.

[349] Opinion No 1 (n 121) 1497.

[350] Guidelines on Recognition (n 67).

[351] Declaration on Yugoslavia (n 67).

[352] ibid.

plications to the Badinter commission for examination. The commission then had to report their findings to the Peace Conference on Yugoslavia, and assist them in reaching a decision.[353] Croatia, Slovenia, Macedonia, and Bosnia-Herzegovina answered and submitted their applications on 19 and 20 December 1991, whereas Serbia and Montenegro did not respond. But then, Germany bounded ahead despite the common position of the EC members concerning the proceeding, eventually leading to recognition of the Yugoslavian republics. On 19 December 1991, the German government announced that all Yugoslav republics declaring that they want to be recognized as States and fulfilling the requirements laid down in the Declaration on Yugoslavia would be granted recognition still before Christmas.[354] Hence, on 23 December, Germany, being of the opinion that Croatia and Slovenia fulfilled all requirements, recognized the two republics as independent States.[355]

After consideration of the applications, the Badinter commission released numerous opinions on 11 January 1992. Opinion No 2 concerned the question whether the Serbian minorities in Croatia and Bosnia-Herzegovina are entitled to self-determination. With reference to the principle of immutability of existing frontiers (*uti possidetis* principle),[356] the commission denied full self-determination, but, nonetheless, recognized their claim to minority rights and rights accorded to ethnic groups.[357] In Opinion No 3 regarding the question whether the formerly internal frontiers of the SFRY are to be treated as external, the commission came to the conclusion that the boundaries between Croatia and Serbia, between Bosnia-Herzegovina and Serbia,

[353] ibid.

[354] AdG, vol 61, 3650. On the same day, however, the US Secretary of State James Baker stated that 'recognition of any of the republics of Yugoslavia's independent countries at this time would not be conducive or would not contribute to a successful resolution of the crisis.'('Press Briefing: Greek Prime Minister Mitsotakis' Visit to Washington, DC, 12 December 1991' [1991] 2[50] US Department of State Dispatch).

[355] AdG, vol 61, 3650.

[356] Latin for 'as you possess under law'; the complete phrase 'uti possidetis iuris, ita possideatis' translates into 'as you possess under law, so you may possess' (my translation).

[357] Badinter Commission, Opinion No 2, 11 January 1992 (1992) 31 ILM 1497 1498-99.

and between other neighbouring States are to be left unaltered, and also that these frontiers are protected by international law.[358]

In Opinions No 4-7 the commission addressed the recognition of the republics. Opinion No 7 concerned the application of Slovenia,[359] the least contested. The commission concluded that Slovenia implemented all requirements in a satisfactory manner. As a result of this opinion, the EC member States recognized Slovenia on 15 January 1992.[360] Croatia, too, was recognized by the EC member States on 15 January 1992.[361] After considering various documents, including the Croatian constitution and the Declaration of Independence, the commission concluded in Opinion No 5 that Croatia met all of the requirements except one.[362] It was stated that at the time Croatia did not fully implement in its Constitutional Act of 4 December 1991 all provisions of the Draft Convention of 4 November 1991, particularly those in chapter II, Article 2(c) titled 'special status'.[363] Areas, in which national or ethnic minorities form a majority, were to enjoy a special status of autonomy.[364] This deficiency was amended to the overall satisfaction of the commission on 8 May 1992.[365] However, the commission's opinion did not consider the fact that the violent conflict between Croatian and Serbian-controlled Yugoslav People's Army supporting the local Serb forces on Croatian territory was still on-going. But this seemed not to be an obstacle to the subsequent recognition of the country.

---

[358] Badinter Commission, Opinion No 3, 11 January 1992 (1992) 31 ILM 1499, 1500.

[359] Badinter Commission, Opinion No 7 on International Recognition of the Republic of Slovenia by the European Community and Its Member States, 11 January 1992 (1992) 31 ILM 1512.

[360] Statement on the Recognition of Yugoslav Republics', Doc 92/009, Brussels (1992) 8 EPC Bull 71 .

[361] ibid.

[362] Badinter Commission, Opinion No 5 on International Recognition of the Republic of Croatia by the European Community and Its Member States, 11 January 1992 (1992) 31 ILM 1503.

[363] ibid, 1505.

[364] Bertrand G Ramcharan (ed), Treaty Provisions for the Convention of 4 November 1991 (Kluwer Law International,1997 1997).

[365] 'Comments of the Republic of Croatia's Constitutional Law of 4 December 1991, as last amended on May 1992' 31 ILM 1505 1507.

After the EC's decision to recognize the two former Yugoslav republics, many European countries, as well as Australia, Argentina, and Canada followed, and were soon joined by Russia, Japan, the US, China, and India in the course of the next few months.[366] Furthermore, both States were admitted to the United Nations shortly after.[367]

The application of Bosnia-Herzegovina was subject of Opinion No 4.[368] After the examination of all relevant documents, the commission concluded that Bosnia-Herzegovina had accepted and adopted the Declaration on Yugoslavia, the Guidelines and the Draft Convention as well as all other relevant international instruments on human rights. Additionally, the constitution of Serbia-Herzegovina guaranteed minority rights and the authorities assured that there were no territorial claims on neighbouring countries. Nonetheless, on 10 November 1991 the Serbian minority of Bosnia-Herzegovina voted in a plebiscite for the creation of the 'Serbian Republic of Bosnia-Herzegovina'. Hence, the commission believed that the will of the people of Bosnia-Herzegovina to form an independent State had not been established. Therefore the commission suggested a referendum on independence.[369] As a result, the EC members refrained from recognizing Bosnia-Herzegovina at that time.[370] On 29 February and 1 March 1992, a referendum was held in which over 99 per cent of those casting a ballot voted in favour of Bosnian independence.[371] The Serbian minority, how-

[366] Roland Rich, 'Recognition of States: The Collapse of Yugoslavia and the Soviet Union' (1993) 4 EJIL 36, 49.

[367] Admission of the Republic of Slovenia to Membership in the United Nations, UNGA Res 46/236 (22 May 1992) UN Doc A/RES/46/236; Admission of the Republic of Bosnia and Herzegovina to Membership in the United Nations, UNGA Res 46/237 (22 May 1992) UN Doc A/RES/46/237.

[368] Badinter Commission, Opinion No 4 on International Recognition of the Socialist Republic of Bosnia-Hercegovina by the European Community and Its Member States, 11 January 1992 (1992) 31 ILM 1501.

[369] ibid, 1503.

[370] Statement on the Recognition of Yugoslav Republics (n 360).

[371] Daniel Bethlehem and Marc Weller, 'The Conflict in Yugoslavia – A Chronology' in Daniel Bethlehem and Marc Weller (eds), *The 'Yugoslav' Crisis in International Law: General Issues* (CUP 1997) xxxiv.

ever, boycotted the referendum,[372] and bloody clashes among the different national groups occurred even before the promulgation of the result on 6 March.[373] The EC and the US declared their readiness to recognize Bosnia-Herzegovina as an independent State on 10 March in a joint statement,[374] and did this on 7 April 1992.[375] After Turkey and Bulgaria had also recognized Bosnia-Herzegovina, many other countries followed suit,[376] despite the fact that the Serbian minority opposed the Bosnian independence and the civil-war like tensions increased.[377] Macedonia also accepted the invitation and applied for recognition. However a dispute with Greece over the name of 'Macedonia' complicated this claim. Greece accused the former Yugoslavian republic of having irredentist plans towards the northern parts of Greek territory, Aegean Macedonia. Thus, they demanded exclusive property of that name and opposed the recognition of the republic as 'Macedonia'.[378] Thus due to Greek pressure, the EC demanded from Macedonia 'prior to recognition' and, in addition to the other requirements in the Declaration on Yugoslavia, 'to adopt constitutional and political guarantees ensuring that it has no territorial claims towards a neighbouring community State and that it will conduct no hostile propaganda activities versus a neighbouring community State including the use of a denomination which implies territorial claims.'[379] The Badinter commission based its opinion on the declaration of 19 December 1991 by the Macedonian Assembly con-

---

[372] Bethlehem and Weller (n 371) xxxiv.

[373] AdG, vol 62, 36650.

[374] 'US/EC Declaration on the Recognition of the Yugoslav Republics, Doc No 92/080, Brussels/Lisbon' (1992) 8 EPC Bull 139.

[375] EC Declaration on Recognition of Bosnia and Herzegovina (6 April 1992) UN Doc S/23793, Annex; Trifunovska Snežana (ed), President Bush's Statement [on the recognition of Bosnia and Herzegovina, Croatia and Slovenia], Washington 7 April 1992 (Martinus Nijhoff Publishers 1994).

[376] Among them Croatia, Canada, Czechoslovakia, Egypt, Hungary, New Zealand, Poland, and Saudi Arabia (Rich [n 366] 50-51).

[377] AdG, vol 62, 36743.

[378] Matjaž Klemenčič, 'The International Community and the FRY/Belligerents, 1989-1997' in Charles Ingrao and Thomas A Emmert (eds), *Confronting the Yugoslav Controversies: A Scholars' Initiative* (Purdue University Press 2009) 171 et passim.

[379] Declaration on Yugoslavia (n 67); Guidelines on Recognition (n 67) 1486.

cerning recognition and the Macedonian constitution of 27 December 1991 with the amendments of 6 January 1992 reaffirming its abstention of territorial claims. Eventually, the commission found that Macedonia satisfied all requirements of the Guidelines and the Declaration of Yugoslavia. Furthermore, the commission stated that Macedonia renounced all territorial claims and 'the use of the name "Macedonia" cannot therefore imply any territorial claim against another State.'[380] Still, the EC was not satisfied, and while recognizing Slovenia and Croatia, it refrained from granting recognition to Macedonia at that time.[381] However, after discussions at a ministerial meeting on 1-2 May 1992 in Guimarães, Portugal, the EC issued a statement declaring that the EC and its members are willing to recognize Macedonia 'under a name that can be accepted by all parties concerned.'[382] The European Council was even more explicit when declaring to recognize 'that republic' but only 'under a name which does not include the term Macedonia.'[383] The UN Security Council tried to ease the situation by recommending to positively respond to the application for UN membership[384] and to refer to the applicant as 'the former Yugoslav Republic of Macedonia' (FYROM), until the name dispute with Greece has been resolved.[385] Still Macedonia continues to pursue its claim on the use of the name of 'Macedonia'. Moreover, the naming issue with Greece remains unsolved despite international efforts to resolve the conflict.[386] Nevertheless, Macedonia today enjoys not only recognition and full diplomatic bilateral rela-

[380] Badinter Commission, Opinion No 6 on International Recognition of the Socialist Republic of Macedonia by the European Community and Its Member States, 11 January 1992 (1992) 31 ILM 1507, 1511.

[381] Statement on the Recognition of Yugoslav Republics (n 360).

[382] EC Declaration on the Former Yugoslav Republic of Macedonia (2 May 1992) UN Doc S/23880, Annex.

[383] European Council in Lisbon, Conclusions of the Presidency, 26/27 June 1992, SN 3321/2792/Rev2, Annex II, European Declaration on Former Yugoslavia .

[384] Letter dated 30 July 1992 from the President of the Republic of Macedonia addressed to the Secretary-General, UN Doc A/47/876-S/25147 (22 January 1993), Annex.

[385] UNSC Res 817 (7 April 1993) UN Doc S/RES/817 para 2.

[386] See, for example Interim Accord [between Greece and the former Yugoslav Republic of Macedonia] (14 December 1995) UN Doc S/1995/794, Annex.

tions with the majority of States,[387] but also access to the United Nations[388] and candidate status for EU membership.[389]

Serbia and Montenegro did not apply for recognition as newly independent and sovereign States. Instead they adopted a new constitution on 27 April 1992 and issued a declaration proclaiming that they wish to remain in the State of Yugoslavia. Moreover, the new Federal Republic of Yugoslavia (FRY) would continue 'the state, international legal and political personality' and therefore also all international rights and obligations of former the Socialist Federal Republic of Yugoslavia'.[390] The EC together with its members as well as other States expressed reservation to this announcement, particularly regarding the continued membership in international organizations including the UN.[391] The UN Security Council noted that the SFRY's claim to continue UN membership was met with disapproval.[392] Subsequently, the EC and its member States refused to recognize the FRY as the successor of the SFRY.[393]

Regarding the succession of SFRY by the FRY, the Badinter commission issued three opinions on 4 July 1992. In Opinion No 8, the commission

---

[387] See the homepage of the Republic of Macedonia, Ministry of Foreign Affairs (http://www.mfa.gov.mk/index.php/en/foreign-policy/bilateral-relations) accessed 28 February 2015. Despite the naming issue, Greece and Macedonia maintain both a Liaison Office in each others capital.

[388] Admission of the State Whose Application is Contained in Document A/47/876-S/25147 to Membership in the United Nations, UNGA Res 47/225 (27 April 1993) UN Doc A/RES/47/225.

[389] Council of the European Union, Presidency's Conclusions (Brussels, 30 January 2006), 15914/1/05 REV 1, 7.

[390] Declaration by the Representatives of the People of the Republic of Serbia and the Republic of Montenegro (5 May 1991) UN Doc S/23877, Annex, para 1.

[391] EC (Statement of the European Community and its member States (5 May 1992) UN Doc A/46/905, Annex); the US (Letter dated 5 May 1992 from the Deputy Permanent Representative of the United States of America (5 May 1992) UN Doc A/46/906); Hungary (Letter dated 6 May 1992 from the Permanent Representative of Hungary (6 May 1992) UN Doc A/46/911).

[392] UNSC Res 757 (30 May 1992) UN Doc S/RES/757.

[393] European Council Declaration on former Yugoslavia (29 June 1992) UN Doc S/24200, Annex.

found that the process of dissolution of the SFRY, as stated in opinion 1,[394] had been completed and thus the SFRY no longer existed.[395] Based on this, the commission concluded in Opinion No 9 that none of the newly established States could claim sole successorship. In addition, the membership of the SFRY in international organizations had to be terminated, and none of the successor States would be entitled to the exclusive membership rights previously enjoyed by the former SFRY.[396] Hence, the FRY 'cannot be considered the sole successor to the SFRY', according to Opinion No 10. Rather, it is a new State, established by the two successor States, Serbia and Montenegro. In order to be recognized by the EC and its member States, it would have to comply with the requirements of general international law and the Guidelines of 16 December 1991.[397] The UN Security Council, having approved this, advised the General Assembly to decide that the FRY had to apply for membership.[398] The General Assembly decided thereupon against the automatic continuation of the SFRY's membership and instead requested a membership application from the FRY.[399] Still, the FRY's position within the United Nations remained in limbo. It was only on 27 October 2000 that the newly elected president of the FRY, Vojislav Kostunica, sent a letter to the Secretary General requesting admission of the FRY into the UN.[400] The General Assembly accommodated the request upon prior recommendation of the Security Council.[401] Yet, the FRY did not exist much longer.

---

[394]Opinion No 1 (n 121) 1497.

[395]Badinter Commission, Opinion No 8, 4 July 1992 (1992) 31 ILM 1521, 1523.

[396]Badinter Commission, Opinion No 9, 4 July 1992 (1992) 31 ILM 1523, 1524-25.

[397]Opinion No 10 (n 122) 1526.

[398]UNSC Res 777 (19 December 1992) UN Doc S/RES/777.

[399]Recommendation of the Security Council of 19 September 1992, UNGA Res 47/1 (22 September 1992) UN Doc A/RES/47/1.

[400]Letter dated 27 October 2000 from the President of the Federal Republic of Yugoslavia to the Secretary-General, UN Doc A/55/528-S/2000/1043 (30 October 2000), Annex.

[401]UNSC Res 1326 (31 October 2000) UN Doc S/RES/1326; Admission of the Federal Republic of Yugoslavia to Membership in the United Nations, UNGA Res 55/12 (10 November 2000) UN Doc A/RES/55/12.

Already by the beginning of 2003, the FRY was dissolved by a parliamentary decision and transformed into the Union of Serbia and Montenegro.[402] Nonetheless Montenegro sought complete independence, and on 21 May 2006 this was approved by 55.5 per cent of all voters in a public referendum.[403] Several days later, on 3 June 2006, the Montenegrin parliament declared its independence from the Union of Serbia and Montenegro.[404] The European Union and its Member States issued the decision that 'they will develop further their relations with the Republic of Montenegro as a sovereign, independent State, taking full account of the referendum result and the afore-mentioned Parliamentary Acts. Member States will take the subsequent measures implementing this decision nationally in accordance with international law and practice.'[405] After Montenegrin declaration of independence, Serbia proclaimed its independence.[406] Additionally, Serbia assumed the succession of the Union regarding rights and obligations as well as membership in the UN and other international organizations, based on Article 60 of the Constitutional Charter of Serbia and Montenegro.[407]

4.3 The autonomous province of Kosovo

During the dissolution of the SFRY, the autonomous province of Kosovo, a part of Serbia, laid claim to independence. This lead eventually to a violent conflict between Armed Forces of the FRY and the Kosovo Liberation Army (UÇK) at the end of the 1990s. During the course of this con-

[402] Martin Woker, 'Belgrad beschliesst einen Neuanfang Ja zur Verfassung von "Serbien und Montenegro"' *NZZ* (Zürich, 29 February 2003) 1.

[403] dpa, 'Das Resultat der Abstimmung in Montenegro bestätigt' *NZZ* (Zürich, 22 May 2006) 2.

[404] Martin Woker, 'Montenegro erklärt die Unabhängigkeit: Formelle Proklamation des Parlaments in Podgorica' *NZZ* (Zürich, 6 June 2006) 1.

[405] EU Council Conclusions on Montenegro - 2737 External Relations Council Meeting (Luxembourg, 12 June 2006), Doc No CL06-123EN ⟨www.eu-un.europa.eu/articles/en/article_6031_en.htm⟩ accessed 1 February 2014.

[406] Woker, 'Montenegro' (n 404).

[407] Letter from the Minister for Foreign Affairs of the Republic of Serbia to the Secretary-General, Historical Information, Serbia, Note 1 ⟨http://treaties.un.org/pages/HistoricalInfo.aspx?#%22Serbia%22⟩ accessed 1 February 2015.

flict grave violations of human rights of the Kosovar civil population took place. Peace negotiations in 1999 between the FRY and Kosovo in Rambouillet failed due to the FRY's refusal to sign a proposed agreement. The recurring violence was eventually terminated in spring 1999 by a NATO air operation. On 10 June 1999, the UN Security Council adopted Resolution 1244 marking the end of the NATO intervention.[408] With this resolution, FRY forces were demanded to withdraw and Kosovo was placed under transitional UN administration. The United Nations Interim Administration Mission in Kosovo (UNMIK) had, amongst other things, the responsibility to facilitate 'a political process designed to determine Kosovo's future status.'[409] In 2005, the UN Secretary General appointed Kai Eide as his Special Envoy to assess whether the conditions were favourable to initiate the political process to determine the future status of Kosovo. In October 2005, he confirmed that 'the time has come to commence this process.'[410] Based on Eide's report, the UNSC approved the commencement of the process and welcomed the appointment of a Special Envoy to lead the Future Status process.[411] The appointed UN Special Envoy, Martti Ahtisaari, submitted his report on Kosovo's future status together with the Comprehensive Proposal for the Kosovo Status Settlement (known as the Ahtisaari Plan) on 26 March 2007 to the UN Security Council. In his report, Ahtisaari stated that the negotiating parties continued to adhere to their fundamentally opposed positions. While Kosovo would accept nothing short of total independence, Serbia demanded autonomy and integration of Kosovo within Serbian borders. Due to this disparity in positions, it had not been possible to achieve progress in the negotiations. Ahtisaari expressed doubts as to whether it would still be feasible to reach any outcome at all. He ruled out

[408] UNSC Res 1244 (10 June 1999) UN Doc S/RES/1244.

[409] ibid para 11(e).

[410] A Comprehensive Review of the Situation in Kosovo, Annex to Letter Dated 7 October 2005 from the Secretary-General Addressed to the President of the Security Council (7 October 2005) UN Doc S/2005/635.

[411] Statement by the President of the Security Council (24 October 2005) UN Doc S/PRST/2005/51.

entirely the reintegration into Serbia as a feasible option,[412] furthermore he did not perceive the continued international administration of Kosovo under which the UN Security Council placed Kosovo while denying Serbia's continued governance in 1999[413] as sustainable. In conclusion, Ahtisaari recommended independence under transitional international supervision as the only viable option for Kosovo. He stressed, however, that this combination of circumstances made Kosovo a special case.[414] In the supplemental Comprehensive Proposal for the Kosovo Status Settlement, Ahtisaari identified 'provisions necessary for a future Kosovo that is viable, sustainable and stable.'[415] These provisions addressed issues such as the promotion and protection of community rights, decentralization, the establishment of an independent and impartial justice system, and the protection and promotion of religious and cultural heritage. Some provisions dealt with the international civilian and military presence in the country, supporting and supervising the implementation of this Settlement.[416]

A year later, on 17 February 2008, when the assembly of Kosovo declared the country's independence it referred to the full accordance of the Ahtisaari Plan of the declaration.[417] Several States recognized Kosovo's independence straightaway. But unlike the other cases of recognition of the other new Balkan States, the EU members did not act unanimously, nor was

---

[412] Report of the Special Envoy of the Secretary-General on Kosovo's Future Status (26 March 2007) UN Doc S/2007/168.

[413] Res 1244 (n 408).

[414] Report of the Special Envoy (n 412).

[415] ibid Annex: Main provisions of the Comprehensive Proposal for the Kosovo Status Settlement.

[416] Comprehensive Proposal for the Kosovo Status Settlement, Addendum to Letter dated 26 March 2007 from the Secretary-General addressed to the President of the Security Council (26 March 2007) UN Doc S/2007/168/Add.1.

[417] Kosova Declaration of Independence by the Assembly of Kosovo, 17 February 2008 (on file with the UN Office of Legal Affairs) [Dossier No. 192] in Material relating to the Establishment of UMMIK Administration of Kosovo – Actions by Kosovo institutions (Part II-H), Dossier, Prepared Pursuant to the Order of the President of the International Court of Justice of 17 October 2008 ⟨http://www.icj-cij.org/docket/index.php?/docket/index.php?p1=3&p2=4&slu=&case=141&code=kos&p3=0⟩ accessed 1 February 2015.

there a framework document comparable to the Guidelines on the Recognition of New States in Eastern Europe and in the Soviet Union. Rather, it was left to the individual States to decide their relation to Kosovo 'in accordance with their national practice and international law.'[418] Shortly after the declaration, numerous EC members and many other States recognized Kosovo's independence.[419] In their statements, however, the recognizing States welcomed Kosovo's commitment to the Ahtisaari Plan and emphasized its implementation as crucial.[420] Nonetheless, they did not mention this commitment as an explicit prerequisite for recognition. Instead, the reason given for the recognition of the Kosovar independence, if one was given at all, was that it would contribute to peace and stability in the region.[421]

Serbia rejected Kosovo's unilateral step and sought clarification on the legality of this declaration. Therefore, the UN General Assembly, on Ser-

---

[418]Council of the European Union, 2851st Council Meeting, General Affairs and External Relations, Brussels (18 February 2008) 6496/08 (Presse 41), 7.

[419]Examples are Japan, Switzerland, Turkey, and the US.

[420]Letter from the [US] President to the President of Kosovo (18 February 2008) ⟨http://georgewbush-whitehouse.archives.gov/news/releases/2008/02/20080218-3.html⟩ accessed 1 February 2015; Statement of HE Mr Ali Babacan, Minister of Foreign Affairs of the Republic of Turkey, Regarding the Recognition of Kosovo by Turkey (18 February 2008) ⟨http://www.mfa.gov.tr/statement-of-h_e_-mr_-ali-babacan_-minister-of-foreign-affairs-of-the-republic--of-turkey_-regarding-the-recognition-of-kosovo.en.mfa⟩ accessed 1 February 2015; Deutschland erkennt Kosovo an (20 February 2008) ⟨http://archiv.bundesregierung.de/Content/DE/Archiv16/Artikel/2008/02/2008-02-20-deutschland-erkennt-kosovo-an.html⟩ accessed 1 February 2015; Statement by [Japanese] Foreign Minister Masahiko Koumura on the Recognition of the Republic of Kosovo (18 March 2008) ⟨http://www.mofa.go.jp/announce/announce/2008/3/0318.html⟩ accessed 1 February 2015.

[421]For example Lettre du Président de la République adressée à Son Excellence M. Fatmir Sejdiu, Président du Kosovo (18 February 2008) ⟨http://www.ambafrance-si.org/Lettre-de-M-Sarkozy-a-M-Sejdiu⟩ accessed 1 February 2015; Joint statement of Bulgaria, Hungary and Croatia on Forthcoming Recognition of Kosovo' (19 March 2008) ⟨http://www.mfa.gov.hu/kum/en/bal/actualities/spokesman_statements/Kosovo_080319.htm⟩ accessed 1 February 2015; Statement by the President of the Swiss Confederation, Pascal Couchepin, Recognition of Kosovo and the Establishment of Diplomatic Relations (27 February 2008) ⟨http://www.eda.admin.ch/eda/en/home/recent/media/single.html?id=17497⟩ accessed 1 February 2015.

bia's behalf, filed a request seeking an advisory opinion by the International Court of Justice on the question: 'Is the unilateral declaration of independence by the Provisional Institutions of Self-Government of Kosovo in accordance with international law?'[422] In the proceedings, members of the United Nations were given the opportunity to give their opinions upon the accordance of Kosovo's unilateral declaration with international law. The States were divided between the opponents and the supporters of the legality of the declaration of independence. The opponents took the view that Kosovo's declaration of independence was breaking international law, particularly the principle of territorial integrity of Serbia.[423] The declaration would also not be compatible with UNSC Resolution 1244 guaranteeing Serbia's sovereignty and territorial integrity.[424] In this regard, the Chinese representative pointed out that China only refrained from blocking the resolution because the reference to Serbia's[425] sovereignty and territorial integrity was included.[426] Another argument brought forward was that

[422]UNGA Res 63/3 (8 October 2008) UN Doc A/RES/63/3.

[423]eg Public Sitting on the Accordance with International Law of the Unilateral Declaration of Independence by the Provisional Institutions of Self-Government of Kosovo, Verbatim records (**Serbia**), (1 December 2009) Doc No CR 2009/24; Public Sitting on the Accordance with International Law of the Unilateral Declaration of Independence by the Provisional Institutions of Self-Government of Kosovo, Verbatim records (**Argentina**), (2 December 2009) Doc No CR 2009/26; Public Sitting on the Accordance with International Law of the Unilateral Declaration of Independence by the Provisional Institutions of Self-Government of Kosovo, Verbatim records (**Brazil**), (4 December 2009) Doc No CR 2009/28; Public Sitting on the Accordance with International Law of the Unilateral Declaration of Independence by the Provisional Institutions of Self-Government of Kosovo, Verbatim records (**The People's Republic of China**), (7 December 2009) Doc No CR 2009/29; Public Sitting on the Accordance with International Law of the Unilateral Declaration of Independence by the Provisional Institutions of Self-Government of Kosovo, Verbatim records (**Russia**), (8 December 2009) Doc No CR 2009/30; Public Sitting on the Accordance with International Law of the Unilateral Declaration of Independence by the Provisional Institutions of Self-Government of Kosovo, Verbatim records (**Spain**), (8 December 2009) Doc No CR 2009/30.

[424]eg **China** (n 423); Public Sitting on the Accordance with International Law of the Unilateral Declaration of Independence by the Provisional Institutions of Self-Government of Kosovo, Verbatim records (**Cyprus**), (7 December 2009) Doc No CR 2009/29.

[425]At that time still referred to as Federal Republic of Yugoslavia.

[426]**China** (n 423) para 5.

there was no legal basis for a unilateral declaration of independence and secession.[427] Kosovo's status in the SFRY might have allowed the invocation of a right to unilateral secession, however, as the process of dissolution of the SFRY has been completed in 1992,[428] this special status no longer existed. Since then, Kosovo has been an integral part of Serbia, and Serbia's internal law provided for the internal autonomy of Kosovo[429] to which the UNSC resolution also referred.[430] It was furthermore argued that international law does not support unilateral secessions. The Russian delegate reminded the Court that the UN Security Council declared Northern Cyprus' and Rhodesia's declarations of independence illegal.[431] Such striving for independence would be only permissible either for former colonies, in case of racist or foreign domination,[432] or when a minority was severely oppressed and deprived of its fundamental right of internal self-determination.[433] Although Serbia did oppress the Albanian population in Kosovo in the late 1990s, these actions could not, however, be considered as the reason for secession in 2008, when the situation had been completely different. Thus, there was neither a reason nor a right for 'remedial secession'.[434]Altogether, the fact that Kosovo might be a *sui generis* case must not lead to the conclusion that principles of international law are not ap-

[427]**Argentina** (n 423); **China** (n 423); **Russia** (n 423).

[428]Romania pointing to the Badinter Opinion 8 stating that the dissolution of the SFRY has been completed Public Sitting on the Accordance with International Law of the Unilateral Declaration of Independence by the Provisional Institutions of Self-Government of Kosovo, Verbatim records (**Romania**), (10 December 2009) Doc No CR 2009/32; also **Russia** (n 423) para 11.

[429]**Romania** (n 428).

[430]Public Sitting on the Accordance with International Law of the Unilateral Declaration of Independence by the Provisional Institutions of Self-Government of Kosovo, Verbatim records (**Bolivia**), (4 December 2009) Doc No CR 2009/28 para 14.

[431]**Russia** (n 423).

[432]**Serbia** (n 423).

[433]Public Sitting on the Accordance with International Law of the Unilateral Declaration of Independence by the Provisional Institutions of Self-Government of Kosovo, Verbatim records (**Belarus**), (3 December 2009) Doc No CR 2009/27.

[434]**Russia** (n 423) 44; **Romania** (n 428).

plicable.[435] It had been argued instead that Kosovo could even serve as a dangerous precedent, if in the future setting up a UN Administration were to be perceived as the first step to secession.[436] Only continued negotiations between Pristina and Belgrade could settle the future status of Kosovo.[437] Hence, the opponents of Kosovo's independence considered this unilateral declaration contrary to a mutual agreement and, consequently, viewed the UNSC Resolution 1244 as remaining in force until the negotiations come to an end.[438]

The advocates of Kosovar independence disagreed. They held the opinion that the declaration of independence did not contradict international law because there was no rule prohibiting it.[439] Unilateral declarations may be found illegal, but only if made in combination with a breach of other provisions of international law. Examples for non-recognition named were Northern Cyprus' independence established by the use of force by a third

---

[435] **Cyprus** (n 424).

[436] **Serbia** (n 423) para 61.

[437] eg **Argentina** (n 423); **Romania** (n 428).

[438] **Brazil** (n 423); **Spain** (n 423).

[439] Public Sitting on the Accordance with International Law of the Unilateral Declaration of Independence by the Provisional Institutions of Self-Government of Kosovo, Verbatim records (**The Authors of the Unilateral Declaration of Independence, ie Kosovo**), (1 December 2009) Doc No CR 2009/24; Public Sitting on the Accordance with International Law of the Unilateral Declaration of Independence by the Provisional Institutions of Self-Government of Kosovo, Verbatim records (**Albania**), (2 December 2009) Doc No CR 2009/26; Public Sitting on the Accordance with International Law of the Unilateral Declaration of Independence by the Provisional Institutions of Self-Government of Kosovo, Verbatim records (**Austria**), (3 December 2009) Doc No CR 2009/27; Public Sitting on the Accordance with International Law of the Unilateral Declaration of Independence by the Provisional Institutions of Self-Government of Kosovo, Verbatim records (**Bulgaria**), (4 December 2009) Doc No CR 2009/28; Public Sitting on the Accordance with International Law of the Unilateral Declaration of Independence by the Provisional Institutions of Self-Government of Kosovo, Verbatim records (**Denmark**), (7 December 2009) Doc No CR 2009/29; Public Sitting on the Accordance with International Law of the Unilateral Declaration of Independence by the Provisional Institutions of Self-Government of Kosovo, Verbatim records (**Finland**), (8 December 2009) Doc No CR 2009/30; Public Sitting on the Accordance with International Law of the Unilateral Declaration of Independence by the Provisional Institutions of Self-Government of Kosovo, Verbatim records (**Germany**), (2 December 2009) Doc No CR 2009/26.

State and Rhodesia's independence proclaimed by a racist regime.[440] In line with this, it would have been against international law if Kosovo's independence would have been caused by intervention of a third State or the violation of a *jus cogens* rule. But in the view of the supporters for independence no such situation had taken place.[441] In addition, the declaration did not run contrary to UNSC Resolution 1244.[442] This was reaffirmed by the fact that a majority of the UNSC members that voted for UNSC Resolution 1244 later also recognized Kosovo's independence.[443] Another argument put forward was that the population of Kosovo had been subject to severe oppression and discrimination by Serbia.[444] By virtue of this, the people of Kosovo were entitled to independence and self-determination as a means of last resort.[445] Also submitted in favour of Kosovo's independence was the view that the principle of territorial integrity applied only between States, but not on the intrastate level.[446] It has been additionally argued that Kosovo as an autonomous province with 'strong elements of statehood' under the 1974 constitution of SFRY had a right to self-determination of which it was only deprived of after the new constitution in 1990.[447] Besides, be-

[440] **Austria** (n 439) . See sub-s 2.4.3 ('Non-recognition') for reasons for non-recognition.

[441] **Albania** (n 439); Public Sitting on the Accordance with International Law of the Unilateral Declaration of Independence by the Provisional Institutions of Self-Government of Kosovo, Verbatim records (**Norway**), (9 December 2009) Doc No CR 2009/31.

[442] **Bulgaria** (n 439); Public Sitting on the Accordance with International Law of the Unilateral Declaration of Independence by the Provisional Institutions of Self-Government of Kosovo, Verbatim records (**US**), (8 December 2009) Doc No CR 2009/30.

[443] **US** (n 442).

[444] Public Sitting on the Accordance with International Law of the Unilateral Declaration of Independence by the Provisional Institutions of Self-Government of Kosovo, Verbatim records (**Croatia**), (7 December 2009) Doc No CR 2009/29; **Denmark** (n 439).

[445] **Germany** (n 439); **Kosovo** (n 439); Public Sitting on the Accordance with International Law of the Unilateral Declaration of Independence by the Provisional Institutions of Self-Government of Kosovo, Verbatim records (**the Netherlands**), (10 December 2009) Doc No CR 2009/32.

[446] **Finland** (n 439); Public Sitting on the Accordance with International Law of the Unilateral Declaration of Independence by the Provisional Institutions of Self-Government of Kosovo, Verbatim records (**Jordan**), (9 December 2009) Doc No CR 2009/31; **Norway** (n 441); **US** (n 442).

[447] **Croatia** (n 444).

cause it fulfilled the requirements of statehood, Kosovo being a State is a fact.[448] Nevertheless, the Special Envoy's view was that Kosovo is a special case, and thus cannot serve as a precedent. This has been repeated several times.[449]

On 22 June 2010, then, the ICJ issued the verdict that 'the adoption of the declaration of independence of 17 February 2008 did not violate general international law, Security Council Resolution 1244 (1999) or the Constitutional Framework. Consequently the adoption of that declaration did not violate any applicable rule of international law.'[450] In addition, the ICJ confirmed that 'the principle of territorial integrity is confined to the sphere of relations between State.'[451] Overall, and despite the fact that 'declarations do not constitute the legal basis for statehood or recognition,'[452] all States that spoke in favour of the legality of the declaration, subsequently recognized Kosovo's independence. As of today, more than 100 States have recognized Kosovo's independence.[453] Moreover, on 29 April 2013, Kosovo and Serbia signed a document aimed at normalizing their relations.[454] Despite this agreement, as well as Kosovo's view of this as proof of the *de jure* recognition of its independence, Serbia stressed that it will never recognize Kosovo.[455]

---

[448] **Croatia** (n 444); **Germany** (n 439).

[449] eg **Bulgaria** (n 439); **Germany** (n 439); the Netherlands (n 445); **Norway** (n 441).

[450] *Accordance with International Law of the Unilateral Declaration of Independence in Respect of Kosovo* (Advisory Opinion) [2010] ICJ Rep 403, para 122.

[451] ibid, para 80.

[452] **Norway** (n 441) para 17.

[453] Recognized or Announced the Recognition of Republic of Kosova ⟨http://www.kosovothanksyou.com/⟩ accessed 1 February 2015.

[454] Aleksandar Vasovic and Justyna Pawlak, 'EU Brokers Historic Kosovo Deal, Door Opens to Serbia Accession' (*Reuters*, 19 April 2013) ⟨http://www.reuters.com/article/2013/04/19/us-serbia-kosovo-eu-idUSBRE93I0IB20130419⟩ accessed 1 February 2015.

[455] ibid.

4.4 The discrepancy between practice and doctrine of recognition

The preceding chapter provided an overview of the process of recognition of the former republics of the USSR, together with the Baltic States, as well as the recognition of the former republics of the SFRY along with the one of Kosovo. The EC and its members were forced to act in response to the dissolution of the USSR and the crisis on the Balkan Peninsula in the 1990s and the subsequent questions regarding the origin of new States. In considering the best course of action, however, it soon emerged that the traditional criteria for determining statehood and hence recognition as the simple acknowledgment of facts failed to meet the needs to tackle this situation. As a result, effectiveness of the three traditional State requirements was present but not the main point of concern for the EC and its members. Likewise the principle of *ex factis jus oritur* appeared to have been less essential. Still these principles were deemed necessary for recognition. But nonetheless, they no longer seemed sufficient.
Instead, several other, additional requirements and considerations, some of them written down in documents like the Guidelines on the Recognition of New States in Eastern Europe and in the Soviet Union, the Declaration on Yugoslavia, and in the Ahtisaari Plan were deemed equally or even more important. Particular weight was placed on a commitment to human rights and the protection of minorities. The notion of self-determination of peoples was another central principle. This was expressed through both an explicit commitment to the principle by the recognizant States themselves, as well as through their demands for democratic referenda through which the populations of the entities seeking recognition were able to express their wish for independence and for democratic structures of the entities' respective political systems. In close context with and, at the same time, opposed to self-determination are the principles of *uti possidetis*, the inviolability of borders, and of territorial integrity. The contradiction is apparent in the inconsistent application by the recognizing States. While recognizing South Ossetia and Abkhazia with reference to the right of self-determination of the people living there, Russia continues until today to oppose the recog-

nition of Kosovo's independence, while attaching more importance on the territorial integrity of Serbia. In contrast, other States like Finland, Jordan and the US, emphasized the special circumstances of Kosovo and thus placed more weight on self-determination than on the territorial integrity of Serbia, holding that the latter is only applicable on the interstate, but not on the intrastate level. At the same time, they refused to recognize many autonomous oblasts and regions referring to the territorial integrity and inviolability of borders of the States concerned. It is further noteworthy that States refusing to recognize Kosovo's independence are often faced with independence-seeking regions themselves, such as Spain, Russia, and China. Concomitantly, many States having spoken in favour of Kosovo were themselves once in a situation where they strived for independence. Examples of this are Croatia, the Netherlands, and the US. The obligation of (nuclear) disarmament, the pledge to non-proliferation, and the demand to settle any possible conflicts through peaceful means have been further requirements for recognition. Moreover, the recognition but also non-recognition of these entities striving for independence was often collectively scheduled and executed, as in the case of the former republics of Yugoslavia and the USSR. This procedure, however, is not to be confused with collective recognition because it has been ultimately the individual States recognizing the entities as States.

After the examination of the recognition cases above, it becomes evident that there is a striking discrepancy between the doctrine and practice of State recognition. The numerous recognition processes in the post-Cold War era were based on the fulfilment of various additional requirements, rather than on the principle of sheer effectiveness. By imposing such additional requirements the recognizing States linked together recognition with further interests and issues. Yet, this contradicts the predominant view of recognition doctrine that not only sets the classic State criteria as the sole requirements for recognition, but also precludes its dependency on any further conditions. Regarding the question on how the recognition of States developed, it is assumed that recognition, over the course of its evolution, served as a powerful means in international politics, through adding and changing the requirements, for the enforcement of the interests of the recognizing States.

III An Explanatory Approach

5 Theoretical foundations

Based on the previous findings, the question arises – how has the concept of recognition of States evolved. The following sets out to solve this question first, by outlining the theoretical foundations of 'social constructivism' and the 'English school of international relations theory'. Based thereupon the explanatory model – the 'recognitional fitness' – will be conceptualized.

5.1 Constructivism

In the academic discipline of international relations, 'social constructivism', or simply 'constructivism', is a relatively young branch that emerged in the early 1990s. The main concern of this theory is the relationship between actors and structures while focusing on the role of ideas and beliefs. The two basic claims are '(1) that the structures of human association are determined primarily by shared ideas rather than material forces and (2) that the identities and interests of purposive actors are constructed by these shared ideas rather than given by nature.'[456] These two claims point to the essence of this theoretical approach: its emphasis on ideas makes it an 'idealist view' as opposed to the 'materialist conceptions' of (neo-)realism and (neo-)liberalism. The second claim of constructivism represents a 'structuralist' or 'holist' approach as it stresses the emergence of social structure by means of social interaction as opposed to the 'individualist' notion that structural development could be reduced to the individual level. Consequently, the constructivist approach can be understood as 'structural' or 'holist idealism'.[457]

---

[456] Alexander Wendt, *Social Theory of International Politics* (CUP 1999) 1.
[457] ibid, 1.

Constructivism emerged as a reaction to the dominant mainstream theories (neo-)realism and (neo-)liberalism. Scholars of classic realism,[458] as well as of neorealism,[459] perceive the international system as anarchical, in that it lacks a central authority able to enforce peace and stability. Hence, States as independent, uniform, and sole actors in this Hobbesian 'state of nature' are always concerned with their survival, and compete for relative power. Their primary concern is 'high politics', ie military security, only then followed by economic, social or environmental issues of 'low politics'. Because of this set list of preferences, adherents of the realist theory perceive States as rational actors. The relation between them is given by the structure of anarchy as a constant zero-sum game – the amount of power and influence gained by one State is lost by another. Co-operation between these rational actors is only possible when a single actor exceeds all the other actors in power and influence. According to realist theory, this is the only situation when co-operation between States under the condition of anarchy is possible: when a hegemon is able to sustain this security and co-operation.

'(Neo-)liberal institutionalists', or just '(neo-)liberals',[460] accept certain realist premises, namely, that States are the most important actors in global affairs, that they act essentially egoistically and rationally and that their behaviour is shaped by the anarchic structure of the system. It is due to their shared commitment to rational choice theory that both liberalism and realism are called rationalist approaches.[461] Furthermore, both approaches hold that actors' behaviour is focused on gains. Yet in the realist view, actors are

[458] Such as Edward Hallett Carr, *The Twenty Years' Crisis, 1919-1939: An Introduction to the Study of International Relations* (Macmillan 1939); Hans J Morgenthau, *Politics Among Nations: The Struggle for Power and Peace* (Alfred Knopf 1948).

[459] Like Stephen M Walt, *The Origins of Alliances* (Cornell University Press 1987); John J Mearsheimer, *The Tragedy of Great Power Politics* (WW Norton & Company 2001); Kenneth N Waltz, *Theory of International Politics* (Random House 1979).

[460] eg Robert O Keohane, *After Hegemony: Cooperation and Discord in the World Political Economy* (Princeton University Press 1984); Robert O Keohane and Joseph S Nye, *Power and Interdependence: World Politics in Transition* (Little Brown & Co 1977).

[461] Alexander Wendt, 'Anarchy Is What the States Make of It: The Social Construction of Power Politics' (1992) 46 IO 391.

interested in *relative* gains, ie more power, wealth or influence than the potential or real adversary. Liberals, by contrast, understand that actors seek *absolute* gains, which are independent of other actors' gains. Therefore, liberal approaches challenge the notion that co-operation between States is not possible. They argue that while engaging with the pursuit of their interests, States as rational actors constantly seek out the most efficient and effective way to realize their interests. If the most efficient way to achieve an objective is to co-operate with others, then States will do so. As a result, co-operation between actors in order to achieve an intended goal seems likely, even under the condition of anarchy.

Until the 1980s, the debate between (neo-)realism and (neo-)liberalism dominated international relations scholarship. The sudden end of the Cold War, however, issued a major challenge to these theories. Neither theory had been able to predict or explain this fundamental change in global affairs.[462] This failure was one of the central factors inducing the emergence of constructivism.[463] This school of thought provides an alternative explanatory model for research in international relations while questioning and dismissing most of the rationalist claims. Despite certain theoretical distinctions, methodological disagreements, and different priorities in research, there is broad consensus among constructivist scholars regarding the central concepts and ideas defining and distinguishing the constructivist approach.[464]

---

[462] Michael Barnett, 'Social Constructivism' in John Baylis, Steve Smith, and Patricia Owens (eds), *The Globalization of World Politics: An Introduction to International Relations* (6th edn, OUP 2014) 157.

[463] cf Christian Reus-Smit, 'Constructivism' in Scott Burchill and others (eds), *Theories of International Relations* (5th edn, Palgrave Macmillan 2013) 223.

[464] Such as Emanuel Adler, 'Cognitive Evolution: A Dynamic Approach for the Study of International Relations and Their Progress' in Emanuel Adler and Beverly Crawford (eds), *Progress in Postwar International Relations* (Columbia University Press 1991); Emanuel Adler, *Communitarian International Relations: The Epistemic Foundations of International Relations* (Routledge 2005); Michael Barnett, 'The New United Nations Politics of Peace: From Juridical Sovereignty to Empirical Sovereignty' (1995) 1 GlobGov 79; Barnett, 'Social Constructivism' (n 462); Jan Hurd, 'Constructivism' in Christian Reus-Smit and Duncan Snidal (eds), *The Oxford Handbook of International Relations* (OUP 2008); Reus-Smit (n 463); Wendt, 'Anarchy' (n 461); Alexander Wendt,

The central distinction between the rationalist approaches and constructivism is found in their contrasting views on origin and function of interests and identities as well as on the structural features of the international sphere. In opposition to rationalists, who understand actors' interests and identities determined by *exogenous* factors, constructivists regard interests and identities as formed *endogenously*.[465] Rationalists perceive interests and identities as composed of the distribution of material capabilities, such as military hardware and natural resources that, in turn, have a direct influence on actors' behaviour. Constructivism, however, claims that interests and identities are shaped by intersubjective beliefs, values and ideas.
By referring to the conception of a group or State, of what specifies it and what makes it distinct from others, the constructivist argument claims that these ideas and beliefs constitute the identity of the actors.

> In IR such beliefs include a group of people's notion of themselves as a nation or nationality, their conception of their country as a state, their notion of their state as a independent sovereign, their idea of themselves as different from other peoples in cultural or religious or historical terms, their sense of history and traditions, their political convictions and prejudices and ideologies, their political institutions, and much else.[466]

But ideas and beliefs do not only give possible answers to questions of identity but also to the closely related questions concerning interests. In principle, constructivism does not reject a priori the idea that each State pursues its respective interests. At the same time, it opposes the assumption that the motivation for this behaviour is only found in material incentives, ie formed exogenously. Instead, constructivism claims that interests, since

'Collective Identity Formation and the International State' (1994) 88 AmPolSciRev 384; Alexander Wendt, 'Constructing International Politics' (1995) 20 IS 71; Wendt, *Social Theory* (n 456).

[465] Hurd (n 464); Wendt, 'Collective Identity Formation' (n 464).

[466] Robert Jackson and Georg Sørensen, *Introduction to International Relations: Theories and Approaches* (2nd edn, OUP 2003) 255.

they are part of the identities of the respective actors, stem from ideas and beliefs acquired in social interaction.[467]

A further distinction between rationalism and constructivism can be found in their respective explanations of the behaviour of actors. Rationalist theory maintains that actors act according to a *logic of consequences*,[468] that is, acting in a rational fashion according to a set list of preferences to be achieved. Constructivists, however, maintain that actors follow a *logic of appropriateness*. The term stands for a behaviour that is grounded in the identity of the actor. Instead of following some external material motivations, the reason to act in a certain way is intrinsic. When considering possible options for action in order to achieve a certain aim, the actor conditions its final decision on the ideas, beliefs, and norms its identity is based on. In other words, the constructivist view is that before making any decision an actor asks 'Given who I am, what is the appropriate way to achieve my goals?' – instead of – 'What is the most efficient way to do so?' In this way constructivism underlines the importance of norms to the behaviour of actors.[469]

Thus, how States behave in relation to each other, what politics they pursue, with whom they go to war, and whom they perceive as trading partners, depends upon what ideas and beliefs their identity and interests are based on. In this way, actors establish and shape the social structure of a normative and ideational reality and ultimately the relational structure among them.[470] Through norms, ideas and beliefs, actors give meaning to the material reality of their relation. To give an example: the fact that both the US and North Korea are in the possession of ballistic missiles is part of the material world. However, this fact means different things for a third country like South Korea. For South Korea, the material fact of North Korea's missile

[467] Hurd (n 464).

[468] Among others James G March and Johan P Olsen, 'Institutional Perspectives on Political Institutions' (1996) 93 Governance 147; James G March and Johan P Olsen, 'The Institutional Dynamics of International Political Orders' (1998) 52 IO 943.

[469] Adler, *Communitarian International Relations* (n 464) 92.

[470] The structure is called social for the reason that it originates from ideational factors that are 'not akin to beliefs or psychological states that reside inside our heads. Instead these ideas are... collectively held...' (Barnett, 'Social Constructivism' [n 462] 158).

possession combined with the ideational fact of differing beliefs and norms creates a hostile relation, giving rise to a threat. The very same material fact, that is, that the US is in possession of such missiles, does not have the same meaning for South Korea. Because these two States consider their relations – or relational structure – as friendly, these missiles do not constitute a threat, but rather are perceived as protection against the very same type of weapons employed by North Korea.[471]

The constructivist understanding that international relations are socially constructed challenges the rationalist notion of the nature of the international sphere in several ways. Constructivism not only questions the anarchical structure of international relations as a 'brute' fact, like a natural disaster, but also understands it as dependent on social interaction and interpretation. The structure of international relations, therefore, is not fixed or given while independent from State action. In fact, international structure can be and is constantly changed by State behaviour. Additionally, anarchy does not necessarily have to be qualified as negative. The term only defines a social structure that lacks a central authority.[472] Thus, anarchy can have a different meaning for different actors based on their respective interpretation of the situation. Wendt has described the distinction as follows.

> Anarchy as such is not a structural cause of anything. What matters is its social structure, which varies across anarchies. An anarchy of friends differs from one of enemies, one of self-help from one of collective security, and these are all constituted by structures of shared knowledge.[473]

Hence, constructivists conclude that '[a]narchy is what the states make of it.'[474] At the same time, constructivists emphasize that actors and structures constitute, shape and reshape each other. 'Normative and ideational structures may well condition the identities and interests of actors, but those

[471] A similar illustration is used by Wendt, 'Constructing' (n 464) 73.
[472] Hurd (n 464) 304.
[473] Wendt, 'Constructing' (n 464) 77-78.
[474] Wendt, 'Anarchy' (n 461) 395.

structures would not exist if it were not for the knowledgeable practices of those actors.'[475]

5.2 English school of international relations theory

Closely related to constructivism is the 'English school of international relations theory', also called the 'English school'.[476] While accepting the notion of anarchy in international relations, its central argument is that despite the anarchic structure, States form an international society 'which they shape and are shaped by.'[477] At the same time, its scholars dismiss the idea of a deterministic character of anarchy. The English school approach stands alongside constructivism as *via media* between rationalist approaches and more alternative theories, such as the critical theory. As such, scholars do not completely agree upon the exact position of the English school among international relations theories, particularly its position regarding liberalism. While Dunne locates the school between realism on one hand and liberalism/cosmopolitanism on the other,[478] Buzan puts it between neorealism/neoliberalism and the 'more radical' theories.[479]

In 1991, Martin Wight distinguished three different 'traditions' in inter-

---

[475] Reus-Smit (n 463) 225.

[476] Among the most influential exponents of this approach are Hedley Bull and Adam Watson (eds), *The Expansion of International Society* (OUP 1984); Hedley Bull, *The Anarchical Society: A Study of Order in World Politics* (3rd edn, Palgrave Macmillan 2002); Barry Buzan, *From International to World Society? The English School Theory and the Social Structure of Globalisation* (CUP 2004); Tim Dunne, 'New Thinking in International Society' (2001) 3 BJPIR 223; Tim Dunne, 'The English School' in Christian Reus-Smit and Duncan Snidal (eds), *The Oxford Handbook of International Relations* (OUP 2008); Robert Jackson, *The Global Covenant: Human Conduct in a World of States* (OUP 2000); Andrew Linklater, 'The English School' in Scott Burchill and others (eds), *Theories of International Relations* (5th edn, Palgrave Macmillan 2014); Daniel Philpott, *Revolutions in Sovereignty: How Ideas Shaped Modern International Relations* (Princeton University Press 2001); Adam Watson, 'Hedley Bull, States System and International Society' (1987) 13 RevIntlStud 147; Martin Wight, *International Theory: The Three Traditions* (Leicester University Press 1991).

[477] Buzan (n 476) 8.

[478] Dunne, 'English School' (n 476) 268.

[479] Buzan (n 476) 10.

national theory: 'realism', 'rationalism', and 'revolutionism'.[480] Realism maintains that the anarchical structure is a Hobbesian state of nature. Realist scholars 'emphasize in international relations the element of anarchy, of power-politics, and of warfare.'[481] Rationalist scholars, then, 'concentrate on, and believe in the value of, the element of international intercourse in a condition predominantly of international anarchy.'[482] But at the same time, it is articulated that due to their rationality, actors are able to co-operate by establishing rules and institutions to maintain the co-operation. Lastly, revolutionists

> believe so passionately in the moral unity of the society of States or the international society, that they identify with it, and therefore they both claim to speak in the name of the unity, and experience an overriding obligation to give effect to it... For them, the whole of international society transcends its parts; they are cosmopolitan rather than 'internationalist'...[483]

As a proponent of the English school theory, Bull raises and explores 'an inquiry into the nature of order in world politics' on these three traditions.[484] He identified in Wight's three '*R's*'[485] three competing traditions of thought: the 'Hobbesian' or 'realist', the 'Kantian' or 'universalist', and the 'Grotian' or 'internationalist'. In the Hobbesian view, there is an international system resembling a state of nature where co-operation between States is impossible. To the contrary, the Kantian view denies the primacy of States in international politics and describes a global society of human individuals. In his study, Bull emphasizes the Grotian idea of an international society of States. This notion shares some basic elements with the Hobbesian conception by accepting the premise that sovereign States are the primary actors in international politics. In addition, there is the common assumption of anarchy in international relations. Nevertheless, this

[480] Wight, *International Theory* (n 476).
[481] ibid 15.
[482] ibid, 13.
[483] ibid, 8.
[484] Bull, *Anarchical Society* (n 476) xxxii.
[485] Realism, rationalism and revolutionism.

understanding of the international sphere is neither a complete zero-sum game in which States struggle for power, nor is it a pure harmony without any kind of conflict. The Grotian approach rejects that anarchy is evidence of the non-existence of international order.[486] On the contrary, it is held that there is 'a very high level of order, and surprisingly little interstate violence, in the absence of a higher coercive authority.'[487] Regarding this position, the English school follows the constructivist notion that anarchy is not the cause of, but rather, the result of state action. They conclude that this interstate action creates some kind of – still anarchic – arrangement to maintain this order. In this regard Bull distinguishes between a *system of States* and a *society of States*.

> A *system of States* (or international system) is formed when two or more states have sufficient contact between them, and have sufficient impact on another's decisions, to cause them to behave – at least in some measure – as parts of a whole.[488]

More precisely, States constitute a system when 'there is interaction between them sufficient to make behaviour of each a necessary element in the calculations of the other.'[489] Thus, in order to form a system, there must be interaction, but not necessarily shared rules or institutions.[490] To a certain extent, the idea of a state system resembles the Hobbesian or realist notion.[491] Yet, whereas in the realist view the interaction is regularly conflictive, it does not matter for the English school's notion of what nature this interaction is, ie cooperative or conflictive, direct or indirect.
A *society of States*, on the other hand, has the distinctive feature of shared norms and institutions.

> A *society of States* (or international society) exists when a group of states, conscious of certain common interests and common

[486] Wight, *International Theory* (n 476) 44-47.
[487] Linklater (n 476) 88.
[488] Bull, *Anarchical Society* (n 476) 9.
[489] ibid, 9-10.
[490] Dunne, 'English School' (n 476) 275.
[491] ibid, 276.

> values, form a society in the sense that they conceive themselves to be bound by a common set of rules in their relations with one another and share in the working of common institutions.[492]

According to the constructivists, ideas, values, and beliefs constitute the actors' identity. In the case of an international society, States understand themselves as 'sovereign entities' and recognize other members of the society as the same.[493] Based on their identities, the actors follow their interests that are, on one hand, the protection of their sovereignty and possessions and, on the other hand, the certainty that promises once made will be kept.[494] To ensure the achievement of their interests and regulate interaction, States set up rules and institutions, such as diplomacy and international law, to which they regard themselves and their actions to be bound. While international organizations also constitute such institutions, it is important to note that such organizations, in particular the League of Nations or the UN, are not to be equated with the concept of a society of States as used within the English school. Rather, such institutions are the expression of the shared values and interests of an international society.

An international society corresponds to an exclusive club in which membership is closely tied to the identity of the respective member. 'According to its rules, international societies grant their own members a broader set of privileges – diplomatic immunities, commitments to consultation, restraint from intervention – than they grant to those they deem outsiders.'[495] Additionally, these self-imposed rules determine admission to the society, whereas the admission criteria perform a gate-keeping function.[496] The members of an international society are exclusively sovereign States. As 'sovereignty' is the common identity of these States, the constitution of an international society is founded both on the claim of sovereignty of each

---

[492] Bull, *Anarchical Society* (n 476) 13.

[493] Wendt, 'Collective Identity Formation' (n 464) 388.

[494] Bull, *Anarchical Society* (n 476) 4.

[495] Philpott (n 476) 20.

[496] Öyvind Österud, 'The Narrow Gate: Entry to the Club of Sovereign States' (1997) 23 RevIntlStud 167, 167.

member as well as on the mutual recognition of the others as such.[497] States can be part of both an international society and an international system. At the same time, there are other, non-recognized entities, which are only part of the international system but not members of the international society.[498] That is not to say that members of this society do not interact with these other entities outside the international society, ie in the international system. But these entities are not seen as equals, and as a result not entitled to full privileges.[499]

The English school's motivation to engage with the idea of international society is guided by the interest in the historical development of the international society.[500] The historical societies are commonly identified as the *Christian international society*, the *international society of civilized States* and *the global international society*. However, there is no general conformity among scholars regarding the denomination or exact time frame of these stages. Bull, for example, referred to the international society of civilized States as the European International Society,[501] while Röling used the terms Christian nations, Civilized Nations, and Peace-Loving Nations.[502] Grewe saw the foundation of the international legal community at the end of the 15th century, dividing the Christian-European society of States into the Spanish Age (1494-1648) and the French Age (1648-1815),[503] whereas Steiger located the roots of international law in the 13th century and employed the terms 'Christianity', 'civilized States', 'mankind' and 'world

---

[497] Dunne, 'English School' (n 476) 272.

[498] Calling this 'de facto regimes', the concept of effectively existing but not recognized entities has also been examined by Frowein, *Untersuchung* (n 209); see on this also Frowein, 'De Facto Regime' (n 209).

[499] Philpott (n 476) 272.

[500] Dunne, 'English School' (n 476) 265.

[501] Bull, *Anarchical Society* (n 476) 31ff.

[502] BVA Röling, *International Law in an Expanded World* (Djambatan 1960).

[503] Grewe, *Epochs* (n 10) 142 et passim; similarly Ziegler (n 11) 121 et passim.

citizen' to label the stages of development of international law and those concerned by it.[504]

The formation of an international society requires the pre-existence of an international system; meanwhile an international system can persist without developing into an international society.[505] Moreover, it is assumed that the development of an international society and its history of shifting the boundaries of inclusion and exclusion is grounded in the recognition and non-recognition of entities as sovereign States.

[504] See for example Heinhard Steiger, 'From the International Law of Christianity to the International Law of the World Citizen – Reflections on the Formation of the Epochs of the History of International Law' (2001) 3 JHistIntLaw 180.

[505] Bull, *Anarchical Society* (n 476) 13.

6 Explaining the evolution of State recognition: The concept of recognitional fitness

Given that the members of a society are known, the question remains how an entity does become recognized as eligible for membership in an international society. To answer this, one must return to the original question of this study on how recognition of States evolved historically. Based on the findings of the comparison of the contemporary doctrine and practice, it is assumed that in order to be recognized as sovereign States, and thus members of an international society, entities must correspond with conditions and rules discussed, implemented and practised by the already existing members, ie the sovereign States that mutually recognize each other as such. That is, States have to identify the entity as one of them, based on their shared ideas, values, and beliefs.

The explanatory model to investigate the question on the evolution of State recognition, which will be developed in the following, is termed 'recognitional fitness'. It is based on elements of the above-presented English school approach and incorporates certain aspects of the discussion between the declaratory and the constitutive theory.

A key point of the English school is the distinction between an international system and an international society. In a system, States coexist, and might even have certain amount of contact with each other, but do not share common values, interests, or norms. As an international society, however, a group of States with similar values and interests has a common set of rules to regulate their relations and their behaviour. This society of States granting its members certain privileges resembles an exclusive club with restrictive admission criteria.[506] While the members' conduct and interaction among themselves is based on formal legal equality, their relations with other States outside the society are based upon a regime of unequal rules and practices.

The English school's reasoning is reminiscent of some of the main points of the declaratory, as well as of the constitutive argument. The declaratory

[506] For this notion, see also Österud (n 496).

approach submits that existence of a State is independent of recognition by the other States as long as this State exists as a fact. The constitutive theory's quintessence, however, is that an entity's endowment with full rights and duties is subject to the recognition by other, already existing States. Recognition is thus equivalent to the admission to the international society. In regard to the English school's line of argument it is concluded that the effective but non-recognized States do exist. They are part of the system of States, but because not recognized, they are not members of the society of States, despite a certain degree of de facto recognition due to 'sufficient contact' with other States. Still, the unrecognized States enjoy only a very limited range of rights, if any. Thus, even if the existence of a State is independent of recognition by the others, it will only be able to enjoy its full amount of international rights upon the recognition by the other States, ie its admission to international society. Because an effective State exists prior to and independent of its recognition, the purpose of recognition is not to transform an entity into a State but rather to admit it to the international society. However, if plain effectiveness leads to Statehood, but nevertheless is insufficient to be recognized by the others, the question arises what criteria are and – with regard the original research question – have been necessary and sufficient to be recognized?

One must distinguish between State criteria and recognition criteria. To be recognized, entities not only have to be effective States, but also fulfil additional requirements. It is furthermore assumed that the (self-)image the States have of themselves and of 'their' international society is based on their values and interests, which in turn are reflected in the respective contemporary international law doctrine and, particularly, state practice. This, again, also affects fundamentally the recognition of States, ie the admission of new members to the international society. Thus, a 'candidate entity' has to be identified fit for recognition by members of international society in order to gain admission.

It is submitted that this recognitional fitness consists of three categories of criteria. Assuming that the categories continue to remain the same over time, the criteria are subject to change. *Effectiveness* is one category for recognition. In order to be considered a candidate for recognition in the first place, the entity has to show a certain degree of effectiveness.[507] This effectiveness is basically grounded on the existence of State territory, population and a government with a certain degree of effectiveness, whereby the effectiveness of its external sovereignty might be limited due to non-recognition. Nevertheless, according to the principle *ex factis jus oritur* and the declarative theory, as soon as a State achieves factual existence, it is a State. However, while effectiveness is necessary, it is not sufficient for recognition. If a State's existence, and the resulting recognition, were based merely on effectiveness, this existence, and also its emergence and disappearance, would be outside the scope of law. This again would lead to the situation where questions of a State's existence or non-existence are decided solely by power.[508] Consequently, a State might effectively exist, having acquired its effectiveness by means violating legal norms. Given this possibility, the idea of 'statehood as effectiveness' has been criticized as facticist.[509] While effectiveness remains indispensable for recognition, it is not sufficient and has therefore to be complemented with a further category of criteria.

Legality is the second category of criteria for recognitional fitness. That is, the effective existence of a State must not have occurred contrary to norms of the society of States. While in present international law, such norms are the prohibition of intervention and of the use of force as well as grave violations of human rights, like racism and apartheid,[510] it is principally subject to change what is considered legal and illegal and up to the respective contemporary concept of international law. Pursuant to the notion that the principle *ex iniuria jus non oritur* overrules the principle *ex factis jus oritur*, the members of the international society do not recognize de facto

---

507 On effectiveness, see ch 1 ('The concept of recognition and the principle of effectiveness').

508 Anne Peters, 'Statehood after 1989: "Effectivités" between Legality and Virtuality' in James Crawford and Sarah Nouwen (eds), *Select Proceedings of the European Society of International Law* (Hart 2012) vol 3, 172.

509 ibid, 172.

510 See also on this, sub-s 2.4.3 ('Non-recognition').

entities emerging through the violation of norms of the international society.

It is believed that effectiveness and legality are both necessary, yet not sufficient for recognition. This is reflected in the notion of the international system where 'States' de facto exist, but are not recognized as such and are therefore not admitted to the international society.[511] For this reason it is assumed that there is – and always has been – certain additional elements required for recognitional fitness, brought together in a third category termed *legitimacy*.[512] Legitimacy is chiefly understood as a 'political order's worthiness to be recognized.'[513] Aside from being 'the collective judgement of international society about rightful membership of the family of nations',[514] legitimacy also defines appropriate conduct within international society.[515] This is not to be confused with legal conduct. Whereas legal conduct is most often also legitimate, situations exist where these two attributes conflict. An example for such a situation was the NATO bombing of Serbia in 1999. Since no UNSC resolution authorized this NATO operation, it was illegal. At the same time, as it seemed a means of last resort to stop an assumed genocide, it was considered legitimate by the Independent International Commission on Kosovo.[516]

---

[511]On this see also Frowein, *Untersuchung* (n 209); Frowein, 'De Facto Regime' (n 209).

[512]eg Ian Clark, *Legitimacy in International Society* (OUP 2005) . Previously, such elements have also been called 'standard of civilization' or 'modern requirement'. See Gerrit W Gong, *The Standard of Civilization in International Society* (Clarendon Press 1984); Chris Brown, 'The Modern Requirement? Reflections on Normative International Theory in a Post-Western World' (1988) 17 Millenium - JIntSt 339.

[513]Jürgen Habermas, 'Legitimation Problems in the Modern State' in *Communication and the Evolution of Society* (Beacon Press 1979) 178.

[514]Martin Wight, *Systems of States* (Leicester University Press 1977) 153.

[515]Dunne, 'New Thinking' (n 476) 89; Clark, *Legitimacy in International Society* (n 512) 5.

[516]Independent International Commission on Kosovo, *The Kosovo Report: Conflict, International Response, Lessons Learned* (OUP 2000) 186; see on this also Fernando Muñoz Hernández, *Legitimität und Legalität im Völkerrecht: Die völkerrechtstheoretische Debatte um die Legitimität Governance-Strukturen* (PhD thesis, University of Thübingen 2011) 5.

The concept of legitimacy is as central as its content is variable and continues over time to evolve.[517] Legitimacy standards are and have been subject to negotiations among members of international society 'as they seek out an accommodation between those seemingly absolute values, and attempt to reconcile them with a working consensus to which all can feel bound.'[518] Thus, legitimacy should not be regarded as static and absolute, but rather as a constantly shifting concept based on the values and interests of the respective contemporary international society. In other words: 'In a world of States, legitimacy is what states make of it.'[519] Legitimacy criteria are requirements imposed on the recognition candidate in addition to the requirements of effectiveness and legality.[520] Whereas it is questionable whether there are exceptions in which legitimacy can compensate for legality,[521] it is plausible that regarding recognition, legitimacy can substitute a deficit in effectiveness.

In summation, an entity desiring recognition and by this gaining access to the privileged and exclusive club of States, must appear fit for recognition by the already existing States, ie the club members. This 'recognitional fitness' consists of three categories of criteria: effectiveness, legality, and legitimacy. Furthermore, there is a distinction between state criteria and recognition criteria. Whereas according to the declaratory approach, simple effectiveness suffices as state criterion, legality and legitimacy are additionally required for recognition.

With this as the foundation, the following part will outline and study the development of State recognition focusing on some representative examples. In the studied era, spanning roughly from the mid-seventeenth cen-

---

[517] Inis L Claude Jr, 'Collective Legitimization as a Political Function of the United Nations' (1966) 20 IO 367, 369; Mlada Bukovansky, *Legitimacy and Power Politics: The American and French Revolutions in International Political Culture* (Princeton University Press 2002) 212.

[518] Clark, *Legitimacy in International Society* (n 512) 29-30.

[519] Ian Clark, 'Legitmacy in a Global Order' (2003) 29 RevIntlStud 75, 81.

[520] See on this sub-s 2.2.3 ('Conditional and unconditional recognition').

[521] Orakhelashvili rules this out (Alexander Orakhelashvili, 'International Law, International Politics and Ideology' in Alexander Orakhelashvili [ed], *Research Handbook on the Theory and History of International Law* (Edward Elgar 2011) 374).

tury until the end of the twentieth century, three international societies are identified: the Christian international society, the international society of civilized States, and the global international society.[522] Every society will be analyzed using the explanatory model of 'recognitional fitness'.

[522] All dates referenced throughout this work are given according to the Gregorian Calendar.

IV The Recognition of States through the Ages

7 Admission to the Christian international society

7.1 The Christian international society

This analysis begins essentially with the admission to the Christian international society of States since 1648, the year of the Peace of Westphalia. Nonetheless, because certain developments that eventually led up to the recognition of some of following examples originated earlier, it is necessary to commence before 1648.

While 1648 represents the majority consensus, it should be noted that some experts place the origin of the Christian international society at the end of the 15th century.[523] Its intellectual and normative foundation as well as its basis of value was Roman-Catholic Christianity. Christianity united Europe politically as well as intellectually and religiously.[524] The Christian international society was not initially, nor for a long time, based on sovereign, independent States in a modern sense.[525] Rather it consisted of a various duchies, counties, and other types of realms covered with a complicated net of vassalage, feudal obligations and jurisdictions, unified and dominated by the Holy Roman Emperor and the Papacy.[526]

Christianity was also the source of law. The members of the Christian international society understood themselves bound to Divine or Natural law.[527] Christianity likewise determined who was within circle, ie the international society, to which this law applied. Hence, these legal standards were only applied among the Christian nations, but not in relation to non-Christian peoples ('heathens').[528] Although the beginning of the Reformation in the 16th century meant the commencing disintegration of the Catholic Church's

---

[523] On this Bull, *Anarchical Society* (n 476) 26ff; Grewe, *Epochs* (n 10) 142 et passim; Röling (n 502) 17-25; Steiger identifies the beginning of this epoch even in the 13th century. See Steiger, 'Reflections' (n 504) 183ff.

[524] Bull, *Anarchical Society* (n 476) 27; Steiger, 'Reflections' (n 504) 184.

[525] Bull, *Anarchical Society* (n 476) 28.

[526] Adam Watson, 'European International Society and Its Expansion' in Hedley Bull and Adam Watson (eds), *The Expansion of International Society* (OUP 1984) 13.

[527] Bull, *Anarchical Society* (n 476) 27-28; Röling (n 502) 21.

[528] Bull, *Anarchical Society* (n 476) 27-28; Röling (n 502) 18.

dominance, the fundamentally Christian – even though denominationally divided – foundation of the international society subsisted for several centuries.[529] With the conclusion of the Westphalian Peace in the mid-17th century, however, the dominance of Emperor and Papacy suffered another setback.

The 'Peace of Westphalia' formally ended the Thirty Years' War (1618–1648), a series of different conflicts about religious and political power in Europe, in which the majority of the States at the time were involved. It was a religious conflict between Protestants and Catholics, triggered by the Reformation. At the same time, it was a struggle between France and Sweden on the one hand, and the Holy Roman Empire on the other. Finally, it was a conflict between the Emperor and the larger estates aiming for a higher degree of independence.[530]

Schiller has described the 'Peace of Westphalia' as 'one of the most interesting and characteristic monuments of human policy and passions'.[531] It actually stands for a cluster of treaties. The treaty between France and the Holy Roman Empire, negotiated in Münster, is the Peace of Münster (Instrumentum Pacis Monasteriensis [IPM]).[532] The Peace of Osnabrück (Instrumentum Pacis Osnabrugensis [IPO]),[533] is the treaty negotiated in Osnabrück between Sweden and the Holy Roman Empire. Both of these contracts were signed on 24 October 1648 in Münster, Westphalia. Also involved in these treaties were Austria, the Duke of Savoy, England, Denmark and Norway with associated estates including the Duchy of Schleswig, Poland, the Duchy of Lorraine, Italy, the Netherlands, the cantons of Switzerland and the Grisons and the princedom of Transylvania as well as Portu-

---

529 Steiger, 'Reflections' (n 504) 184.

530 Bardo Fassbender, 'Peace of Westphalia (1648)' in Ruediger Wolfrum (ed), *The Max Planck Encyclopedia of Public International Law* (OUP 2012) vol X, 865.

531 Frederick Schiller, *History of the Thirty Years War* (AJW Morrission tr, first published 1788, Harper Brothers 1846) 370.

532 Treaty of Peace between France and the Empire ['Instrumentum Pacis Monasteriensis, (IPM)'] (signed 24 October 1648) 1 CTS 271.

533 Treaty of Peace between Sweden and the Empire ['Instrumentum Pacis Osnabrugensis (IPO)'] (signed 24 October 1648) 1 CTS 119.

gal, Russia and the Republic of Venice.[534] In addition, the peace treaty between Spain and the Dutch Republic from 30 January 1648 ending the Eighty' Years War (1568-1648), in which the Netherlands sought independence from Spain, is also considered part of the Peace of Westphalia.[535] Many international relations and international law scholars understand the Peace of Westphalia as a historical caesura.[536] According to them, it essentially signified the watershed between the decay old European *respublica christiana*, characterized by the dominance of the political and religious union of the Holy Roman Empire and the Christian Church, and the rise of the society of equal States coordinating their interaction through an established set of rules. Establishment of the concept of state sovereignty

---

[534]IPO (n 533) art 17, §§10-11; because IPO art 17 §§10-11 is missing in CTS, it is taken instead from Wilhelm G Grewe (ed), *Fontes Historiae Iuris Gentium* (Berlin and New York, 1988-1995) vol 1, 201.

[535]Treaty of Peace between Spain and the Netherlands (signed 30 January 1648) 1 CTS 1.

[536]Philip Bobbitt, *The Shield of Achilles: War, Peace, and the Course of History* (Knopf 2002) 508; Hedley Bull, 'The Importance of Grotius in the Study of International Relations' in Hedley Bull, Benedict Kingsbury, and Adam Roberts (eds), *Hugo Grotius and International Relations* (Clarendon Press 1990) 76; Cassese, *International Law* (n 19) 22, 24; Richard Falk, 'The Interplay of Westphalia and Charter Conception of International Legal Order' in Richard A Falk and Cyril E Black (eds), *The Future of the International Order: Trends and Patterns* (Princeton University Press 1969) vol I, 43; Grewe, *Epochs* (n 10) 293; Leo Gross, 'The Peace of Westphalia, 1648-1948' (1948) 42 AJIL 20, 26, 28-29; Kalevi Jaakko Holsti, *Peace and War: Armed Conflicts and International Order 1648-1989* (CUP 1991) 26, 39; Jackson (n 476) 165; Martin Kintzinger, 'From the Late Middle Ages to the Peace of Westphalia' in Bardo Fassbender and Anne Peters (eds), *The Oxford Handbook of the History of international Law* (OUP 2012) 607; Malanczuk (n 109) 9; Philpott (n 476) 89; Gianfranco Poggi, *The Development of the Modern State: A Sociological Introduction* (Hutchinson 1978) 89; Robert F Randle, *Issues in the History of International Relations: The Role of Issues in the Evolution of the State System* (Praeger 1987) 36; Heinhard Steiger, 'Concrete Peace and General Order: The Legal Meaning of the Treaties of 24 October 1648' in Klaus Bussmann and Heinz Schilling (eds), *1648: War and Peace in Europe* (Westfälisches Landesmuseum für Kunst und Kulturgeschichte 1998) vol 1: Politics, Religion, Law and Society, 445; Adam Watson, *The Evolution of International Society: A Comparative Historical Analysis* (Routledge 1992) 186; Stephan Verosta, 'History of International Law, 1648-1815' in Ruediger Wolfrum (ed), *The Max Planck Encyclopedia of Public International Law* (OUP 2012) vol IV, 823.

is widely seen as the main attainment of the Peace of Westphalia.[537] According to this perception, often summarized under the term *Westphalian system*,[538] States became the main actors with full sovereignty within their borders. As a result, new political and legal concepts arose, such as legal equality of States and State sovereignty based on exclusive territorial jurisdiction. So that the sovereignty of the weaker States was not undermined by the more powerful ones, the concept of balance of power was installed. Also, State consent became the only valid source of international law. The concept of non-intervention, ie no external power is entitled to interfere in the internal affairs of a State is perceived as another central outcome of the Peace of Westphalia, and as a consequence of the principles of sovereignty and equality of States.[539]

This position is not universally adopted. Other scholars denied the view of the Peace of Westphalia as a clean break by calling it a myth,[540] or, simply, wrong.[541] Others, again, did not go as far but still expressed various reservations about its alleged extraordinary role.[542] They remarked that the

---

[537] eg Holsti (n 536) 39; Norman Paech and Gerhard Stuby, *Völkerrecht und Machtpolitik in den internationalen Beziehungen: Aktualisierte Ausgabe* (VSA-Verlag 2013) 53; Walter Simons, *The Evolution of International Public Law in Europe since Grotius* (Yale University Press 1931) 6.

[538] See on this Rainer Grote, 'Westphalian System' in Ruediger Wolfrum (ed), *The Max Planck Encyclopedia of Public International Law* (OUP 2012) vol X, 870.

[539] ibid, 871.

[540] Andreas Osiander, *The States System of Europe, 1640-1990: Peacemaking and the Conditions of International Stability* (Clarendon Press 1994) 78; Andreas Osiander, 'Sovereignty, International Relations, and the Westphalian Myth' (2001) 55 IO 251, 251; Benno Teschke, *The Myth of 1648: Class, Geopolitics, and the Making of Modern International Relations* (Verso 2003).

[541] Stephen D Krasner, 'Westphalia and All That' in Judith Goldstein and Robert O Keohane (eds), *Ideas and Foreign Policy: Beliefs, institutions, and Political Change* (Cornell University Press 1993) 235; Yet, Krasner amended his statement calling the Peace of Westphalia 'a break point with the past' nonetheless, see Stephen D Krasner, *Sovereignty: Organized Hypocrisy* (Princeton University Press 1999) 82.

[542] Jeremy Black, *European International Relations 1648-1815* (Palgrave 2002) 74; Derek Croxton, 'The Peace of Westphalia of 1648 and the Origins of Sovereignty' (1999) 21 Int Hist Rev 569, 574; Fassbender, 'Westphalia' (n 530) 866; Grote (n 538) 872; Ulrich Scheuner, 'Die grossen Friedensschlüsse als Grundlage der Europäischen Staatsordnung

Peace of Westphalia does not stand for a turning point in history because not only were the developments towards independent entities with clear defined territories commenced already from 1500 onwards, but also the Holy Roman Empire did not cease to exist for another 150 years. It is furthermore pointed out that the Peace of Westphalia cannot be considered the breakthrough of sovereignty.[543] Despite that the concept was already employed by Jean Bodin in *Les six livres de la République* (1576),[544] and in Thomas Hobbes' *De Cive* (1642),[545] as well as in official documents before and after 1648, the term as such was not specifically used in the Westphalian treaties.[546] In practice, the independence and sovereignty of several States, such as Sweden, France and England, had already been established before the Peace of Westphalia.[547]

The sovereignty of the German estates was only limited. In 1555, the Religious Peace of Augsburg established the principle of *cuius regio, eius religio*[548] allowing each territorial ruler to determine the denomination within his territory for himself and his subjects. The treaties of Münster and Osnabrück confirmed this principle in essence,[549] yet, added for the subjects the right to emigrate,[550] the freedom to adopt another denomination without being prevented, to worship at home and in their neighbourhood and to educate their children in schools of their confession or at home.[551] Hence, while bestowing the individual subjects with denominational rights, it limited the State's sovereignty.[552] It was not only with regard to religious af-

---

zwischen 1648 und 1815' in Konrad Repgen and Stephan Skalweit (eds), *Spiegel der Geschichte: Festgabe für Max Braubach zum 10. April 1964* (Verlag Aschendorff 1964) 223.

543 Croxton (n 542) 574, 584.

544 Jean Bodin, *Les six livres de la République* (first published 1576, Librairie générale française 1983).

545 Thomas Hobbes, *De Cive: The English Version* (Clarendon Press 1983).

546 Grote (n 538) 872; Fassbender, 'Westphalia' (n 530) 868.

547 Grote (n 538) 872.

548 'whose realm, his religion'.

549 IPO (n 533) art 5 §1; confirmed in IPM (n 532) §47.

550 IPO (n 533) art 5 §30.

551 ibid, art 5 §34.

552 Croxton (n 542) 575; also Grote (n 538) 872.

fairs, but also in foreign policy, that the individual States remained affiliated to the Empire. The estates had the right to conclude treaties and make alliances among themselves or with foreigners in order to sustain peace and security provided that these alliances were not directed against the Emperor or the Empire.[553]

Another point of reservation concerns the advancement of international law. The rise of the international society after 1648 is often equated with the emergence of modern international law or the so-called law of nations. Yet, it has been indicated that also the doctrinal development already reached its first apex before the Peace of Westphalia.[554] Already the exponents of the Spanish scholastics, above all Francisco de Vitoria and Franscisco Suárez, concerned themselves with questions regarding various emerging interstate problems and developed new doctrinal approaches, particularly regarding war and peace. Moreover, with the work of Hugo Grotius, referred to as the 'father of international law',[555] international law became a separate legal discipline already before the end of the Thirty Years' War.[556]

Overall, despite that certain developments got under way before 1648, the Peace of Westphalia still signifies a prominent evolutionary stage of the international society. Particularly with regard to State recognition, the year 1648 serves as temporary delimitation of the Christian international society. Before then, when there existed mainly hereditary monarchies, the question of recognizing States and governments was not highly relevant. The transfer of sovereignty was seen as an internal process on which other States usually were not supposed to take a stance.[557] Now, because the recognition

---

[553] IPO (n 533) art 5 §1; IPM (n 532) §65; also on this Grote (n 538) 872.

[554] Bardo Fassbender, 'Die verfassung- und völkerrechtliche Bedeutung des Westfälischen Friedens von 1648' in Ingo Erberich and others (eds), *Frieden und Recht* (Boorberg 1998) 21.

[555] eg Peter Haggenmacher, 'Hugo Grotius (1583-1645)' in Bardo Fassbender and Anne Peters (eds), *The Oxford Handbook of the History of international Law* (OUP 2012) 1098.

[556] Fassbender, 'Bedeutung' (n 554) 22.

[557] Grewe, *Epochs* (n 10) 343-44.

of the Dutch and Swiss independence in the Peace of Westphalia proved to be a novelty, the year 1648 is used here as a caesura.

7.2 Recognition of States in Christian international society doctrine

In legal scholarship, the issue of recognizing new States and the requirements for it were initially, ie prior to the independence of the Netherlands and Switzerland, not subject of debate. Furthermore, Georg Jellinek's 'three elements',[558] in particular a defined territory, did not matter in the Christian international society doctrine. Rather, based on the idea of the social contract, the concept 'State' was conceived as a voluntary association of men under a common government.[559] Hence, Grotius defined a State as 'a complete association of free men, joined together for the enjoyment of rights and for their common interest.'[560] Also for Vattel States were 'political bodies, societies of men who have united together and combined their forces, in order to procure their mutual welfare and security.'[561]
As a result, the discussion on recognition concerned first and foremost the question whether subjects were allowed to rebel against and to dispose of their ruler. Vitoria held that despite that the ruler obtains its governmental power from its commonwealth, its monarchical power derives from God. In consequence, when the commonwealth had transferred the power to the king it can no longer demand it back.[562] However, if the king proves to be

[558] See s 2.1 ('Requirements for recognition').

[559] Daniel-Erasmus Khan, 'Territory and Boundaries' in Bardo Fassbender and Anne Peters (eds), *The Oxford Handbook of the History of International Law* (OUP 2012) 234.

[560] Hugo Grotius, *De Jure Belli ac Pacis Libri Tres* (Francis W Kelsey ed, first published 1625, Clarendon Press 1925) vol 2, book 1, ch I, 44.

[561] Emer de Vattel, *Le droit des gens ou principes de la loi naturelle appliqués à la conduite et aux affaires des nations et des souverain* (first published 1758, Carnegie Institution 1916) book 1, Introduction, 3; on this also Khan (n 559) 234.

[562] Francisco De Vitoria, 'On Civil Power' in Anthony Pagden and Jeremy Lawrance (eds), *Francisco De Vitoria: Political Writings* (first published 1528, CUP 1991) 14-16 and 31.

a tyrant, the commonwealth still has the right to defend itself.[563] But regardless of this, because the king derives its power from God, it would be still a sacrilege to revolt.[564] Ayala argued similarly, stating that under no circumstances can the subjects rebel against their king, unless he is a tyrant who forcibly and illegally usurped the throne.[565] But a rightful ruler may not be killed or disposed of by his people. Only the Pope as 'God's regent on earth' is allowed to depose a king abusing his power because he derived his power from God. Suárez shared the view that a rightful ruler has to be obeyed and cannot be deprived of his power unless he becomes a tyrant.[566] But in Suárez' opinion, it is not only the Pope, but also the community of the subjects acting as a whole, who may dispose the king in order to defend itself and preserve the State as a means of last resort. Despite having the right to disposition of the king, the subjects are still subordinate to the Pope, who first has to examine the cause, and eventually may deter the community from the undertaking. At the same time, the Pope has the power to command the community to depose the sovereign.[567] A revolt is, therefore, not 'intrinsically evil'. For the reason that the tyrant 'waging unjustly war' is an aggressor against the State or parts of it, the State or parts of it have the right to defend themselves.[568] Grotius, then again, rejects the notion that

[563] Francisco De Vitoria, 'On Law: Lectures on Summa Theologica I-II. 90-105' in Anthony Pagden and Jeremy Lawrance (eds), *Francisco De Vitoria: Political Writings* (CUP 1991) 199-200.

[564] Anthony Pagden and Jeremy Lawrance, 'Introduction' in Anthony Pagden and Jeremy Lawrance (eds), *Francisco De Vitoria: Political Writings* (CUP 1991) xx.

[565] Balthazar Ayala, *Balthazaris Ayalae I. C. et Exercitus Regii apud Belgas Supremi Juridici: De Jure et Officiis Bellicis et Disciplina Militari Libri III* (John Westlake ed, John Pawly Bate tr, first published 1582, Carnegie Institution 1912) vol 2, 14-20.

[566] Francisco Suárez, 'De Legibus, ac Deo Legislatore' in James B Scott (ed), *Selections from Three Works of Francisco Suárez, S.J.* (first published 1612, Clarendon Press; H Milford 1944) vol 1 (Photogaphic reproduction from the original Editions), 383-84 and 386-87.

[567] Francisco Suárez, 'Defensio Fidei Catholicae, et Apostologicae Adversus Anglicanae Sectae Errores' in James B Scott (ed), *Selections from Three Works of Francisco Suárez, S.J.* (first published 1612, Clarendon Press; H Milford 1944) vol 2, 718-20.

[568] Francisco Suárez, 'De Triplici Virtute Theologica, Fide, Spe, et Charitate' in James B Scott (ed), *Selections from Three Works of Francisco Suárez, S.J.* (first published 1621,

because power is vested in the people they have the unexceptional right to punish an abusive king.[569] Rebellion against the authority is permissible only in very rare cases of 'extreme and imminent peril',[570] for example, if a ruler transgresses against the laws and the State, if the king renounces his governmental authority, if he alienates his kingdom, or if he turns into an enemy against his own people.[571] Against this, Milton argued, that since rulers obtain their power for the common good from the people being born free, it is their right to depose him, if he acts as a tyrant.[572]

Only in the 18th century, the examinations did get under way as to what conditions the recognition of newly independent entities and the admission to the international society were appropriate. Vattel, for instance, generally supported the view of effective independence being sufficient.[573] Nevertheless, in case there is an internal conflict over power, third States may not interfere.[574] A community, however, is permitted to 'withdraw itself from his obedience' if the ruler turns into a tyrant. In this, Vattel saw the justification for the secession of the Netherlands from Spain.[575] Thus the Swiss Confederation split rightfully from the Empire and obtained its independence long before its acknowledgement.[576] Moser shared the opinion that no state is allowed to get involved in the internal affairs of another State.[577] As a consequence, third States have to withhold recognition of a new State that had achieved its independence through armed revolution and secession

Clarendon Press; H Milford 1944) vol 1 (Photogaphic reproduction from the original Editions), vol 2, 854-55.

[569] Grotius (n 560) vol 2, book I, ch II, 103 and ch III, 138ff.

[570] ibid, ch III, 148.

[571] ibid, ch III, 156.

[572] John Milton, *The Tenure of Kings and Magistrates* (Printed by Matthew Simmons 1649) 14-15.

[573] Vattel (n 561) vol 1, book I, ch I, 18; on this also Grewe, *Epochs* (n 10) 345-46.

[574] Vattel (n 561) ch III, 38.

[575] ibid, ch IV, 47.

[576] ibid, ch XVII, 190-91.

[577] Johann Jacob Moser, *Grund-Sätze des jetzt üblichen Europäischen Völcker-Rechts in Friedens-Zeiten* (2nd edn, bey Johann August Raspe 1763) 521.

from its former sovereign. Only after the old sovereign has relinquished its sovereignty, is it permitted to grant recognition.[578]

Steck, too, made the legality and the recognition of independence of a seceding entity from its mother country dependent upon the recognition and renunciation of its sovereignty by the latter, whereas the mere declaration of independence does not suffice.[579] Before this renunciation of the mother State, however, it is not permitted for third States to recognize the independence of this province, although it might be even factually independent. The State concerned would perceive such behaviour as hostility.[580] 'Eine stärkere Beleidigung lässt sich allerdings nicht gedenken, als ein abgefallenes, ein sich vom Mutterlande lossreissendes Volk für entlediget seiner Verbindungen mit demselben, für frey, für unabhängig zu erkennen.'[581]

Martens supported the opinion that in case of a revolution a third State is in principle not allowed to intervene and that initially the previous ruler is presumed to be still the legitimate sovereign. But because there might be cases where a revolution had been justifiable, then a neutral third State does not 'insult international law or neutrality' by treating an effectively independent province as such notwithstanding that the counterpart might believe to be able to complain for not having yet given up its claim of sovereignty over the seceded entity. But once the State had expressed or implied recognition of the seceding province, third States can no longer reject to recognize the new State.[582]

---

[578] Moser, *Grund-Sätze des jetzt üblichen Europäischen Völcker-Rechts in Friedens-Zeiten* (n 577) 102-6.

[579] Johann Christian Wilhelm von Steck, *Versuche über verschiedene Materien politischer und rechtlicher Kenntnisse* (Berlin und Stralsund, 1783) 49 and 51.

[580] ibid, 54.

[581] ibid, 55. 'A more serious offence is not thinkable than recognizing a seceding people that abandons its mother State as free, independent, and as absolved of its obligations' (my translation).

[582] Georg Friedrich von Martens, *Einleitung in das positive Europäische Völkerrecht auf Verträge und Herkommen gegründet* (bey Johann Christian Lieterich 1796) 89-91.

7.3 The Netherlands

Spain recognized the Dutch independence in the Treaty of Peace of 30 January 1648.[583] In the process towards the Dutch independence between the mid-16th century and 1648, three essential stages are identifiable: the Act of Abjuration (*Plakkaat van Verlatinge*) in 1581,[584] the Treaty of Antwerp of 1609 (also known as the Twelve Years Truce),[585] and, eventually, the Peace of Münster in 1648.[586]
In the mid-16th century, the population of the Low Countries – roughly stretching over the territories of modern day Netherlands, Belgium, and Luxembourg – became increasingly discontent with its Spanish master.[587]

---

583 See on these developments in more detail for example Paul Arblaster, *A History of the Low Countries* (2nd edn, Palgrave Macmillan 2012); Christoph Driessen, *Geschichte der Niederlande: Von der Seemacht zum Trendland* (Verlag Friedrich Pustet 2009); Martin van Gelderen, *The Political Thought of the Dutch Revolt, 1555-1590* (CUP 1992); Jonathan Israel, *The Dutch Republic: Its Rise, Greatness, and Fall, 1477-1806* (Clarendon Press 1995); Jonathan Israel, 'The Dutch-Spanish War and the Holy Roman Empire' in Klaus Bussmann and Heinz Schilling (eds), *1648: War and Peace in Europe* (Westfälisches Landesmuseum für Kunst und Kulturgeschichte 1998) vol 1: Politics, Religion, Law and Society; Michael North, *Geschichte der Niederlande* (4th edn, CH Beck 2013); Günter Vogler, *Europas Aufbruch in die Neuzeit, 1500-1650* (Eugen Ulmer 2003).

584 Edict of the States General of the United Netherlands by which they declare that the king of Spain has forfeited the sovereignty and government of the afore-said Netherlands, with a lengthy explanation of the reasons thereof, and in which they forbid the use of his name and seal in these same countries, 26 July 1581 ['Act of Abjuration'], reprinted in EH Kossman and AF Mellink (eds) Texts concerning the Revolt of the Netherlands, *Texts concerning the Revolt of the Netherlands* (OUP 1974) .

585 Articles of Truce ['Treaty of Antwerp'], reprinted in *Articles, of a Treatie of Truce. Made and concluded in the towne and citie of Antvverp, the 9. of April 1609. betweene the commissioners of the most excellent Princes, Arch-dukes Albert and Isabella Clara Eugenia, as well in the name of the Catholicke Kings Maiestie, as in their owne. Together with the commissioners and deputies the renowmed Lords, the Estates Generall of the Vnited Prouinces of the Low-countryes: and that through the mediation and with the aduice of the Lords Ambassadors of the most Christian King, and of the King of Great Britaine* (Printed [by John Windet] for George Potter and Nicholas Bourne and are to bee sold at his shoppe vnder the Royall Exchange 1609) .

586 Treaty of Peace between Spain and the Netherlands (n 535).

587 North (n 583) 29-31.

One reason was of religious nature. At the beginning of the 16th century, Reformation spread in the Low Countries, first, as Lutheranism and eventually as Calvinism.[588] The Roman-Catholic Church perceived the increasing expansion of Reformation as a threat and heresy. It was therefore that Emperor Charles V, and later his son Philip II, king of Spain, believed it was their duty to repress Protestantism. For this, new bishoprics, in addition to the already existing ones, were established and 'heretics' were fiercely prosecuted by the inquisition. Another reason for growing discontentedness of the population was political. Towards the middle of the 16th century, Spain sought increased 'Hispanicisation' of its power in the Low Countries by filling central positions with Spanish officials instead of local high nobility. In particular, the essential role of Cardinal Antoine Perrenot de Granvelle as major adviser of Philip II and later of Philip's half-sister and appointed governess general for the Low Countries Margaret of Parma irritated the Dutch nobility. As a third reason, there was an increasing financial burden on the population through imposition of high taxes caused by the battles against France and the Ottomans.[589]

In April 1566, the nobility of the Low Countries approached Margaret of Parma with a petition to relax the anti-heresy laws and end the inquisition. The pejorative reference of the petitioners as beggars (*Geuzen*) by a hostile courtier served as the origin of the party name of the rebel movement in the time to come.[590] In the autumn, however, the discontent of the population erupted in iconoclasm and aggression against the clergy. Philip's response came a year later in 1567 when he sent troops under the command of Duke of Alva, Fernando Alvarez de Toledo, to the Low Countries in order to counter the insurgency with intensified inquisition and an emergency tribunal, which soon became known as the 'Council of Blood'.[591] Among the thousand convicted and executed for treason and

[588] For a detailed insight on the rise of Reformation in the Netherlands, see Israel, *Dutch Republic* (n 583) 74-105.

[589] North (n 583) 29-31.

[590] Driessen (n 583) 24.

[591] Arblaster (n 583) 119-20.

heresy were also moderate noblemen like Laamoral, the Count of Egmond, and Philippe de Montmorency, Count of Horn, both Catholics tolerant of Protestantism. Duke Alva's clampdown drove many Protestants into exile, and also many Catholic oppositionists fled. Among them William of Orange who, in 1568 after having sought refuge in Dillenburg, joined the armed insurrection against King Philip. A newly introduced tax ('Tenth Penny') and the oppressive governance by the Duke of Alva resulted in an open revolt by the population in 1572. The revolt was supported by the so-called 'sea-beggars' (*Watergeuzen*). These privateers had been issued letters of marque by William of Orange and operated mainly from the ports of England. In April 1572 they successfully seized the town of Brill. After this first territorial conquest, the rebels conquered and held further towns and territories in the provinces of Holland and Zeeland.[592] But despite these achievements, Alva's troops kept the upper hand and pacified most southern provinces.[593]

In 1576 the situation fundamentally changed. The enduring war against the rebellious Low Countries together with that against the Ottoman Empire was a growing burden for Spain to the point that its treasury became insolvent in 1575. This meant that Spain could no longer pay its troops. The soldiers began to mutiny and the army to disintegrate. The mutinies were followed by widespread pillaging culminating in the sack of Antwerp in 1576 (also known as the 'Spanish Fury') in which thousands were raped, massacred and the city was plundered. Moreover, the successor of Alva as the governor general of the Low Countries, Don Luis de Requesens, died in the same year leaving behind a power vacuum. In order to defend themselves against the Spaniards and to settle religious disputes, the southern Catholic provinces, as well as the Protestant provinces, Zeeland and Holland agreed in November 1576 to the 'Pacification of Ghent'.[594] In the following year, the Estates General negotiated with the new gover-

[592] Vogler (n 583) 87.

[593] Israel, 'Dutch-Spanish War' (n 583) 113.

[594] Pacification of Ghent (signed at Ghent, 8 November 1576), reprinted in EH Kossman and AF Mellink (eds), Texts concerning the Revolt of the Netherlands, *Texts concerning the Revolt of the Netherlands* (OUP 1974) ; Israel, *Dutch Republic* (n 583) 184-85.

nor general of Spain, Don Juan de Austria, the Perpetual Edict in which Don Juan recognized the Pacification of Ghent and obligated himself to withdraw the Spanish troops. Yet, still in the same year, Don Juan revoked the Perpetual Edict and attacked the Protestant provinces anew and defeated the jointly raised forces of the Low Countries in 1578 at Gembloux.[595]

In early 1579, the Catholic, southern provinces Artois, Hainaut and Walloon Flanders left the alliance set up by the Pacification of Ghent and founded the Union of Arras with the objective to establish a separate peace with Philip II. The Protestant provinces in the North (Friesland, Groningen, Guelders, Holland, Overijssel, Utrecht, and Zeeland) joined in response the Union of Utrecht in order to carry on the resistance against Spain. They also declared Don Juan's deposition and offered the position of governor general to Philip's nephew, Matthias, the Archduke of Austria, who in 1581 already returned to Austria after failing to establish himself in the Low Countries. Also in 1581, the members of the Union of Utrecht declared their independence from the Spanish Crown with the Act of Abjuration.[596] Referring to natural law, it was argued that due to the continuous oppression of his subjects in the Low Countries, Philip II forfeited his sovereignty and, in consequence, would be abandoned. In his stead, 'another powerful and merciful prince to protect and defend these provinces' would be elected.[597] As new sovereign and replacement of Mathias the members of the Union of Utrecht chose Francis, Duke of Anjou. But Francis, too, abdicated in 1583, after he attempted unsuccessfully to seize Antwerp, dissatisfied with the limited power the provinces accorded him. Thereafter, it was decided not to rely anymore on foreign rulers. Instead William of Orange was made the *stadholder*, ie the executive officer of the Estates General.[598] After the issuing of the Act of Abjuration, Prince Philip II aimed to recapture the separatist provinces. Yet, the northern provinces fought back, first under the guidance of William

[595] Arblaster (n 583) 123.
[596] Act of Abjuration (n 584).
[597] ibid , 224, also 217, 225.
[598] Arblaster (n 583) 125.

of Orange and later, after his assassination in 1784, under his son, Maurice of Nassau. After the passing of Philip II in 1598 and the expulsion of the Spanish troops from the North, the United Provinces and Spain concluded the Treaty of Antwerp (1609) agreeing on a ceasefire lasting for 12 years, the 'Twelve Years Truce'.[599] This treaty included the Spanish concession to treat the Dutch provinces 'in qualitie, and as holding, accounting, and esteeming them to be free Countreys, Prouinces and Estates, whereunto they pretend not any Right or Title of Soueraigntie'.[600] Although this treaty did not yet contain the ultimate renunciation of Spanish sovereignty claims and therefore not the *de jure* recognition of the Dutch independence, it was the first time the Spanish Crown recognized the provinces *de facto*.[601]

Neither party to the treaty was able to get all their original demands from this agreement. The Spanish side denied the Dutch demands to recognize the Act of Abjuration as well as to tolerate Protestantism. The provinces, too, rejected several demands from Spain: they refused to relinquish their colonies in America, to liquidate the Dutch East India Company (*Vereenigde Oost-Indische Compagnie, VOC*) or even limit its activities,[602] or to refrain from funding the Chartered West India Company (*Geoctroyeerde West-Indische Compagnie, GWIC*).[603] Furthermore, the Spanish request for religious freedom of Catholics in the Protestant provinces was denied.[604]

As a result of this, the tensions soon grew again, and after the expiration of the ceasefire the war resumed in 1621. The Spanish army once again attacked the northern provinces and succeeded in 1625 under Ambrogio Spinola to seize the town of Breda. In the same year, Maurice of Nassau died. It was his half-brother, Frederick-Henry, who then took

[599] More precisely, the treaty was agreed upon between the States General on one side, and the new governess general and daughter of Philip II, Isabella Clara Eugenia, and her husband, Albert VII, Archduke of Austria, on the other Treaty of Antwerp (n 585).

[600] ibid art 1.

[601] On this also Grewe, *Epochs* (n 10) 185.

[602] The VOC has been established in 1602 in order to consolidate all already existing trade companies.

[603] The GWIC was eventually founded in 1621.

[604] Israel, 'Dutch-Spanish War' (n 583) 116; Vogler (n 583) 99.

Maurice's place. Under his command, the Dutch troops captured not only a Spanish silver fleet (1628), but also seized numerous towns and cities particularly Wesel and s-Hertogenbosch in 1629, and Maastricht in 1632 and eventually recaptured the town of Breda in 1637.[605] This series of successes came in addition to Spain's involvement in the Thirty Years' War against France after the French invasion of the Catholic provinces in 1635.

But it was not until 1647 when a delegation of the Estates General travelled to Münster to enter into peace negotiations with the Spanish Crown. By 1648 most provinces were willing to conclude peace, except for the envoy of Zeeland who was nonetheless unable to prevent it.[606] On 30 January 1648 the parties eventually reached an agreement and ratified it on 25 May. In the Peace of Münster, which drew substantially from the content of the Treaty of Antwerp (1609),[607] Spain formally recognized the independence and sovereignty of the northern provinces and abandoned any claim to power over them.[608] Moreover, it was determined that the territorial allocation remained as at time present.[609]

However, an indication that only this treaty and not the Treaty of Antwerp was regarded as the formal recognition of the Dutch independence by Spain was the refusal of the other States at the Münster conference, particularly France, to treat the Dutch delegation initially as representatives of an independent State by calling them 'excellencies'.[610] The Dutch delegation for their part yet insisted on this title. In an Imperial decision then the granting of the title was made conditional upon the Spanish consent to recognize the provinces' independence. Hence, with the Spanish-Dutch peace treaty in

---

[605] Arblaster (n 583) 150-53; Israel, *Dutch Republic* (n 583) 506-32.

[606] Arblaster (n 583) 154.

[607] Paul Brood, 'The Twelve Years Truce: Textual Explanations' in Randall Lesaffer (ed), *The Twelve Years Truce (1609): Peace, Truce, War and the Law in the Low Countries at the Turn of the 17th Century* (Brill 2014) 12 et passim.

[608] Treaty of Peace between Spain and the Netherlands (n 535) art 1.

[609] ibid, art 3.

[610] Frowein, 'Die Entwicklung der Anerkennung von Staaten und Regierungen im Völkerrecht' (n 148) 146-47.

January 1648 this issue was resolved, and the Netherlands found entrance as participants into the Treaty of Osnabrück.

7.4 The Swiss Confederation

The year 1648 also denotes the recognition of the Swiss Confederation.[611] This loose confederation of the 13 States (cantons) evolved from the end of the 13th until the 16th century and existed until the invasion of France at the close of the 18th century. The territory of the Swiss Confederation was part of the Holy Roman Empire. However, already from the 13th century, the territories Uri, Schwyz and Unterwalden and the towns Bern, Solothurn, and Zürich – later followed by others – were able to obtain certain privileges and liberties from the Emperor, for example, the permission to hold

[611] See on this Edgar Bonjour, 'Die Loslösung der Eidgnossenschaft vom Reich und J.R. Wettstein' (1948) 8 SM 481; Franz Egger, 'Johann Rudolf Wettstein and the International Recognition of Switzerland as a European Nation' in Klaus Bussmann and Heinz Schilling (eds), *1648: War and Peace in Europe* (Westfälisches Landesmuseum für Kunst und Kulturgeschichte 1998) vol 1: Politics, Religion, Law and Society; Julia Gauss, 'Die westfälische Mission Wettsteins im Widerstreit zwischen Reichstradition und Souveränitätsidee' (1948) 28 ZSG 177; Frida Gallati, 'Die formelle Exemtion der Schweiz vom Deutschen Reich im Westälischen Frieden 1648' (1948) 28 ZSG 453; Marco Jorio 'Westfälischer Frieden', *Historisches Lexikon der Schweiz* (2013) ⟨http://www.hls-dhs-dss.ch/textes/d/D8908.php⟩ ; Thomas Maissen, *Die Geburt der Republic: Staatsverständnis und Repräsentation in der frühneuzeitlichen Eidgenossenschaft* (2nd edn, Vandenhoeck & Ruprecht 2008) 187-214; Volker Reinhardt, *Die Geschichte der Schweiz: Von den Anfängen bis heute* (CH Beck 2011); Bernhard Christ, 'Die Loslösung der Alten Eidgenossenschaft vom Heiligen Römischen Reich Deutscher Nationen' in Historisches Museum Basel (ed), *Wettstein – Die Schweiz und Europa 1648* (Christoph Merian Verlag 1998); for IPO, art 6 and IPM §61 in particular, see Karl Mommsen, 'Bodins Souveränitätslehre und die Exemption der Eidgenossenschaft' in *Discordia Concors: Festgabe für Edgar bonjour zu seinem siebzigsten Geburtstag am 21. August 1968* (Helbing 1968) vol 2, 441; Karl Mommsen, *Auf dem Wege zur Staatssouveränität: Staatliche Grundbegriffe im Basler juristischen Doktordisputationen des 17. und 18. Jahrhunderts* (Francke 1970); Konrad Müller, 'Die Exemtion der Eidgenossen 1648: Ein Beitrag zur Erklärung des Exemtionsartikels im Westfälischen Frieden' (1946) 4 SBAG 216.

blood court inflicting the death penalty.[612] These privileges were anxiously renewed with regularity. At the same time, the gradual dissociation between the Swiss Confederation and the Empire commenced culminating in the *de facto* independence of the Confederation after the decisions of the Imperial Diet of Worms (1495) and the Peace of Basel (1499) terminating the Swabian War.[613] The independence of the Confederation and its allied towns and territories (*zugewandte Orte*) also manifested in the in the gradual refusal to pay imperial taxes and to participate in the imperial diet. Nonetheless, the formal separation of the Empire – let alone the recognition of such a separation – was never an issue in spite of the increasing factual independence of the Confederation.[614]

In the middle of the 17th century, two circumstances gave cause to redefine the relationship of the Confederation to the Holy Roman Empire. There was the immediate danger that the Alsace, neighbouring Basel in the North, was to become part of the Kingdom of France. Furthermore, the Imperial Chamber Court (*Reichskammergericht*) in Speyer repeatedly permitted appeals against judgments from the Basel municipal court. The Imperial Chamber Court justified its competence with reference to the fact that Basel, as well as some of the allied towns and territories, was still included in the *Reichsmatrikel*[615] of 1521 and the Procedural order of the Imperial Chamber Court (*Reichskammergerichtsordnung*) of 1555 and for this reason still belonged to the imperial territory.[616] But Basel denied the competence of the Imperial Chamber Court and sought to clarify its legal status and that of the Swiss Confederation towards the Empire. In the first instance, Basel approached the Swiss Diet (*Tagsatzung*) in 1643. After several unanswered notes of protest to the attention of the Emperor, Basel sug-

---

612 René Pahud de Mortanges, *Schweizerische Rechtsgeschichte: Ein Grundriss* (Dike 2007) 54.

613 Pahud de Mortanges (n 612) 55-56; Egger (n 611) 423.

614 Gallati (n 611) 453.

615 The Reichsmatrikel was a quota table forming the basis of the civil and military tax system for the expenses of Holy Roman Empire met by contributions from the estates' treasuries. (See for example Steven W Rowan, 'The Common Penny (1495-99) as a Source of German Social and Demographic History' [1977] 10 CEH 148, 149).

616 Jorio (n 611).

gested a diplomatic mission guided by the mayor of Basel, Johann Rudolf Wettstein, to the peace negotiations in Westphalia in order to represent the interests of the Confederation. But this plan found only limited approval among the confederates. Because the Catholic cantons withheld their support, Wettstein embarked on 14 December 1646 only with the mandate of the four protestant towns (Zürich, Bern, Basel, and Schaffhausen) and the two allied protestant towns Biel and St. Gallen, but nonetheless with the backing of the French ambassador in Solothurn Jacques Lefèvre de Caumartin, and the head of the French delegation and duke of Neuchatel Henri II. d'Orléans-Longueville. Caumartin at first hesitated to support a separate Swiss delegation to Westphalia due to his concerns that the Swiss cause might conflict with French interests. But once he learned that the French territorial gains had been secured, he eventually changed his mind.

Wettstein's initial intention was simply to obtain reaffirmation of the imperial privileges and the mere exemption from imperial jurisdiction. But instead of being forwarded to the Emperor, Wettstein's petition was sent to the representatives of the Imperial Estates (*Reichsstände*). They decided to request an expert opinion from the Imperial Chamber Court. The Court concluded that no part of the Empire might join another State or become a republic, unless upon approval by the head of State or in the sole exception that the head of State neglected his duties towards his subjects. But Basel left the Empire and joined the Swiss Confederation of its own accord and without the permission of either the Emperor or the Imperial Estates. Therefore, Basel remained to be regarded as a part of the Empire, as long as it does not secede in a correct fashion from latter.[617] The Estates recommended to grant Basel exemption from the jurisdiction of the Imperial Chamber Court due 'to certain substantial reasons' that were not further defined.[618] The Swiss Confederation in total, though, did not get mentioned.

[617] 'Bericht des K.K. Kam̃ergerichts an den Kaiser Ferdinand III. vom 9 Feb./20. Jan 1647', in Ludwig Friedrich von Jan (ed), *Staatsrechtliches Verhältnis der Schweiz zu dem deutschen Reiche von dem Ursprung der Eidgenossenschaft bis zum Ende des achtzehnten Jahrhunderts* (Monath und Kussler 1801-1803) vol 3 (Urkundenbuch); paraphrased according to Gallati (n 611) 466.

[618] 'aus gewissen erheblichen ursachen' ('Bericht der kaiserlichen Plenipotenz an den Kaiser d. d. Osnabrügg den 3 May 1647', in Ludwig Friedrich von Jan [ed], *Staatsrechtliches*

However, Wettstein, not satisfied with this answer, responded in February 1647 with a clarification (*Recharge*) of his request. Also, he eventually received a new negotiating mandate now signed by all thirteen confederates, ie also by the Catholic ones. By altering the foundations of his request, he explained that his precedent petition did not actually concern a confirmation or an extension of the special privileges but rather requested that the Confederation, based on its freedom and, be continually to be left alone and in peace.[619] Moreover, that the Imperial Chamber Court in Speyer must discontinue all pending suits against Basel and that it may never again prosecute Basel, nor any other members of the Swiss Confederation or its allies. The Confederation shall furthermore be determined to defend its freedom and sovereignty with force.[620]
In the course of the next several months, Wettstein succeeded to gain and intensify the support for his cause by France and Sweden, as well as plenipotentiaries of the Emperor. Because the Emperor wanted to prevent an even closer relationship between France and the Confederation, he issued a decree in October 1647. In this, based on the acknowledgement that the thirteen States of the Confederation had already been free and independent for some time, he awarded the desired exemption.[621] This decree, however, was

Verhältnis der Schweiz zu dem deutschen Reiche von dem Ursprung der Eidgenossenschaft bis zum Ende des achtzehnten Jahrhunderts (Monath und Kussler 1801-1803) vol 3 (Urkundenbuch)).

619 'Eine lobliche Eydgnossenschaft bey Ihrem freyen souuerainen Stand und Herkommen fürbass ruhig und ohnturbiert zu lassen' (Johann Rudolf Wettstein, *Acta und Handlungen betreffend gemeiner Eydgnosschafft Exemption, und was deren, durch die Cammer zu Speyr, darwider vorgenommenen Turbationen halb so wol bey den Westphälischen Fridens-Tracktaten als am Kayserl: Hoof und anderswo negocirt und verrichtet worden* (J J Genath 1651) lit D, 28).

620 ibid, lit D, 28.

621 'Decretum Exemptionis für die dreyzehen Ortt der Aydtgnossenschaft, und für die Statt Basel vom 16 May 1647', in Ludwig Friedrich von Jan (ed), *Staatsrechtliches Verhältnis der Schweiz zu dem deutschen Reiche von dem Ursprung der Eidgenossenschaft bis zum Ende des achtzehnten Jahrhunderts* (Monath und Kussler 1801-1803) vol 3 (Urkundenbuch).

predated for mid-May 1647.[622] This was meant to give the impression that the Emperor's decision was the result of his own free will and not of external pressures. The Confederation ought not to believe that they owed this decree in any way to the French, which suggested already in June a draft of text for the Swiss article of exemption for the Westphalian treaties.[623] The content of the Imperial decree, then, found a year later entrance into both Peace Treaties in a slightly modified and shortened version. Article 6 of the Treaty of Osnabrück,[624] and §61 of the Treaty of Münster[625] both congruently read that

> the said City of Bazil, and the other Swiss Cantons to be in possession of a quasi full Liberty and Exemption from the Empire [*in possessione vel quasi plenae libertatis et exemptionis ab imperio*], and so no way subject to the Tribunals and Sentences of the said Empire...

The meaning of this for the recognition of the Swiss sovereignty has been disputed for a long time. Some view the above passage as evidence that the recognition of sovereignty had been rejected with the argument that it stands for exemption from imperial jurisdiction only.[626] Others, however, are of divergent opinions.[627] It has been pointed out that *exemptio* has its origin in canon law, and stands primarily for the exemption from a certain jurisdiction. Yet it has to be distinguished between *exemption intra imperio* and *exemptio extra* or *ab imperio*. The first term stands for the loss of imperial immediacy by a member of the Empire that has been absorbed

[622] There seems to be a little confusion with the exact date of the decree. While some name the 16 (eg Gallati [n 611] 471; Ludwig Friedrich von Jan [ed], *Staatsrechtliches Verhältnis der Schweiz zu dem deutschen Reiche von dem Ursprung der Eidgenossenschaft bis zum Ende des achtzehnten Jahrhunderts* (Monath und Kussler 1801-1803) vol 1, 255), others (eg Christ [n 611] 43) set the date on the 14. Also in the final text of the article of exemption in both treaties, 14 May is referred to as the issue date.

[623] Gallati (n 611) 471.

[624] IPO (n 533).

[625] IPM (n 532).

[626] Jan, *Verhältnis* (n 622) vol 2, 158-63 et passim.

[627] Christ (n 611) 38; Mommsen, 'Souveränitätslehre' (n 611) 442ff.

by another, superior member. The *exemptio extra* or *ab imperio*, on the other hand, signifies the complete separation from the Empire by a member. It can occur when the member has had its territory occupied or has been ceded to another power. Another possibility for an *exemptio ab imperio* is a break-away by the member on its own initiative. This, though, is considered illegal and will endure only as long as the Empire is able to reverse this exemtion.[628] It has also been emphasized that the expression *possessio vel quasi* should not be interpreted as a limitation on the *possessio* because it is simply a technical term. Whereas the term *possessio* refers to the possession of material property, *possessio vel quasi* corresponds to the possession of intangible property.[629] In accordance with Wettstein's line of reasoning, ie having based his request on the already existing sovereignty,[630] it has furthermore been suggested that the Peace of Westphalia ultimately only confirmed the *de facto* independence which already existed.[631] But overall it is understood that this Article stands for the recognition of the formal Swiss independence by the signing parties of the treaties.[632]

7.5 The United States of America

The independence of the US and its recognition by other States has been engendered by tax disputes between the previous American colonies and the British Crown commencing in the 1760s. Due to the Seven Years'

[628] Christ (n 611) 38; Mommsen, 'Souveränitätslehre' (n 611) 442ff.

[629] Gallati (n 611) 477; Müller (n 611) 220.

[630] 'bey Ihrem freyen souuerainen Stand und Herkommen...' (Wettstein [n 619] lit D, 28).

[631] Christ (n 611) 44; Müller (n 611) 227; already Johann Stephan Pütter, *Historische Entwickelung der heutigen Staatsverfassung des Teutschen Reichs* (Vandenhoeck 1786) vol 2, 52-53.

[632] For example Bonjour (n 611) 481; Egger (n 611) 423; Gallati (n 611) 477; Jorio (n 611); Reinhardt (n 611) 223; also already Johann Jakob Moser, *Die gerettete völlige Souverainete der löblichen Schweitzerischen Eydgenossenschafft, oder, Gründlicher Beweis, dass in dem Westphälischen Frieden von dem H. Römischen Reich der löbl. Eydgenossenschafft nicht nur die Exemtion... eingeraumt und zugestanden worden seye...: mit Beylegung deren nöthigen Actorum publicorum* (Tubingen, gedruckt bey Joh Heinrich Philipp Schramm 1731) 49.

War (1756-1763),[633] the British Empire was faced with enormous costs. To tackle them, Great Britain introduced new taxes to its colonies on the American continent, causing a challenge to the sovereignty, and legitimacy of the British rule in the colonies.[634]
Among the new tax laws, the Stamp Act in particular was met with broad resistance.[635] The Stamp Act introduced a stamp tax not only for all kinds of legal and official documents, but also for other paper products such as newspapers, pamphlets, playing cards and calendars. In response, the Stamp Act Congress, an inter-colonial assembly of 27 representatives from 9 colonies, adopted the Declaration of Rights (and Grievances) in October 1765.[636] They enunciated that as subjects of the British crown, they enjoy certain rights, the rights of Englishmen. One of these rights guaranteed that there are no taxes introduced against their consent.[637] But as the colonists were not represented in the British parliament, taxes cannot be imposed on them ('no taxation without representation'). Only the locally elected government in the colonies was allowed to collect taxes.[638] Great Britain eventually abandoned the Stamp Act, but issued shortly after, on 4 March 1766, the American Colonies Act, claiming full sovereignty to raise taxes in the colonies.[639] Hence, in 1773, the British parliament passed the Tea Act in order to improve the desolate financial state of the East India Company (EIC). Despite the fact that tea became cheaper this way, the Act created various protest campaigns culminating in the Boston Tea Party on 16 March 1773.[640] At this, outraged colonists disguised themselves as members of the Mohawk tribe, boarded royal ships anchored at

[633] Also known as the French and Indian War.

[634] R Jackson Wilson, *The Pursuit of Liberty: A History of the American People* (Alfred A Knopf 1984) 151.

[635] Stamp Act 1765 (5 Geo 3 c 12) .

[636] Declaration of Rights in *Journal of the First Congress of the American Colonies, in Opposition to the Tyrannical Acts of the British Parliament.* Held at New York, October 7, 1765 (New York, 1845) , para 3.

[637] ibid, paras 1-3.

[638] ibid, paras 4-5.

[639] American Colonies Act 1766 (6 Geo 3 c 12) , also known as the Declaratory Act.

[640] Wilson, *Pursuit* (n 634) 159.

the Boston Harbour and threw the cargo, boxes of tea, into the sea. A similar incident occurred in New York on 22 April 1774.[641] The British Crown answered with a series of acts, collectively called the Intolerable Acts, intended to punish the colonies economically and politically. The Boston Port Act (31 March 1774)[642] shut down the Boston harbour making its reopening conditioned on the compensation of the damages caused. Additional measures included interventions into local jurisdictions,[643] the curtailing electoral rights,[644] and the requirement to provide housing for British soldiers.[645] A further measure, even though not part of the Intolerable Acts,[646] was the concession of religious freedom to the Catholics in the province of Quebec, which offended the (mostly Protestant) colonists.[647] On 5 September 1774, the First Continental Congress convened in order to coordinate the resistance against these sanctions imposed by the British Crown. In the Declaration and Resolves of the First Continental Congress of 14 October 1774,[648] the inter-colonial assembly condemned the British measures against the colonies as 'impolitic, unjust, and cruel as well as unconstitutional, and most dangerous and destructive of American rights', referred again to the 'rights of the Englishmen'[649] and repeated their entitlement not to be taxed against their consent.

In the meantime, the British view grew that the colonies can only be kept down with force. Thus, they attacked the towns of Lexington and Concord in Massachusetts in April 1775, in an attempt to dissolve the assembly

[641] Hellmuth Günther Dahms, *Grundzüge der Geschichte der Vereinigten Staaten* (4th edn, Wissenschaftliche Buchgesellschaft 1997) 30.

[642] Boston Port Act 1774 (14 Geo 3 c 19) .

[643] Administration of Justice Act 1774 (14 Geo 3 c 39)

[644] Massachusetts Government Act 1774 (14 Geo 3 c 45) .

[645] Quartering Act 1774 (14 Geo 3 c 54) .

[646] Wilson, *Pursuit* (n 634) 160.

[647] Quebec Act 1774 (14 Geo 3 c 83) .

[648] 'Declaration and Resolves of the First Continental Congress', in Henry Steele Commager (ed), *Documents of American History* (7th edn, Appleton-Century-Crofts 1962).

[649] As in Declaration of Rights in *Journal of the First Congress of the American Colonies, in Opposition to the Tyrannical Acts of the British Parliament.* Held at New York, October 7, 1765 (New York, 1845) (n 636) para 3.

illegally in session and confiscate the assumed arms cache.[650] After the establishment of the Continental Army by the colonists and the appointment of George Washington as commander-in-chief in June 1775, King George III declared that the colonies are in the state of rebellion and called for the suppression of the uprising.[651] The desire for independence from the British mother country by the colonies has been embodied in pamphlets such as Thomas Paine's *Common Sense*.[652] Calling King George III a 'Royal Brute',[653] and 'hardened, fullen tempered Pharaoh of England',[654] Paine made a passionate plea for an 'open and determined declaration of independence.'[655] Eventually and under increasing pressure by the colonies,[656] the Second Continental Congress, being in session since 10 May 1775, adopted on 4 July 1776 the Declaration of Independence. This new document was the Americans' answer to the 'history of repeated injuries and usurpations, all having in direct object the establishment of an absolute Tyranny.'[657]

Already before this declaration, the Congress organized a delegation to France to inquire the principal conditions in case 'the Colonies should be forced to form themselves into an independent State... France would probably acknowledge them as such, receive their ambassadors, enter into any treaty or alliance with them, for commerce or defense, or both.'[658] The idea behind this was to provide France with an opportunity to intervene into British affairs as revenge for the near complete loss of its colonies in the

[650] Volker Depkat, *Geschichte Nordamerikas: Eine Einführung* (Böhlau Verlag 2008) 215-16.

[651] ibid, 216.

[652] Thomas Paine, *Common Sense: Addressed to the Inhabitants of America* (Philadelphia, 1776).

[653] ibid 32.

[654] ibid, 27.

[655] ibid, 43.

[656] Dahms (n 641) 32.

[657] Declaration of Independence (4 July 1776) 1 Stat 1 , 1.

[658] 'Franklin et al, Committee of Secret Correspondence, to Silas Deane, Philadelphia, March 3, 1776', in Francis Wharton (ed), *The Revolutionary Diplomatic Correspondence of the United States* (Washington Printing Office 1889) vol 2, 73.

western hemisphere in the Treaty of Paris (1763)[659] after its defeat in the Seven Years' War.[660] Yet, France initially held that it would grant recognition to the colonies only when their independence has been effectively established.[661] Nevertheless, there was the concern that a belated recognition, ie after the potential recognition by Great Britain, would result in the disappearance of commercial preference as well as of the chance for revenge.[662] The victorious success of the revolutionary forces in Saratoga on 17 October 1777,[663] and the growing demand for reconciliation in Great Britain, however, prompted France to reconsider its stance towards American independence. It was concluded that the circumstances were favourable to negotiate with the colonies about formal relations.[664] France recognized the independence of the United States on 6 February 1778 through the conclusion of a treaty of amity and commerce,[665] and of a treaty of alliance.[666] In the latter, France guaranteed to the United States 'their liberty, Sovereignty, and Independence absolute, and unlimited.'[667] In addition, France and the US concluded a secret supplementary agreement providing that if Spain recognized the US independence, it would also be eligible to join the two other treaties on the same conditions.[668]

On 15 March 1778, France notified Great Britain about the conclusion of these treaties. It was pointed out that the treaties with the US, which was in full possession of their independence, did not include any exclusive ad-

---

659 Definitive Treaty of Peace and Friendship between France, Great Britain and Spain ['Treaty of Paris (1763)'] (signed 10 February 1763) 42 CTS 279.

660 Goebel (n 101) 74.

661 ibid, 76, 79.

662 ibid, 74-80.

663 Capitulation between Great Britain and the United States (signed 16 October 1777) 46 CTS 383.

664 Goebel (n 101) 90.

665 Treaty of Amity and Commerce between France and the United States (signed 6 February 1778) 46 CTS 417.

666 Treaty of Alliance between France and the United States (signed 6 February 1778) 46 CTS 447.

667 ibid, art 11.

668 Separate and Secret Act between France and the United States (signed 6 February 1778) 46 CTS 457.

vantages for France. Instead, the United States reserved the right to treat all nations on the same basis of equality and reciprocity.[669] In a supplemental exposition in 1779, France explained the motives of its conduct. The complaint was made that despite the declared intention to adhere to peace, the British Crown continued its harassment and violence against trade and navigation of the French subjects.[670] The United States, however, was eventually forced to have recourse to arms in order to obtain the rights and freedom. Nonetheless, it is not the concern of the French king either to judge the British quarrelling with its former colonies or to treat the Americans like rebels.[671] The United States had declared and effectively established their independence, which even Great Britain had somehow recognized by acquiescing certain acts implying sovereignty.[672] Great Britain argued in response that France had violated the Treaty of Paris (1763) with its conduct.[673] In case a foreign enemy had taken possession in the British colonies and France had confirmed such a hostile act, the whole of Europe would have disapproved of such an injustice.[674] Yet, as 'domestic rebels' have annexed the colonies, disposed of the law of the British sovereign, and sought foreign powers for alliances to acknowledge their independence, these foreign powers must not recognize this independence since rebellion cannot create more rights than war.[675] Hence Great Britain regarded the conduct of France as a declaration of war. In its answer, France defended its act with the argument that at the time of the French notification to Great Britain the

[669] Karl de Martens, 'Déclaration remise par le marquis de Noailles, ambassadeur de France près la cour de Londres, à lord Weymouth, secrétaire d'État de S. M. Britannique; du 15 mars 1778' in *Nouvelles causes célèbres du droit des gens* (Brockhaus & Avenarius 1843) vol I, 406-7.

[670] Karl de Martens, 'Exposé des motifs de la conduite du roi de France relativement à l'Angleterre, en 1779' in *Nouvelles causes célèbres du droit des gens* (Brockhaus & Avenarius 1843) vol I, 425-26.

[671] ibid, 427.

[672] ibid, 430.

[673] Karl de Martens, 'Mémoire justificatif publié par la cour de Londres, en réponse à l'exposé des motifs de la conduite de la France' in *Nouvelles causes célèbres du droit des gens* (Brockhaus & Avenarius 1843) vol I, 446-47.

[674] ibid, 455.

[675] ibid, 458-59.

US had already been in possession of its independence. Besides, the king of France was entitled to view this independence as existent without being obliged to examine its legality and no law banned him from forming alliances with the Americans.[676]

> Au surplus, que les États-Unis aient eu ou non le droit d'assurer la souveraineté de l'Angleterre, que la possession, où ils sont de leur indépendance, soit légitime ou non; ce n'est point à la France à discuter ces deux questions. Le roi n'est point le juge des querelles domestiques de l'Angleterre. Ni le droit des gens, ni les traités, ni la morale, ni la politique ne lui imposent l'obligation d'être le gardien de la fidélité, que les sujets anglais peuvent devoir à leur souverain. Il suffit pour la justification de S. M., que les colonies, qui forment une nation considérable tant par le nombre de leurs habitants que par l'étendue de leurs domaines, aient établi leur indépendance, non-seulement par un acte solennel, mais aussi par le fait, et qu'elles l'aient maintenue contre les efforts de leur mère patrie.[677]

There is, however, the view that the US independence had not yet been effective when the treaties between France and the US were concluded in 1778. The final decision in the war of independence was brought about

---

[676] Karl de Martens, 'Observations de la cour de Versailles, sur le mémoire justificatif de la cour de Londres' in *Nouvelles causes célèbres du droit des gens* (Brockhaus & Avenarius 1843) vol I, 481.

[677] 'Besides, whether the United States have or have not the right to assure [their] sovereignty from England, whether the possession of their independence is legitimate or not, it is not for France to discuss these two questions. The king is not the judge of domestic quarrelling of England. Neither the right of the people, nor treaties, nor morality, nor politics impose on him the obligation to be the guardian of the loyalty that British subjects may owe to their sovereign. It is sufficient for the justification of his Majesty that the colonies, which form a considerable nation, both by their number of inhabitants as well as by the extent of their dominions, have established their independence, not only by a solemn act but also by fact, and have maintained it against the efforts of their mother country.' (my translation) (ibid, 484).

through the enforced surrender of Great Britain by France after the Battle of Yorktown in October 1781.[678] Hence, the recognition of US independence based on its effectiveness by means of the Treaty of Amity and Commerce, and of the Treaty of Alliance in 1778 ought to be considered premature.[679] Great Britain recognized the US independence eventually in November 1782, first in a preliminary peace agreement,[680] then confirming this in the Treaty of Paris on 3 September 1783.[681]

Another State, besides France, to recognize the independence of the United States before Great Britain was the Netherlands.[682] The preliminary Dutch assurances for recognition of the US, which were accidentally discovered, eventually led to a British declaration of war on the Netherlands. Shortly after this, the Netherlands recognized the United States officially. However, whereas in the Treaty of Amity and Commerce[683] as well as in the Convention concerning Recaptured Vessels,[684] both signed on 8 October 1782, there is no explicit declaration of recognition on behalf of the Netherlands, the emphasis in the preamble of the Treaty of Amity on the 'most perfect Equality and Reciprocity, for the Basis of Their Agreement' corresponds to this. Also Morocco aiming to promote its foreign trade acted before the British recognition. It granted American vessels – together with ships of other European countries – free access to its ports on 20 December 1777, thereby already implicitly recognizing the independence of United States.[685] It was only on 28 June 1786 that Morocco formally entered into

[678] Hillgruber (n 9) 12.

[679] ibid, 12.

[680] Provisional Articles of Peace between Great Britain and the United States (signed 30 November 1782) 48 CTS 223, art 1.

[681] Definitive Treaty of Paris between Great Britain and the United States ['Treaty of Paris (1783)'] (signed 3 September 1783) 48 CTS 487.

[682] Goebel (n 101) 93-95.

[683] Treaty of Amity and Commerce between the Netherlands and the United States (signed 8 October 1782) 48 CTS 137.

[684] Convention concerning Recaptured Vessels between the Netherlands and the United States (signed 8 October 1782) 48 CTS 169.

[685] Priscilla H Roberts and James N Tull, 'Moroccan Sultan Sidi Muhammad Ibn Abdallah's Diplomatic Initiatives toward the United States, 1777-1786' (1999) 143 PAPhS 233, 235-39.

the Treaty of Peace and Friendship with the US.[686] Other States, however, only brought themselves to recognize the US independence, after its acceptance by the British Crown. Before this, the recognition of the colonies and their treatment as a sovereign State was considered hostile behaviour. Such an act was expected to entail grave consequences including a declaration of war by the State concerned.[687]

The Spanish Court, an ally of France, supported the United States in their war against Britain. Nonetheless, for a long time Spain refused to recognize the British colonies as independent out of concern that the approving principles would eventually work against Spanish interests as a colonial power in the Americas.[688] It was only after the conclusion of peace with Great Britain in 1783[689] that Spain took up formal relations with the United States.[690] Prussia, bound to be loyal to Great Britain due to Anglo-Prussian Subsidy Treaty,[691] was also unable to grant recognition before its alliance partner did. Hence, only in 1785, Prussia and the United States signed the Treaty of Amity and Commerce.[692] Sweden recognized the US independence in April 1783 by concluding the Treaty of Amity and Commerce.[693] Austria, Russia and Tuscany, however, firmly rejected recognizing US independence, because for them granting this recognition would have corresponded with 'the sanctioning of the abhorrent principles of revolution.'[694]Only in 1824 the Saint Petersburg Convention was concluded between Russia and the United States, presuming mutual recognition[695]

[686]Treaty of Peace and Friendship between Morocco and the United States (signed 23 June, 6 July, and 15 July 1786) 9 Bevans 1278 .

[687]Fabry (n 8) 34-35.

[688]Goebel (n 101) 86-87.

[689]Treaty of Peace between Great Britain and Spain (signed 3 September 1783) 48 CTS 481.

[690]Hillgruber (n 9) 14.

[691]Treaty between Great Britain and Prussia (signed 11 April 1756) 41 CTS 179.

[692]Treaty of Amity and Commerce between Prussia and the United States (signed 10 September 1785) 49 CTS 331.

[693]Treaty of Amity and Commerce between Sweden and the United States (signed 3 April 1783) 48 CTS 269.

[694]Goebel (n 101) 93.

[695]Convention regarding Navigation, Fishing, and Trading on the Pacific Ocean and along the northwest Coast of America (signed 17 April 1824) 11 Bevans 1205.

while the Treaty of Commerce and Navigation between Austria and the US was not signed until 1829.[696]

7.6 Interim conclusion: The recognitional fitness of the Christian international society

The admission to the international society trough recognition at the time of the Peace of Westphalia and after is characterized by different aspects. The examples investigated were recognitions within the Christian international society. They differ insofar as the first two examples, the recognition of the Netherlands and Switzerland, occurred within the Christian international society in Europe, whereas the third, the recognition of the US independence, signified a spatial extension of the international society beyond the European continent.

Initially, the Christian character of the international society is also clearly identifiable in treaties. In the preamble of both the Treaty of Osnabrück and the Treaty of Münster, as well as of the Treaty between Spain and the Netherlands, there are invocations to God ('In nomine & ad honorem Dei') and numerous references to the entire Christianity ('ad communem salutem... universae Christianitatis'). In the documents concerning the US recognition, this emphasis on the Christian foundation of the international society vanished.

Alongside other reasons for recognition, such as economical (the US recognition by Morocco to stimulate its foreign trade) or political nature (the US recognition by France to take revenge on Great Britain), the main issue of State recognition in this international society is whether a State has only to be effective or whether it had additionally to be legal. The predominant view in doctrine and State practice was that legality had to be obtained through the declared renunciation of the sovereignty claims by the mother country over its estates concerned. Before the mother State waived its claims over a certain territory, other States were not permitted to recognize the recently independent State. Otherwise, this behaviour by third

[696] Treaty of Commerce and Navigation between the United States of America and His Majesty the Emperor of Austria (signed 27 August 1829) 5 Bevans 202.

States would be considered an involvement in the original State's inner affairs, and consequentially, illegal. Nevertheless, the opposite view, that as soon as an entity gained its factual independence, it was fit for recognition regardless of the recognition of its former sovereign, was occasionally held. This was illustrated by the example of France's recognition of the US independence.

8 Admission to the international society of civilized States

8.1 The international society of civilized States

At the turn of the 19th century, the international society underwent a multifaceted change. Since the 16th century the society had been limited to the Christian-European States. Only the admission of the US at the end of the 18th century led to a spatial extension of the society over the Atlantic. Moreover, with the beginning of the new century, natural law gave way to positivism as the dominant concept in scholarship and practice. Natural law doctrine had assumed a universally applicable, common law originating in nature and Divine will. By way of contrast, the positivist doctrine of the 19th century held that international law was solely based on the consent of the States, ie the members of the international society. Contemporaneously the gradual replacement of Christianity as ideational foundation of the international society by the concepts of 'civilization' and 'civilized States' occurred observable in court decisions, literature and treaties where the notion quickly gained much traction.[697]
However, already from the mid-1700s the term 'civilized States' found sporadic entrance into court decisions, even if not yet in terms of international law.[698] Mention of 'civilized nations' became more frequent in 18th century

[697] See Antony Anghie, 'Finding the Peripheries: Sovereignty and Colonialism in Nineteenth-Century International Law' (1999) 40 HarvIntlLJ 1; Bull, *Anarchical Society* (n 476) 31ff; Jörg Fisch, *Die europäische Expansion und das Völkerrecht: Die Auseinandersetzungen um den Status der überseeischen Gebiete vom 15. Jahrhundert bis zur Gegenwart* (Franz Steiner 1984) 285ff; Gong (n 512); Gustavo Gozzi, 'History of International Law and Western Civilization' (2007) 9 ICLR 353; Arnulf Becker Lorca, 'Universal International Law: Nineteenth-Century Histories of Imposition and Appropriation' (2010) 51 HarvIntlLJ 476; Liliana Obregón, 'The Civilized and the Uncivilized' in Bardo Fassbender and Anne Peters (eds), *The Oxford Handbook of the History of International Law* (OUP 2012); Röling (n 502) 26ff; James Sloan, 'Civilized Nations' in Ruediger Wolfrum (ed), *The Max Planck Encyclopedia of Public International Law* (OUP 2012) vol II, 211; Georg Schwarzenberger, 'The Standard of Civilisation in International Law' (1955) 8 CLP 212, 216ff.

[698] *Harrison v Doctor Burwell* (1667) 124 ER 1039 , 1058.

rulings, albeit still reflecting the contemporary notion of international law as originating in natural law. Illustrative of this is a passage from a 1765 decision of the Court of King's Bench stating that '[t]he jus gentium arises from natural reason, interpreted by the practice of all civilized nations'.[699] Since the 19th century, general references to civilized nations in conjunction with international law became common practice,[700] as well as to its origin being the consent of the States.[701]
In treaties, too, the transformation from the Christian-European to the society of civilized nations began to be noticeable, even though invocations of the Holy Trinity were still found as for example in agreements related to the end of the Napoleonic Wars and the Congress of Vienna.[702] This reference alludes to the Christian-European root of the newly emerging society, and the fact that initially it had been simply the former members of the old society constituting the newly established one.[703] In this regard, however, Bluntschli held that, although the contemporary law of civilized nations had its origin in the Christian nations, it is not bound to the Christian faith. Instead international law connected Christians, 'Mohammedans', Brahmanists, Confucians, 'admirers of the stars', believers, and nonbelievers.[704] This emerging shift in the way of thinking is also identifiable in treaties, such as the Declaration relative to the Universal Abolition of the

---

[699] *The King v Guerchy* (1765) 96 ER 315 , 316; similarly *Scrimshire v Scrimshire* (1752) 161 ER 782 , 789; also Georg Friedrich von Martens, *A Compendium of the Law of Nations: Founded on the Treaties and Customs of the Modern Nations of Europe* (Cobbett and Morgan 1802) 2ff.

[700] For example in Great Britain *The Emperor of Austria v Day and Kossuth* (1861) 66 ER 263 , 281; in the US *US v Arredondo* 31 US 691 , 712; *US v Percheman* 32 US 51 , 87.

[701] *The Queen v Keyn* (1876) 2 ExD 63 , 68.

[702] For example Definitive Treaty of Peace and Amity ['Peace of Paris (1814)'] (signed 30 May 1814) 63 CTS 172; Treaty between Austria and Russia (signed 21 April 1815) 64 CTS 135; Act of the Congress of Vienna (signed 9 June 1815) 64 CTS 453; Definitive Treaty of Peace ['Treaty of Paris (1815)'] (signed 20 November 1815) 65 CTS 251.

[703] Oppenheim, *International Law: A Treatise* (n 98) 210; Josef Laurenz Kunz, *Die Anerkennung von Staaten und Regierungen im Völkerrecht* (W Kohlhammer 1928) 91.

[704] Bluntschli (n 133) 55.

Slave Trade (1815).[705] In addition to invoking 'all the Powers of Christianity', reference is made to 'the public voice, in all civilized countries' and 'the knowledge of Europe, and of all civilized countries.'[706] Yet, exceptions, such as the Holy Alliance Treaty (1815), still existed in this development.[707] Its three signatories Austria, Prussia, and Russia attempted to secure the established power balance in Europe and to base it on a Christian law of nations. Ultimately, this endeavour proved to be a failure soon after its inception.[708]

Contemporary legal doctrine considered only civilized States as members of the international society. They were perceived as owing the 'principate over the world' but also upholding 'a legal principle that for the mutual relations of civilized States the territories inhabited by savages or semi-savages are not to be regarded and treated as States but instead as res nullius...'[709] Initially, international law was considered only to apply to States that were assumed civilized, ie Christian-European.[710] 'The area within which the law of nations operates is supposed to coincide with the area of civilization.'[711] These States were regarded as the original members of the international society.[712]

---

[705] Declaration relative to the Universal Abolition of the Slave Trade (signed 8 February 1815) 63 CTS 473.

[706] 'toutes les Puissances de la Chrétienté'... 'la voix public... dans tous les pays civilisés'... 'à la connoissance de l'Europe et de toutes les Nations civilisées de la terre' (my translation).

[707] Holy Alliance between Austria, Prussia, and Russia (signed 11 September 1815) 65 CTS 199.

[708] Bluntschli (n 133) 55-56.

[709] 'der Principat über die Welt'... 'das Rechtsprincip, dass Reviere, in denen Wilde und Halbwilde hausen, nicht als Staatsterritorien anzusehen und zu behandeln sind, vielmehr für die gegenseitigen Beziehungen der Civilisirten als res nullius... in Betracht kommen' (my translation) (Ferdinand von Martitz, 'Das Internationale System zur Unterdrückung des Afrikanischen Sklavenhandels in seinem heutigen Bestande' [1886] I AöR 3, 16-17).

[710] Wheaton, *Elements of International Law* (n 111) 16.

[711] Lawrence (n 111) 59.

[712] ibid, 84.

In contrast to the civilized States stood the uncivilized States, also called barbaric,[713] rude,[714] savages, and semi-savages.[715] Occasionally, a distinction was made, aside from that between civilized and uncivilized States, between different levels of uncivilized. Certain States, such as Siam, China or Morocco, were seen as somewhat more civilized, and therefore called 'barbaric' or 'semi-civilized', while all the others outside the international society were simply seen as 'savages' and 'non-civilized'.[716] As non-members of the international society, international law did not apply to them, nor were they expected to observe it. They stood outside its realm. Moreover, for the reason that the will of the civilized States had been construed as the sole source of international law, uncivilized States were not able to participate in its creation and advancement. Furthermore, for the non-European, non-Christian, and hence uncivilized States, the basic distinction between civilized and uncivilized resulted in an exclusion from political power and participation in decision-making. For the members of the society of civilized States, by contrast, it served the enforcement of their interests by means of domination and colonization of the non-member States.[717]

Nevertheless, despite the fact that international legal doctrine deemed the application of international law between a civilized and any uncivilized States generally impossible,[718] different kinds of 'agreements', such as the 'unequal treaties', 'capitulations', and 'protectorate treaties' were concluded.[719] All of these kinds of treaties had several attributes in common

---

[713]Joseph Hornung, 'Cilivisés et barbares' (1885) XVII RDILC 5, 447, 539; John Stuart Mill, 'A Few Words on Intervention' in *Dissertations and Discussions: Political, Philosophical and Historical* (William V Spencer 1864) vol 3, 252; James Lorimer, 'La doctrine de la reconnaissance: Fondement du droit international' (1884) 16 RDILC 334, 350ff.

[714]Travers Twiss, *The Law of Nations Considered as Independent Political Communities: On the Rights and Duties of Nations in Time of Peace* (Clarendon Press & Longman 1861) 119-20.

[715]Charles Calvo, 'Civilisation' in *Dictionnaire de droit international public et privé* (G Pedone-Lauriel 1885) vol 1, 148; Martitz (n 709) 16-17.

[716]Lorimer (n 713) 335ff; Liszt (n 111) 1ff.

[717]Lorca (n 697) 495; Röling (n 502) 28; Sloan (n 697) 211.

[718]Mill (n 713) 252.

[719]Gong (n 512) 8.

regardless of their different substance. Typically, one contracting side was a civilized State from Europe or the US, while the other was an uncivilized State. These treaties were often formed under force or threat, and they served characteristically to the advantage of the civilized State and to the disadvantage of the uncivilized State.[720]

Members of the international society concluded treaties on equal terms regularly, but only among each other. In order to acquire equal treaties, uncivilized States strived to obtain membership in the society of civilized States. But an admission seeking State was not in the position to declare its membership in the society by itself.[721] Instead the admission to the international society was attainable only through the recognition by the member States. But '[a]s the basis of international law is the common consent of the civilised States, statehood alone does not include membership of the Family of Nations.'[722] Required for recognition was the attainment of a certain standard of civilization determined by the members of the society.[723]

At the same time, the prevailing view was that uncivilized States had no right to recognition, but were only entitled to guardianship.[724] The civilized States, on the other hand, had, according to contemporary doctrine of the time, a duty to support the uncivilized States in their efforts to become civilized.[725] This was repeatedly confirmed in treaties. The General Act of

---

720 Christine Bell, 'Capitulations' in Ruediger Wolfrum (ed), *The Max Planck Encyclopedia of Public International Law* (OUP 2012) vol I; Anne Peters, 'Unequal Treaties' in Ruediger Wolfrum (ed), *The Max Planck Encyclopedia of Public International Law* (OUP 2012) vol X; Mirja Trilsch, 'Protectorates and Protected States' in Ruediger Wolfrum (ed), *The Max Planck Encyclopedia of Public International Law* (OUP 2012) vol VIII.

721 Fritz Stier-Somlo, 'Völkerrechtsgemeinschaft' in Karl Strupp (ed), *Wörterbuch des Völkerrechts und der Diplomatie Wörterbuch des Völkerrechts und der Diplomatie* (Walter de Gruyter 1929) 188.

722 Oppenheim, *International Law: A Treatise* (n 98) 108-9.

723 John Fischer Williams, 'La doctrine de la reconnaissance en droit international et ses développements récents' (1933-II) 44 RdC 199, 226; also on this Bull, *Anarchical Society* (n 476) 31ff.

724 'elles ont droit, non à la reconaissance, mais à la tutelle.'(Lorimer [n 713] 16).

725 Calvo (n 715) 148.

the Conference of Berlin concerning the Congo (1885), for example, stated that

> [a]ll Powers exercising rights of sovereignty or an influence in the Said territories engage themselves to watch over the conservation of the indigenous populations and the amelioration of their moral and material conditions of existence and to strive for the suppression of slavery and especially of the negro slave trade; they shall protect and favor without distinction of nationality or of worship, all the institutions and enterprises religious, scientific or charitable, created and organized for these objects or tending to instruct the natives and to make them understand and appreciate the advantages of civilization.[726]

The significance of civilization as a core concept of international law and politics endured until the first half of the 20th century. The Hague Convention II (1907),[727] like The Hague Convention I (1899),[728] spoke in its preamble of 'the solidarity uniting the members of the society of civilized nations.' After World War I, Article 22 of the Covenant League of Nation determined that

> [t]o those colonies and territories which as a consequence of the late war have ceased to be under the sovereignty of the States which formerly governed them and which are inhabited by peoples not yet able to stand by themselves under the strenuous conditions of the modern world, there should be applied the principle that the well- being and development of such peoples form a sacred trust of civilization and that securities for the performance of this trust should be embodied in this Covenant. The best method of giving practical effect to this principle is

[726] The General Act of the Conference of Berlin concerning the Congo (signed 26 February 1885) 3 AJIL Supp 7, art 6.

[727] The Convention for the Pacific Settlement of International Disputes ['Hague Convention I'] (signed 29 July 1899) 2 MPTMH 1115.

[728] The Convention for the Pacific Settlement of International Disputes ['Hague Convention II'] (signed 18 October 1907) 2 MPTMH 1197.

> that the tutelage of such peoples should be entrusted to advanced nations who by reason of their resources, their experience, or their geographical position can best undertake this responsibility, and who are willing to accept it, and that this tutelage should be exercised by them as Mandataries on behalf of the League.[729]

Furthermore, the Statute of the Permanent Court of Justice specified in its Article 38 that, aside from international conventions and international custom, the 'general principles of law recognized by civilized nations' ought to be applied.[730]

8.2 Recognition of States in international society of civilized States doctrine

In international doctrine the issue of admission to international society of civilized States was subject to dispute. 'Being civilized' was essential for membership in international society. 'Civilization' was closely associated with development regarding industrial, technical, and scientific progress as well as with a specific, ie European, state of mind regarding morals, values and customs, education, art and culture.[731] However, aside from the fact that civilization was considered of high importance for the admission into

---

[729] Covenant of the League of Nations (signed 28 April 1919, entered into force 10 January 1920) 13 AJIL Supp 128.

[730] Statute of the Permanent Court of International Justice (signed 16 December 1920, entered into force 20 August 1921) 6 LNTS 379, para 3; also still found in Statute of the International Court of Justice (signed 26 June 1945, entered into force 24 October 1945) 33 UNTS 993.

[731] Calvo (n 715) 148; James Mackintosh, *The Miscellaneous Works of the Right Honourable Sir James Mackintosh* (Longman, Brown, Green, and Longmans 1846) vol 3, 459; also on this Obregón (n 697) 917-18; Schwarzenberger, 'The Standard of Civilisation in International Law' (n 697); for an extensive and in-depth account of the concept, see Jörg Fisch, 'Zivilisation, Kultur' in Otto Brunner, Werner Conze, and Reinhart Koselleck (eds), *Geschichtliche Grundbegriffe: Historisches Lexikon zur politisch-sozialen Sprache in Deutschland* (Klett-Cotta 1997) vol 7.

international society,[732] the actual features constituting civilization were rather ambiguous. As a result, the precise requirements necessary for a State to be recognized, and hence admitted to the international society were not consistently and exhaustively defined.[733]
Lawrence, for example, specified that it was necessary for an entity seeking recognition as a State to possess 'a certain size and importance' as well as 'a fixed territory, within which an organized government rules in a civilized fashion, commanding the obedience of its citizens and speaking with authority on their behalf in its dealings with other states.'[734] Hence, 'the state to be admitted shall be to some extent civilized after the European model.'[735] However, he had to admit, that 'the exact amount of civilization required cannot be defined beforehand', but instead every case must be judged separately.[736] Oppenheim outlined three requirements for the admittance to the international society. First, a State had to be civilized and in constant interaction with other States. Second, the State had to agree 'to be bound for its future conduct by the rules of International Law.' Lastly, the other members had to agree to the admission into the society.[737] Whereas the civilization of the State to be recognized did not have to be particularly Christian, it had to be alike in order to 'understand and act in conformity with the principles of the Law of Nations.'[738] For Rivier, too, the international society was not closed off but accessible to all States as soon as they reach the required level of civilized behaviour.[739] Unfortunately, he also left unspecified what this 'required level' actually entailed. While emphasizing that States can be recognized without being part of the international soci-

[732]eg Hall (n 111) 83.

[733]Koskenniemi even regarded the existence of an actual standard of civilization simply as a myth. (Martti Koskenniemi, *The Gentle Civilizer of Nations: The Rise and Fall of International Law 1870-1960* (CUP 2002) 134-35).

[734]Lawrence (n 111) 87.

[735]ibid, 84-85.

[736]ibid, 85.

[737]Oppenheim, *International Law: A Treatise* (n 98) 31.

[738]ibid, 31.

[739]Alphons Rivier, *Lehrbuch des Völkerrechts* (2nd edn, Enke 1899) 5.

ety,[740] Rivier perceived the application of international law to States outside the international society as a problem.[741] Hence, even though effective sovereignty was, according to Rivier, the *sine qua non* for *de facto* recognition that is necessary to conclude treaties, the actual *de jure* recognition and with this the admission to the international society was dependent on the attainment of civilization based on the Christian-European notion. Westlake, however, regarded a stable government able to protect Europeans so they may 'carry on the complex life to which they have been accustomed' as the ultimate test for civilization.[742] Yet in any case, a new State must accept and obey the law of international society.[743] The existence or non-existence of constitutionally established institutions capable of fulfilling international legal duties, signified for Verdross, the difference between civilized and uncivilized States.[744]

Another attribute of civilization considered was the abolition of slave trade.[745] Since the Declaration relative to the Universal Abolition of the Slave Trade in 1815,[746] slave trade was not only deemed a 'scandal to humanity',[747] but declared illegal. In accordance with this, Phillimore remarked that 'by general practice, by treaties, by the law and ordinances of civilized States, as well as by the immutable laws of eternal justice, it [the slave trade] is now indelibly branded as a legal as well as a natural crime.'[748]

---

740 ibid, 92-94.

741 ibid, 5-6.

742 John Westlake, *Chapters on the Principles of International Law* (CUP 1894) vol 1, 141; see also John Westlake, *International Law* (CUP 1904) 46, 50.

743 Westlake, *International Law* (n 742) 49.

744 Alfred Verdross, *Die Verfassung der Völkerrechtsgemeinschaft* (Springer 1926) 118-19.

745 See on this also Seymour Drescher and Paul Finkelman, 'Slavery' in Bardo Fassbender and Anne Peters (eds), *The Oxford Handbook of the History of International Law* (OUP 2012) 906, considering the perpetuation and abolition of slave trade as the 'decisive markers of civilization'.

746 Declaration relative to the Universal Abolition of the Slave Trade (n 705).

747 Mill (n 713) 238; similarly Bluntschli (n 133) 19-20.

748 Robert Phillimore, *Commentaries upon International Law* (Butterworths 1854-1861) vol 1, 246-47.

The admission of entities that separated from their mother countries presented a different issue of recognition addressed by scholarly consideration. In this regard, Rivier described a sovereign State as an autonomous, independent community permanently organized in a territory.[749] Sovereignty, being the crucial prerequisite for recognition by other States, was expressed on one hand by freely adopting a constitution, and on the other, by having the right to conduct war, to conclude treaties, and to establish diplomatic missions.[750] Similarly, and particularly with regard to secession, Phillimore held the view that in order to be recognized, the new State had to be consolidated, able to maintain relations with other States, in possession of absolute independence and a government acknowledged by its people, and have the competence to meet its international obligations.[751] The ability and willingness of the government to comply with the already existing requirements of the international society had also for Holtzendorff been the decisive factor for recognition.[752] Besides the effectiveness criteria such as having a stable, constitutional government and the willingness and ability to comply with international law and obligations, the view already held by the scholars of the Christian international society remained that premature recognition of the independence of the seceding part is an interference into the mother country's internal affairs, and therefore illegal.[753] Yet there is no consensus in doctrine whether preceding recognition by the mother country would be an absolute necessity to the recognition by third States.[754]

---

[749] Rivier, *Lehrbuch des Völkerrechts* (n 739) 88.

[750] ibid, 89-94.

[751] Phillimore (n 748) vol 2, 34.

[752] Franz von Holtzendorff, *Handbuch des Völkerrechts: Auf Grundlage Europäischer Staatspraxis - Bd. 2 Die völkerrechtliche Verfassung und Grundordnung der auswärtigen Staatsbeziehungen* (Verlag von JF Richter 1887) 24.

[753] eg Holtzendorff (n 752) 24-26; Johann Ludwig Klüber, *Europäisches Völkerrecht* (Cotta 1821) vol 1, 49-50; Leone Levi, *International Law* (D Appleton and Company 1888) 86; Oppenheim, *International Law: A Treatise* (n 98) 112; Rivier, *Lehrbuch des Völkerrechts* (n 739) 93.

[754] Emphasizing its necessity, eg Klüber (n 753) vol 1, 50; Rivier, *Lehrbuch des Völkerrechts* (n 739) 93; denying it, eg Holtzendorff (n 752) 25; Phillimore (n 748) vol 2, 23.

Aside from the requirements, the consequences of recognition were another topic that evolved in the era of the international society of civilized States. Particularly, the question discussed was whether recognition was compulsory for the establishment of new States. Whereas one side, the constitutivist, claimed it was necessary, the other side, comprised of the adherents to the declaratory approach, denied the State constituting impact of recognition. They held that the establishment of a State occurred independently, and that recognition was a mere declaratory act by the other States.[755]

8.3 Brazil

At the dawn of the 19th century the Spanish and Portuguese colonial empires were shaken to the very foundations by the desire for freedom of the resident populations, more than 300 years after their subjection. But while the independence of the former Spanish colonies was preceded by bloody revolutions,[756] Brazil achieved its independence relatively peacefully and obtained international recognition as an independent State soon after.

After Napoleon Bonaparte came into power in 1799 and had crowned himself emperor of the French in 1804, he attempted to conquer the entire European continent and Great Britain. As part of his strategy he imposed an embargo on all imported British goods to the continent by establishing the Continental Blockade with the promulgation of the Berlin decree.[757] But because the Portuguese regent, Dom João, did not want to jeopardize the good relations with Great Britain, an ally and trading partner for cen-

[755] See on this debate, s 2.3 ('Consequences of recognition').

[756] For an account on the revolutions for independence of the Spanish colonies, see for example Jorge I Dominguez, *Insurrection or Loyalty:The Breakdown of the Spanish American Empire* (Harvard University Press 1980); John Lynch, *The Spanish American Revolutions 1808-1826* (2nd edn, WW Norton & Company 1986); William S Maltby, *The Rise and Fall of the Spanish Empire* (Palgrave MacMillan 2009) 172-92.

[757] 'Décret de Berlin' (1806) 2 de Clerq 194.

turies,[758] he refused to obey the French decree.[759] As a reprisal for Portugal's refusal, French troops invaded Portugal in November 1807. But Great Britain was not able to comply with its alliance obligations due to its own battles with Napoleon. Consequently, the entire Portuguese court evacuated Lisbon on ships heading for its colony on the Latin American continent. Great Britain supported this evacuation with naval assistance during the passage. The fleet first arrived at Bahia in January 1808, but continued its journey in February to Rio de Janeiro, the administrative centre of the colony.[760]

A major problem was posed by the fact that now all trade links between Brazil and the mother country were cut off due to the French occupation of Portugal. This was problematic as Brazilian trade relations were exclusive with Portugal, and the Brazilian economy depended on it. Furthermore, after the escape from Portugal, the Portuguese Court was in financial straits and was forced to take on debt from Great Britain. As a result, the regent opened the Brazilian ports for trade with friendly nations, even before he landed in Rio, most notably for Great Britain.[761] But Portugal went even further and made additional concessions. In February 1810, three treaties were concluded granting special taxes and tariffs in matters of commerce and navigation to Great Britain.[762]

After Napoleon's defeat in 1814, the demand in Portugal grew for the regent to return home. The evacuation of the royal family was initially

[758] cf Treaty of Peace, Friendship, and Alliance between England and Portugal (signed 16 June 1373) I BFSP 462; Treaty of Peace, Commerce, and Alliance between Great Britain and Portugal (signed 29 January 1642) I BFSP 473.

[759] Joseph Smith and Francisco Vinhosa, *History of Brazil, 1500-2000: Politics, Economy, Society, Diplomacy* (Longman 2002) 38.

[760] Thomas E Skidmore, *Brazil: Five Centuries of Change* (2nd edn, OUP 2010) 41-43.

[761] Roderick J Barman, *Brazil: The Forging of a Nation, 1798-1852* (Stanford University Press 1988) 45-46.

[762] Treaty of Commerce and Navigation between Great Britain and Portugal (signed 19 February 1810, entered into force 19 June 1810) I BFSP 513; Treaty of Friendship and Alliance between His Britannic Majesty and his Royal Highness the Prince Regent of Portugal (signed 19 February 1810) I BFSP 547; Convention for the Arrangement of Packets, between His Britannic Majesty and His Royal Highness the Prince Regent of Portugal (signed 19 February 1810) I BFSP 557.

only intended as a temporary measure, but Dom João was reluctant to set out on the long journey back to Lisbon, and the longer he remained the more reluctant he became. Instead he elevated Brazil to the equal status of Portugal by founding the United Kingdom of Portugal, Brazil, and the Algarves.[763] In August 1820, Portuguese liberals enacted a liberal revolution demanding the introduction of a constitutional monarchy and convening a national parliament (*cortes*) in January 1821 to draw up a liberal constitution. As pressure on João to return increased,[764] he eventually went back to Portugal motivated finally by his fear of losing the throne otherwise. However, he left behind his 23-year old son, Dom Pedro, as the new ruler of Brazil.[765] But the *cortes* demanded more. Not only should Brazil be stripped of its new status, but also Pedro, as heir of the throne, would have to return to Portugal. These claims, however, were met with opposition from the local elites in Brazil, rejecting the restoration of the previous conditions. Thus, on 9 January 1822 Pedro received a petition by the people of Brazil urging him to stay.[766] Pedro not only responded positively to this petition, but also declared the independence of Brazil on 7 September 1822. At the river Ipiranga near São Paulo, he ended more than three centuries of Brazilian subjection to Portuguese dominance with the outcry 'death or independence'.[767] Soon after, on 1 December 1822, Dom Pedro was crowned Emperor Pedro I of the Empire of Brazil.

Three main parties were initially involved in the quarrel over the recognition of this newly established independence: Brazil, the former colony, Portugal, the former mother country, and Great Britain as ally and trading partner of Portugal. Unlike other Latin American colonies, the central issue for British recognition of Brazil's independence was the slave trade. For the Portuguese, and thus, for the Brazilian economy, slaves were deemed essential, and Brazil was at the time the largest importer of African

[763] Skidmore (n 760) 44.
[764] He was crowned King João IV after the death of his mother Marie I.
[765] Smith and Vinhosa (n 759) 40-41.
[766] Skidmore (n 760) 45.
[767] This declaration became famous as the 'cry of Ipiranga' (*Grito do Ipiranga*).

slaves on the Latin American continent.[768] Slaves worked on plantations growing sugar, later cocoa, coffee, and cotton as well as in the gold and diamond mines.[769] Meanwhile, at the dawn of the 18th century, the Abolitionist movement in Great Britain gained influence. In 1807 the Slave Trade Act passed, abolishing slave trade in most of the British Empire.[770] In the Declaration relative to the Universal Abolition of Slave Trade[771] in 1815 Great Britain, Austria, France, Portugal, Russia, Spain, and Sweden committed themselves to the abolition of slave trade. Furthermore, Great Britain, eager to stop slavery internationally, included either the abolition of slave trade into numerous bilateral agreements with other States,[772] or even negotiated specific treaties regarding the matter.[773] In several treaties in 1810, 1815, and 1817, Great Britain also obligated Portugal to the gradual abolition of slave trade.[774]

For Great Britain, the issue of recognizing Brazil bore a specific significance because the commercial treaty of 1810 with Portugal, concerning

[768] João Joé Reis and Herbert S Klein, 'Slavery in Brazil' in *The Oxford Handbook of Latin American History* (OUP 2011) 181.

[769] Robert M Levine, *The History of Brazil* (Greenwood Press 1999) 18-19.

[770] An Act for the Abolition of the Slave Trade 1807; Slavery as such, however, was only banned in 1833 by the Slavery Abolition Act 1833.

[771] Declaration relative to the Universal Abolition of the Slave Trade (n 705).

[772] For example with Denmark (Treaty of Peace between His Britannic Majesty and His Majesty the King of Denmark [signed 14 January 1814] I BFSP 234); with France in additional articles to the Treaty of Paris (Peace of Paris (1814) [n 702]); with the Netherlands (Convention between Great Britain and the Netherlands, relative to the Dutch Colonies; Trade with the East and the West Indies [signed 13 August 1814] II BFSP 370).

[773] For example Treaty between Great Britain and Spain, for the Abolition of the Slave Trade (signed 23 September 1817) IV BFSP 33.

[774] Treaty of Friendship and Alliance between His Britannic Majesty and his Royal Highness the Prince Regent of Portugal (signed 19 February 1810) I BFSP 547; Treaty between Great Britain and Portugal, for the Restriction of the Portuguese Slave-Trade, and for the Annulment of the Convention of Loan 1809, and Treaty of Alliance 1810 (signed 22 January 1815) II BFSP 348; Additional Convention between Great Britain and Portugal, for the Prevention of Slave Trade (signed 28 July 1817) IV BFSP 85.

to a large extent trade advantages in Brazil, was to expire in 1825.[775] But after the recent events in Brazil, it became evident that the extension of these trade advantages – in the future to be granted by Brazil – was connected with British recognition of Brazil's independence. While keen for British recognition, Brazil was, at the same time, highly aware of the significance of slave trade for its economy. In November 1822, unofficial talks between Great Britain and Brazil took place. In the course of these talks, the Brazilian representative, Felizberto Caldeira Brant Pontes, indicated that Brazil might consent to abolish its slave trade in return for Britain's recognition.[776] But it turned out that Brant was not in the position to negotiate such an accord.[777] Regardless, the British Foreign Secretary, George Canning, a supporter of the Abolitionist movement, intended to make the abolition of slave trade a necessary requirement for Great Britain's recognition of Brazil.[778]

Great Britain, therefore, considered crucial a resolution of the conflict between its long-time ally and its new important trading partner. However, the negotiations for reconciliation between Brazil and Portugal reached a dead end before they even started. Whereas Brazil refused to negotiate without a priori recognition of its independence, Portugal rejected negotiations without previous confirmation of its sovereignty over Brazil.[779]

It became evident that this dilemma could only be solved with outside intervention. Hence, after some preparation and negotiation, talks between Portugal and Brazil commenced in July 1824 in London with British-Austrian mediation. But even after five conferences, the stalemate could not be

[775] Treaty of Commerce and Navigation between Great Britain and Portugal (signed 19 February 1810, entered into force 19 June 1810) I BFSP 513 art 33.

[776] Canning to Chamberlain, 15 February 1823 in Charles Kingsley Webster (ed), *Britain and the Independence of Latin America 1812-1830: Select Documents from the Foreign Office Archives* (OUP 1938) vol 1, 220, 221.

[777] Chamberlain to Canning, 2 April 1823 in ibid, vol 1, 222.

[778] Canning to Chamberlain, 15 February 1823 in ibid, vol 1, 220, 221.

[779] Alan K Manchester, 'The Recognition of Brazilian Independence' (1951) 31 HAHR 80, 85-86.

solved.[780] In order to reach an agreement, after all, Canning proposed the establishment of a federative union, where the ruler alternatively resides in Rio or Lisbon having a deputy sovereign in the other capital. But his suggestion did not meet with approval, thus the stalemate continued.[781] At the subsequent conference, in November 1824, Portugal came forward with a counter proposal. Among other things, it was suggested that the king of Portugal should be declared senior emperor of Brazil. This, however, was unacceptable to both Portugal and Great Britain.[782] It additionally came to light that Portugal approached Russia, Spain, Prussia and France, behindAustria's and Britain's back, for support that prompted Canning to an immediate termination of the talks.[783]

Although Great Britain was eager to untangle the situation once and for all it still was in a quandary. On the one hand, the extension of the commercial treaty of 1810 was subject to the British recognition of the Brazilian independence. On the other hand, there was a risk that upon recognition as independent, Brazil might attack Portugal. This, again, would make Great Britain fulfil its obligation and defend Portugal against any attacking foreign power.[784] In a new attempt to find a solution, Canning suggested to settle the matter by mediation through a special envoy, Charles Stuart.[785] Convinced that withholding recognition of the independence would not undo this independence, Canning ordered Stuart first to Lisbon in order to convince the king that there existed no alternative than granting substantial independence to Brazil, and then, either as bearer of a royal edict or as envoy plenipotentiary of Portugal to negotiate the terms of independence with Brazil. It was paramount for Stuart to alert Portugal that if these negotiations failed to achieve the desired result within a reasonable time, Great Britain would take up its own negotiations in order to extend

[780] Harold Temperley, *The Foreign Policy of Canning, 1822-1827: England, the Neo-holy Alliance and the New World* (G Bell and Sons 1925) 217.

[781] William W Kaufmann, *British Policy and the Independence of Latin America, 1804-1828* (Yale University Press 1951) 186-87.

[782] Temperley (n 780) 218.

[783] Canning to Villa Real, 19 November 1824 in Webster (n 776) vol 2, 254, 255.

[784] Canning to Chamberlain, 12 January, 1825 in ibid, vol 1, 248, 251-52.

[785] Canning to Chamberlain, 15 January, 1825 in ibid, vol 1, 255, 256.

the 1810 commercial treaty.[786] After having received a *Carta Patente* (letters patent) with which Portugal transferred the full sovereignty over Brazil to Pedro, Stuart departed from Lisbon and reached Rio in July. Soon after, having settled some discords, a treaty was signed in August in which Portugal recognized Brazil's independence.[787] In an additional convention dealing with mutual claims, Portugal committed Brazil to pay two million pounds.[788]

After the conclusion of these treaties, Stuart proceeded to his second assignment. This time as a representative of Great Britain, he was to negotiate with Brazil a two-year extension of the commercial treaty of 1810. Additionally, this convention had to include the immediate and effective abolition of slave trade.[789] But Stuart, inebriated by his success, was not able to resist the temptation to deviate from his instructions. Instead of an extension of the previous treaty, he negotiated an all-new commercial treaty as well as a separate treaty to abolish slave trade both of which were signed on 18 October 1825. But Canning, disproving of the liberties taken by Stuart, rejected the ratification of these documents because they failed to conform to British interests in several ways.[790] Thereupon Canning recalled Stuart from Brazil and sent Robert Gordon as new envoy, to resume negotiations with Brazil.[791] In November 1826, Gordon concluded new treaty of commerce securing British trade advantages in Brazil for another 15 years.[792] Furthermore, he negotiated a new treaty

---

[786]Canning to Stuart, 14 March 1825 in ibid, vol 1, 262.

[787]Treaty between His Most Faithful Majesty and His Imperial Majesty, concerning the Recognition of the Empire of Brazil (signed 29 August 1825) XII BFSP 674, art 1.

[788]Convention between Portugal and Brazil, for the Settlement of Claims (signed 29 August 1825) XIII BFSP 933.

[789]Canning to Stuart, 12 May 1825 in Webster (n 776) vol 1, 279.

[790]Canning to Stuart, 1 December 1825 in Webster (n 776) vol 1, 290; Canning to Stuart, 10 January 1826 in Webster (n 776) vol 1, 294; Canning to Granville in Edward J Stapleton (ed), *Some Official Correspondence of George Canning* (Longmans 1887) vol 2, 16.

[791]Canning to Stuart, 2 February 1826 in Webster (n 776) vol 1, 295, 296.

[792]Treaty of Amity and Commerce between Great Britain and Brazil (signed 17 August 1827, entered into force 10 November 1827) XIV BFSP 1008.

concerning the termination of slave trade,[793] equating any involvement in the trade after 1830 with piracy.[794] Despite this, Brazil only banned overseas slave trade eventually in 1850,[795] and prohibited slavery altogether in 1888.[796]

Soon after the Portuguese recognition, other States followed suit. In early 1826 France signed a treaty of commerce explicitly recognizing Brazil's independence,[797] as did Austria,[798] Prussia,[799] the hanseatic cities,[800] and the Netherlands.[801] A formal treaty of commerce between the US and Brazil, however, was only concluded in December 1828,[802] after the US had already recognized Brazil in May 1824, and thus preceding Great Britain.[803]

---

[793] Convention between Great Britain and Brazil, for the Abolition of the African Slave Trade (signed 23 November 1826, entered into force 13 March 1827) XIV BFSP 609.

[794] Yet, nowhere in these agreements is the explicit mention of the British recognition of Brazil's independence found because Canning regarded this superfluous given the circumstances. In fact, the conclusion of these treaties implied the recognition of Brazil.(Canning to Stuart, 1 December 1825 in Webster [n 776] vol 1, 290, 293).

[795] Law of the Legislature of Brazil, for the Suppression of the Slave Trade (4 September 1850) XXXIX BFSP 1060 .

[796] Law Declaring Slavery to be Abolished in Brazil (13 May 1888) LXXIX BFSP 259 .

[797] Treaty of Friendship, Navigation, and Commerce, between France and Brazil (signed 8 January 1826) XIII BFSP 805.

[798] Treaty of Commerce and Navigation between Austria and Brazil (signed 16 June 1827) XV BFSP 923.

[799] Traité d'Amitié, de Navigation, et de Commerce, entre Sa Majesté le Roi de Prusse et Sa Majesté l'Empereur du Brésil (signed 9 July 1827) XVI BFSP 1201.

[800] Treaty of Commerce and Navigation between Brazil and Lubeck, Bremen and Hamburgh (signed 17 November 1827) XIV BFSP 715.

[801] Treaty of Friendship, Commerce, and Navigation, between Brazil and the Netherlands (signed 20 December 1828) XIV BFSP 557.

[802] Treaty of Peace, Friendship, Commerce, and Navigation, between The United States and Brazil (signed 12 December 1828) XV BFSP 944/1245.

[803] Arthur Preston Whitaker, *The United States and the Independence of Latin America, 1800-1830* (The Johns Hopkins Press 1941) 553-55.

8.4 The Ottoman Empire

The recognition and, thus, admission of the Ottoman Empire to the international society in the mid-19th century emerged from different circumstances than those found in the examples earlier examined. Unlike most other newly recognized States, which used to be part of another State, the Ottoman Empire had been an independent State for centuries. Therefore it was not the recognition of a newly established entity, but rather the admission of an already existing State.

Already from the 14th century, the Empire occupied and ruled over a third of the European continent at times.[804] Thus, for a long time there had been regular contact between the powers of the European society of States and the Ottoman Empire. Not only were there diplomatic exchanges, but also numerous treaties, often in the form of capitulations.[805] Therefore the Ottoman Empire, according to the English school, was, while part of the system of States, not part of society of States.[806] A similar argument was made by Martens in his *Einleitung in das positive europäische Völkerrecht* (1796). While not perceiving them as being part of the 'European association', he still classified the 'Ottomans' among the 'entirely sovereign States.'[807] Nevertheless, Wheaton reported that the 'Ottoman Empire was not represented in the Congress [of Vienna] nor included in the system of public law established by it.'[808] Only in the Treaty of Paris (1856), did its admission to the international society find its explicit expression.[809]

---

[804] Thomas Naff, 'The Ottoman Empire and the European States System' in Hedley Bull and Adam Watson (eds), *The Expansion of International Society* (Clarendon Press 1984) 144.

[805] Bell (n 720) 1123-24; Umut Özsu, 'Ottoman Empire' in Bardo Fassbender and Anne Peters (eds), *The Oxford Handbook of the History of International Law* (OUP 2012) 433ff.

[806] See on this, s 4.2 ('English school of international relations theory').

[807] Martens, *Einleitung in das positive Europäische Völkerrecht auf Verträge und Herkommen gegründet* (n 582) 27-29.

[808] Henry Wheaton, *History of the Law of Nations in Europe and America: From the the Earliest Times to the Treaty of Washington, 1842* (Gould Banks & Co 1845) 556.

[809] Peace of Paris (1856) (n 51).

The background for the Treaty of Paris had been the Crimean War (1853-1856).[810] This conflict had been fought between Russia and the Ottoman Empire, supported by France, Great Britain and Piedmont-Sardinia.[811] Its main venue was on the Crimean Peninsula, but also on the Danube, in the Caucasus, in Finland, the White Sea and even in the Pacific on the Kamchatka Peninsula.[812] The conflict originated from a dispute over rights to pilgrimage sites and population in the Holy Lands between French Catholics, who saw their interests safeguarded by Napoleon III, and the Greek Orthodox Church, which viewed itself under the protection of the Russian Tsar Nicholas I. The outbreak of Crimean War, however, was triggered by the Russian demand for the protectorate over the entire orthodox Christianity on Ottoman territory.[813] Not only did the Sublime Porte refuse this, but also England and France rejected this Russian attempt of concealed seizure of Ottoman territory.[814] The object of the European powers was to reduce the Russian predominance in the Orient and to establish an 'oriental balance of power' according to the balance of power in Europe.[815] After its outbreak in 1853 with the Russian occupation of Moldavia and subsequent battles by both sea and land, the war reached its climax and termination with the Siege of Sevastopol (1854-1855),[816] marking the ultimate defeat of Russia.

---

[810]On the Crimean War see eg Andrew Robarts, 'Crimean War' in Gábor Ágoston and Bruce Masters (eds), *Encyclopedia of the Ottoman Empire* (Facts on File 2009) 161-63; M Şükrü Hanioğlu, *A Brief History of the Late Ottoman Empire* (Princeton University Press 2008) 78-82; Klaus Kreiser, *Der osmanische Staat* (2nd edn, Oldenbourg 2008) 39; for an comprehensive examination, see Candan Badem, *The Ottoman Crimean War* (Brill 2010).

[811]Theodor Schieder, 'Paris Peace Treaty (1856)' in Ruediger Wolfrum (ed), *The Max Planck Encyclopedia of Public International Law* (OUP 2012) vol VIII, 67.

[812]Winfried Baumgart, 'Der Krimkrieg 1863-1856: Ein Überblick' in Georg Maag, Wolfram Pyta, and Martin Windisch (eds), *Der Krimkrieg als erster europäischer Medienkrieg* (LIT Verlag 2010) 209.

[813]Robarts (n 810) 161.

[814]Heinz Kramer and Maurus Reinowski, *Die Türkei und Europa: Eine wechselhafte Beziehungsgeschichte* (Kohlhammer 2008) 68.

[815]Baumgart (n 812) 216.

[816]The capital of the Crimea.

The Crimean War formally ended with the Treaty of Paris (1856). In Article 7, it was declared that 'the Sublime Port admitted to participate in the advantages of the Public Law and System (*Concert*) of Europe.'[817] Furthermore, it was guaranteed 'to respect the Independence and the Territorial Integrity of the Ottoman Empire ... and will, in consequence, consider any act tending to its violation as a question of general interest.'[818]
The background and intention of Article 7 are found in the protocols of the conferences held during the war as well as in protocols of the conference.[819] Its determination, and eventually the explicit admission of the Ottoman Empire into the European society is recorded in a protocol of a conference between Austria, France, Great Britain and Prussia, on 9 April 1854. It stated that

> [l]'integrité territorial de l'Empire Ottoman est et demeure la condition *sine qua non* de toute transaction destinée à rétablir la paix entre les Puissances belligérantes, et les Gouvernments représentés par le Sousignés s'engagent à rechercher en commun les guaranties les plus propres à rattacher l'existence de cet Empire à l'equilibre général de l'Europe. [820]

For this purpose, Austria, France, and Great Britain defined so-called 'guarantees', which they accorded to Russia as a memorandum.[821] These guarantees demanded the suspension of the protectorate exercised by Russia over Moldavia, Wallachia, and Serbia, the ensuring of free navigation on the

---

[817]Peace of Paris (1856) (n 51) (English translation according to II MPTMH 947, 948).
[818]ibid.
[819]A detailed analysis of these materials also in Hugh McKinnon Wood, 'The Treaty of Paris and Turkey's Status in International Law' (1943) 37(2) AJIL 262, 265ff.
[820]'The territorial integrity of the Ottoman Empire is and remains the condition sine qua non of every transaction intended to re-establish peace between the belligerent Powers, and the Governments represented by the signatories commit themselves to search together for the most suitable guaranties to associate the existence of this Empire to the general balance of Europe.' (my translation)('Protocol of Conference between Austria, France, Great Britain, and Prussia' [1854] XLIV BFSP 82, 83).
[821]'Memorandum Communicated by the Plenipotentiaries of Austria, France, and Great Britain, to Prince Gortchakoff' (1854) XLV BFSP 53 .

Danube, the revision of the Treaty of Adrianople[822] in order to finish the Russian preponderance on the Black Sea, and the revocation of the Russian claims for the protectorate on Ottoman territory together with collective efforts of the European powers for protection of Christian minorities within the realm of the Sublime Porte without any interference of the Ottoman independence.[823] Thus, the intention of the admission to the international society was to protect the territorial integrity and the sovereignty of the Ottoman Empire from the grasp of Russia. This, again, together with the other guarantees was thought to prevent a Russian gain in power, and, thus, to sustain the balance of power.

It is noticeable, however, that there is no record of any consideration found – neither in the documents and protocols of conferences before or during the war,[824] nor of the conference in Paris[825] – whether the Ottoman Empire fulfilled any standards of civilization. Neither were there requirements in this regard in the Treaty of Paris concerning the admission of the Ottoman Empire to the international society.

In contemporary doctrine at the time, however, it was undecided if and when the Ottoman Empire became a member of the international society. Some scholars expressed doubts that only the Treaty of Paris in 1856 admitted the Ottoman Empire to the international society. Wheaton, for example, held the view that the law of nations would principally apply to Christian-European States only.[826] He believed, nonetheless, already before the treaty of 1856, that the 'independence and integrity of the Ottoman Empire have been long regarded as forming essential elements in the European balance

---

[822]Treaty of Adrianople (signed 14 September 1829) 80 CTS 84.

[823]Memorandum to Prince Gortchakoff (n 821) 53-54.

[824]'Protocols of Conferences held before and during the Crimean War' XLIV BFSP 82 and 1049; 'Notes Exchanged between Great Britain and Austria, respecting the Conditions to Be Imposed for the Re-establishment of Peace with Russia' (1854) XLIV BFSP 88; 'Protocols of the Conferences held at Paris, relative to the Conclusion of the General Treaty of Paris' XLVI BFSP 63.

[825]Protocols held at the Conference at Paris, between the Plenipotentiaries of Austria, France, Great Britain, Prussia, Sardinia, and Turkey, Relative to the Conclusion of a General Treaty of Peace (February-April 1856) XLVI BFSP 63 .

[826]Wheaton, *Elements of International Law* (n 111) 16.

of power, and, as such, have recently become the objects of conventional stipulations between the Christian States of Europe and that Empire, which may be considered as bringing it within the pale of the public law of the former.'[827] Similarly by virtue of numerous treaties concluded with the European States, Phillimore considered the Ottoman Empire already in 1854 subject 'not only to the principles of general International Law, but to the provisions of the European Code.'[828]

Others, like Heinrich Oppenheim,[829] Despagnet,[830] and Hornung[831] were of the opinion that it was the Paris Peace Treaty that admitted the Ottoman Empire into the European public international law. Bluntschli stated correspondingly that only the Paris Peace Treaty meant the admission of Turkey as a legitimate member. Before then, Turkey had been excluded from the European society of States, despite inevitable conclusions of treaties with the Sublime Porte for centuries.[832] Heffter pointed out that since the crusades, the Muslim and the European States are connected by treaties, but that apart from this their conduct with each other was regulated by mere convenience. Only since accession to the European society through the Treaty of Paris, was the Sublime Porte bound to European international law.[833]

However, there were other scholars who were sceptical whether the Treaty of Paris truly made the Ottoman Empire fully belong to the international society.[834] Westlake, for example, argued that the Ottoman Empire had, indeed, been formally admitted to the international society in 1856, but due

---

[827] ibid, 21.

[828] Phillimore (n 748) vol 1, 101.

[829] Heinrich Oppenheim, *System des Völkerrechts* (Krøner 1866) 57.

[830] Frantz Despagnet, *Cours de droit international public* (2nd edn, Librairie de la Société du Recueil Sirey 1899) 58.

[831] Hornung (n 713) 10.

[832] Bluntschli (n 133) 17.

[833] August Wilhelm Heffter, *Das europäische Völkerrecht der Gegenwart: Auf den bisherigen Grundlagen* (4th edn, Schroeder 1861) 15.

[834] See on this also Gong (n 512) 106ff; Herbert Arthur Smith, *Great Britain and the Law of Nations: A Selection of Documents Illustrating the Views of the Government in the United Kingdom upon Matters of International Law* (London, 1932-1935) vol 1, 16-17; Wood (n 819) 262.

to big differences in civilization, the admission remained only partial.[835] A corresponding opinion held by Lorimer stated in 1884 that the Turks are only partly recognized, and submitted that they were unable to fulfil their international duties and, moreover, may not even belong to the 'races progressives'.[836] Also Rivier noted that although the Ottoman Empire entered the European Concert with Article 7 of the Treaty of Paris, it is still not equal to the other members.[837] He saw the reason for this in the enduring validity of the disadvantageous capitulations.[838]

Notwithstanding the divergence of these three positions on the admission, ie recognition, and membership of the Ottoman Empire, they all were to a certain extent correct. The first position held was right insofar as there had indeed been treaties concluded between the Sublime Porte and European powers long before 1856. This required recognition, at least implicitly, of the Porte's partial subjection to law of nations and the ability to conclude treaties. However, still at the end of the 19th century, the view had been held that treaty relations could actually be established with semi-civilized States outside the international society. But because these States were not recognized as belonging to international society, the law of nations only with regard to and within the scope of the particular treaty would apply to them. In other international intercourse with semi-civilized States outside contractual relations – and in intercourse with all other non-civilized States – the international society of civilized States had been seen to be bound only to the principles of Christianity and humanity.[839] In contrast, the position stating that only the Treaty of Paris admitted the Ottoman Empire to the society of nations is sustained by the fact that Article 7 is the first *multilateral* and *explicit* recognition of the Ottoman Empire. The third position disputed that the peace treaty of 1856 actually resulted in the recognition of Turkey as an equal member of the international society. The grounds for this view were twofold. Whereas one line of argument referred to a lack of

[835]Westlake, *International Law* (n 742) 40, 47.
[836]Lorimer (n 713) 336.
[837]Rivier, *Lehrbuch des Völkerrechts* (n 739) 5.
[838]ibid, 303-8.
[839]Liszt (n 111) 3-4.

civilization and development leading to the Ottomans' inability to perform international duties, another pointed to the continuous capitulations putting Turkey in an inferior and disadvantaged position. Only after the Greco-Turkish War (1919-1923) was Turkey able to change this. In the Treaty of Lausanne (1923) Great Britain, France, Italy, Japan, Greece, Romania, and Yugoslavia of the one part, and Turkey of the other part agreed eventually upon 'the complete abolition of the Capitulations in Turkey in every respect.'[840]

8.5 New States on the Balkans: Romania, Serbia and Montenegro

The recognition of Romania, Serbia, and Montenegro was closely connected to the so-called Eastern Question.[841] This term stands for a series of complex problems arising from the decline of the Ottoman Empire and the resulting conflicting interests of the European powers on the Balkan Peninsula. A main reason for the crisis of the Ottoman Empire was Turkish-Russian rivalry on the Balkans and on the territories around the Black Sea. This caused several wars between the Ottoman and the Russian Empire, four of which were fought in the 19th century.[842] In addition, emerging from the ideas of the French revolution and Romanticism, nationalism sparked the desire of the numerous peoples on the Balkans, whose territory had been under Ottoman control for centuries, to create their own State.

8.5.1 Romania

The modern Romania originated from the union of the Wallachia and Moldavia, the Danubian Principalities, in 1861. Since the 14th and 15th century, they had been under the suzerainty of the Sublime Porte. Nonetheless, both nations enjoyed a certain amount of freedom regarding their internal affairs.

---

[840] Treaty of Lausanne (signed 24 July 1823) 28 LNTS 11.

[841] For a full account on the Eastern Question, see Matthew Smith Anderson, *The Eastern Question, 1774-1923: A Study in International Relations* (Macmillan 1982); AL Macfie, *The Eastern Question: 1774-1923* (Rev edn, Pearson 2004).

[842] 1806-1812, 1828-1829, 1853-1856 (Crimean War), and 1877-1878.

Towards the end of the 18th century, Russia gained more and more influence in the area. After the Russian-Ottoman War (1806-1812), however, Russia had to vacate the previously occupied principalities. In return the Ottoman Empire had to cede Bessarabia to Russia.[843] After another war between Russia and the Ottoman Empire (1828-1829) Russia consolidated its influence and voice as a protector of the Wallachia and Moldavia in the Treaty of Adrianople (1829).[844] This growing Russian influence on the principalities aroused resistance in 1848, culminating in a revolution demanding a united, independent State of their own. This revolt, however, was crushed by Ottoman and Russian forces soon after.[845]

The Russian protectorate was eventually terminated in the Treaty of Paris (1856)[846] ending the Crimean War (1853-1856). While the principalities remained under Ottoman suzerainty, their privileges and immunities were put under the guarantee of the contracting Powers.[847] Furthermore, the Ottoman undertook to preserve the independent, national administration of the principalities, as well as their freedom of worship, legislation, trade and navigation.[848] The leaders of the 1848 revolt continued to demand the union of the two principalities. In May 1858, the signatory States of the Treaty of Paris met anew for a conference in Paris to discuss the situation in the principalities. Finally, they signed the Convention of Paris in which they agreed on a loose union called the United Principalities of Wallachia and Moldavia.[849] This union still was subject to Ottoman suzerainty. At the same time, the principalities retained the freedom of internal administration and each was now allowed to elect their respective prince (*hospodar*). But contrary to the Paris Convention, which provided for the election of two separate princes – one for each principality – the people of both

[843]Treaty of Bucharest (signed 28 May 1812) 62 CTS 25.

[844]Treaty of Adrianople (signed 14 September 1829) 80 CTS 84.

[845]Ioan Bolovan, 'Romanians in the Period of Reforms and Democratic revolutions (1820-1859)' in Ioan-Aurel Pop and Ioan Bolovan (eds), *History of Romania: Compendium* (Romanian Cultural Institute 2006) 468-74.

[846]Peace of Paris (1856) (n 51).

[847]ibid art 22. See also s 7.4 ('The Ottoman Empire').

[848]ibid, art 22.

[849]Convention of Paris (signed 19 August 1858) XLVII BFSP 107.

Wallachia and Moldavia elected the very same person as their *hospodar* in 1859: Alexandru Ioan Cuza. In 1861 he united the two principalities into the State of Romania and made Bucharest its capital.[850] The participant States of the Paris Conference acknowledged this *fait accompli* with some surprise, but accepted it.[851]

As part of the Russian-Ottoman War (1877-1878), Romania and Russia concluded an agreement in April 1877 that permitted the Russian troops to pass through Romanian territory. Shortly after this, Romania also declared war on the Ottoman Empire,[852] soon followed by Romania's declaration of independence.[853] The European powers had already in some cases concluded provisional treaty agreements[854] with Romania in which reference was made to Romania as a State.[855] Nevertheless, despite taking note of this declaration, they refused to recognize *de jure* Romania's independence.[856] The recognition by the Sublime Porte was only granted in the Treaty of

---

[850] Gheorghe Iacob, 'Romanians during the Emergence of Nation-States (1859-1918)' in Ioan-Aurel Pop and Ioan Bolovan (eds), *History of Romania: Compendium* (Romanian Cultural Institute 2006) 502; Keith Hitchins, *Rumania 1866-1947* (Clarendon Press 1994) 12-13.

[851] Protocol of the Conference between the Plenipotentiaries of Austria, France, Great Britain, Prussia, Russia, Sardinia and Turkey, recognizing Prince Couza as Hospodar of Moldavia and of Wallachia (signed 6 September 1859) LVII BFSP 520.

[852] Despatch from the Roumanian Minister for Foreign Affairs to the Roumanian Agent at Paris, announcing the existence of a State of War with Turkey (14 May 1877) 4 Hertslet 2618 .

[853] Roumanian Declaration of Independence (3 June 1877) LXVIII BFSP 871 .

[854] Declaration between France and Roumania, for regulating, provisionally, the Commercial Relations between the Two Countries (signed 5 November 1876) LXVII BFSP 665; Declaration between Great Britain and Roumania, for regulating Provisionally the Commercial Relations between the Two Countries (signed 30 November 1876) LXVII BFSP 50; Convention de Commerce et de Navigation entre la Russie et la Roumanie (signed 27 March 1876) LXVII BFSP 67; Convention de Commerce entre l'Allemagne et la Roumanie (signed 14 November 1877) LXVII BFSP 120.

[855] In the agreement between Romania and Russia, for example, mentioning of the 'relations commerciales entres les deux États' is found.

[856] See the diplomatic correspondence concerning the declaration of independence of Romania between the powers in AN Makarov and Ernst Schmitz (eds), *Digest of the Diplomatic Correspondence of the European States, 1871-1878* (Carl Heymann 1937) 90-96.

San Stefano (1878), concluded after the war, and by other Powers after the Congress of Berlin.

8.5.2 Serbia

Serbia had been almost permanently – apart from two short periods of Austrian occupation in the 18th century – under Ottoman rule since the 15th century. In 1804 the peasants and the nobles of Serbia launched an insurrection triggered by a brutal massacre of the village elders (*knez*).[857] Đorđe Petrović, also known as Karađorđe (Black George), took the lead in this uprising, which was not yet targeted against the Sublime Porte as such, but rather against the violent and perceived illegitimate arbitrary rule of the Janissaries in the *Sandžak*[858] Belgrade.[859] Despite the attempts of the Sultan to negotiate with the rebels, no settlement could be reached. Initially only a local matter, it developed quickly into a region-wide revolution against Ottoman rule and for a Serbian independence. The Serbs sought to build an alliance with the Russian Empire, which was at war with the Ottomans since 1806. But because Russia was threatened by an imminent French invasion, it concluded the Treaty of Bucharest with the Ottoman Empire in 1812 to end the war.[860] In this agreement, the Ottoman Empire committed itself to a general amnesty for the Serbian rebels, who were guaranteed their freedom.[861] But despite this commitment, the Ottoman troops marched into Serbian territory and countered the uprising. Karađorđe and many of his followers fled abroad. A few years later, in 1815, the second Serbian uprising broke out. The new leader of the Serbs was Miloš Obrenović who was soon recognized as prince of the Serbs by the Ottoman Empire. With a combination of smart military tactics and diplomatic skills, he attained for

[857] Misha Glenny, *The Balkans 1804-2012: Nationalism, War and the Great Powers* (Granta 2012) 8.

[858] *Sandžak* is the term used for an certain administrative district of the Ottoman Empire.

[859] Stevan K Pavlowitch, *A History of the Balkans: 1804-1945* (Longman 1999) 28.

[860] Treaty of Bucharest (signed 28 May 1812) 62 CTS 25.

[861] ibid, art 7.

Serbia the status of an autonomous principality of the Ottoman Empire.[862] The status of autonomous Serbia together with its rights and privileges were then endorsed internationally in a separate act of the Convention of Ackerman (1826)[863] and in the Peace of Adrianople (1829).[864] Nevertheless it was undisputed for the European powers that Serbia was still part of the Ottoman Empire. Therefore Serbia's position under Ottoman rule was reconfirmed, not only in these treaties but also later in the Paris Peace Treaty (1856).[865]

In June 1862 another conflict between Serbia and the Sublime Porte arose. In the course of this conflict, Ottoman canons shot at Belgrade, consequentially all Ottoman inhabitants were banned from the city.[866] In order to consider this situation the plenipotentiaries of Great Britain, Austria, France, Prussia, Russia, Sardinia, and the Ottoman Empire met for a conference in Constantinople. Their aim was it to re-establish the relations between Serbia and the Sublime Porte. In essence, the participants of the conference reassured the suzerainty of the Ottoman Empire together with the autonomy of the principality. Hence, there was a consensus among the powers, that it is the duty of the Serbs

> de donner de leur côté à la Sublime Port, par des témoignages irrécusables, la confiance que, dans le développement légitime de cette autonomie ils ne cherchent pas les moyens de relacher les liens qui les unissent à l'Empire Ottoman...[867]

---

[862] Mark Biondich, *The Balkans: Revolution, War, and Political Violence since 1878* (OUP 2011) 20; Glenny (n 857) 19.

[863] Convention between Russia and Turkey for the Implementation of the Treaty of Bucharest etc ['Convention of Ackerman'] (signed 7 October 1826) 76 CTS 412.

[864] Treaty of Adrianople (signed 14 September 1829) 80 CTS 84.

[865] Peace of Paris (1856) (n 51) art 28.

[866] Pavlowitch (n 859) 82.

[867] 'to give from their side through incontestable evidence the assurance that in the legitimate development of this autonomy, they do not seek the means to release the ties that bind them to the Ottoman Empire...' (my translation) (Protocole contentant l'Arrangement, relatif à la Servie, définitivement arrêté entre la Sublime Porte et les Représentants des Puissances signataires du Traité de Paris de 1856 [signed 4 September 1862] LII BFSP 1141, 1142).

Furthermore, the participants agreed that the Sublime Porte had to reduce its forces in the territory as well as to evacuate and destroy the Ottoman fortresses in Serbia. The Ottoman handed over the last four remaining fortresses in 1867.[868]
In 1875 revolts against the Ottoman rule broke out in Bosnia, Herzegovina, and Bulgaria. The brutality of the Ottoman forces, particularly against the Bulgarian population, caused popular demand for intervention in Serbia and Montenegro.[869] Thus, in June and July 1876 Serbia[870] and Montenegro[871] declared war on the Ottoman Empire. But the Serbian militia was hopelessly outnumbered and militarily inferior to the Ottoman forces. Serbia was only saved from a total defeat by Russia applying pressure on the Ottoman Empire to consent to an armistice.[872] At a conference in Constantinople, the European powers demanded a peace based on the re-establishment of the *status quo ante bellum*,[873] to which Serbia and the Sublime Porte officially agreed to on 16 February 1877.[874] In addition to this, the European powers pressed for the division and reorganization of Bosnia, Herzegovina, and Bulgaria. The Sublime Porte, however, refused to this, as he considered it an intervention into the internal affairs of the Ottoman Empire.[875] For Russia, this rejection was motive for declaring war

[868] Firman of the Sultan relative to the Evacuation of the Servian Fortresses by the Turks (10 April 1867) III Hertslet 1800 .

[869] Pavlowitch (n 859) 108-12.

[870] Serbie: Lettre adressée, le 22 juin 1876, par le Prince Milan au Grand-vizir pour annoncer l'entrée des troupes serbes dans les provinces turques (1878-1879) III NRG2 14 .

[871] Monténégro: Déclaration de guerre à la Turquie, en date du 2 Juillet 1876 (1878-1879) III NRG2 18 .

[872] Ultimatum russe et acceptation de la Turquie; et date du 31 octobre / 1er novembre 1876 (1878-1879) III NRG2 32 .

[873] Protocols of the Conferences at Constantinople (December 1876-January 1877) LXVIII BFSP 1114 , 1192.

[874] Protocol for the Conclusion of Peace (28 February 1877) LXVIII BFSP 810 , 811; Turkish Firman to the Prince of Servia, on the Conclusion of Peace (20 February 1877) LXVIII BFSP 814 .

[875] Protocols of the Conferences at Constantinople (December 1876-January 1877) LXVIII BFSP 1114 (n 873) 1206.

on the Ottoman Empire, once more.[876] Also Serbia, in support of Russia, declared war on the Ottoman Empire in December 1877.[877] Both the Russian-Ottoman war and the Serbian-Ottoman war were terminated by the Treaty of San Stefano in 1778.

8.5.3 Montenegro

Montenegro was also a *Sandžak* of the Ottoman Empire since the end of the 15th century. Nevertheless, Montenegro always claimed a certain amount of autonomy, which it had defended by means of armed resistance.
Until the mid-19th century, the Petrović-Njegoš family held both the highest secular and ecclesiastic powers. Hence, Petar II Petrović-Njegoš was not only prince, but also bishop (*vladika*) of Montenegro. It was his nephew, Danilo I Petrović Njegoš, who eventually divided these two roles, and proclaimed Montenegro a secular principality in 1852.[878] Despite this, Montenegro remained under the suzerainty of the Sublime Porte. Danilo's support for the liberation endeavour in Herzegovina provoked the Sublime Porte. An Ottoman invasion in Montenegro was narrowly and temporarily avoided only through Austrian mediation in 1853.[879]
During the Crimean War, Montenegro stayed neutral. At the Paris Peace Conference after the war, confronted with apprehensions that Russia would plan to reach out to Montenegro, the Russian plenipotentiary declared that 'leur Gouvernement n'entretient avec le Monténégro d'autres rapports que ceux qui naissent des sympathies des Monténégrins pour la Russie et des dispositions bienveillantes de la Russie pour ces montagnards.'[880] The Ottoman representative affirmed that the Porte still considered Montenegro an

[876]Russian Note, Declaring War against Turkey (24 April 1877) LXVIII BFSP 844 .

[877]Declaration of War by Servia against Turkey (14 December 1877) LXVIII BFSP 885 .

[878]Elizabeth Roberts, *Realm of the Black Mountain: A History of Montenegro* (Cornell University Press 2007) 218.

[879]Kenneth Morrison, *Montenegro: A Modern History* (IB Tauris 2009) 25.

[880]'. . . the Government does not entertain with the Montenegrins any other relations than the ones arising out from the sympathies of the Montenegrins for Russia and the benevolent dispositions on behalf of Russia for these mountaineers.' (my translation) (Protocole No 14 (25 March 1856) XLVI BFSP 97 , 102).

integral part of the Ottoman Empire, but had no intention to alter the existing state of things.[881] However, Montenegro's demand for complete independence from Ottoman rule was not included into the Paris Peace Treaty, and the Sublime Porte continued to oppose recognition of an independent Montenegro.[882]

On 31 May 1858 Danilo issued a note to the European powers that demanded the diplomatic recognition of Montenegro, the extension of the frontiers towards Herzegovina and Albania, the definitive settlement of the frontier line towards the Ottoman Empire, and the annexation of the port of Antivari to the principality.[883] In response, the European powers hardly paid any attention to these claims. Later in the year, the continued Montenegrin involvement in Herzegovina's resistance culminated in the Battle of Grahovo between Ottoman and Montenegrin forces.[884] After the rather surprising victory of the inferior Montenegrin forces, the powers returned to Danilo's demands and assigned an international commission to define the boundaries between Montenegro and the Ottoman Empire.[885] This constituted another step towards Montenegro's *de facto* independence.[886]

After Danilo was assassinated in 1860, his successor, Nikola I Mirkov Petrović-Njegoš, continued to support Herzegovina's revolt against the Sublime Porte. This caused the Ottomans to undertake another intervention in Montenegro in 1862 in order to discipline the principality.[887] Montenegro was defeated and forced to accept several restrictions in the Convention of Scutari (1862).[888] Thus, Montenegro was able to keep its autonomy re-

---

881 Protocole No 15 (26 March 1856) XLVI BFSP 104 , 104.

882 Đorđe Borozan, 'Montenegro vom 16. Jahrhundert bis 1918' in Walter Lukan, Ljubinkaq Trgovčević, and Dragan Vukčević (eds), *Serbien und Montenegro* (LIT Verlag 2005) 185; Roberts (n 878) 221.

883 Note to the European Powers (31 May 1856) II Hertslet 1438 .

884 Morrison (n 879) 27.

885 Proces-verbal entre les Reprisentants de l'Autriche, de la France, de la Grande-Bretagne, de la Prusse, de la Russie, de la Turquie, pour la délimitation des Frontiéres d'Albanie, de l'Herzégovine, et du Monténégro (signed 27 October 1858) L BFSP 1001.

886 Borozan (n 882) 185.

887 Morrison (n 879) 27-38; Roberts (n 878) 231-234.

888 Turkish Conditions Imposed upon Montenegro; and Accepted by the Prince ['Convention of Scutari'] (signed 31 August 1862) LXI BFSP 1060.

garding internal administration, but had to acquiesce to Ottoman forces stationed in its territory, and was banned from fortifying its borders.
Prompted by a renewed outbreak of the upheaval in Herzegovina in 1875, Montenegro formed an alliance with Serbia and began to wage war against the already weakened Ottoman Empire.[889] A series of early victories forced the Ottoman Empire to agree to a ceasefire. This ceasefire was short-lived, however, and soon the fighting flared up once again. This time the Ottoman successfully fought back against the Montenegrin troops. Only under pressure from the Russian Empire did the Ottoman forces retire from Montenegro's territory. They were ultimately defeated by Russia in a series of battles at the Shipka Pass in January 1878.[890]

8.5.4 The Treaty of San Stefano and the Treaty of Berlin

In February 1878, the Russian and the Ottoman Empire put an end to their war with the conclusion of the Treaty of San Stefano.[891] With this, the Sublime Porte recognized Romania,[892] Serbia,[893] and Montenegro[894] as independent States.
But the European powers – Great Britain, France and Austria – were concerned about the consequences of this Russian-Ottoman agreement. Particularly, they feared increased power for Russia on the Balkan Peninsula.[895] In order to consider the situation and to adjust the Treaty of San Stefano in accordance with their interests, the signatory States of the Paris Peace

---

[889] Monténégro: Déclaration de guerre à la Turquie, en date du 2 Juillet 1876 (1878-1879) III NRG2 18 (n 871).
[890] Morrison (n 879) 24-29.
[891] Treaty of San Stefano (signed 3 March 1862) II MPTMH 959.
[892] ibid, art 5.
[893] ibid, art 3.
[894] ibid, art 2.
[895] Circulaire adressée aux ambassades britanniques touchant la paix preliminaire de San Stefano, le 1er avril 1878 (1878-1879) III NRG2 256 .

Treaty of 1856 met in Berlin by invitation of German Chancellor Bismarck.[896]

Since the Ottoman Empire no longer opposed to recognize the independence of Romania, Serbia, and Montenegro,[897] the other powers consented in principle to recognize Serbia's independence, yet only with the requirement of religious freedom. In this respect, the French plenipotentiary emphasized that

> la Serbie, qui demande à entrer dans la famille Européenne sur le même pied que les autres États, doit au préalable reconnaitre les principes qui sont la base de l'organisation sociale dans tous les États de l'Europe, et les accepter comme une condition nécessaire de la faveur qu'elle sollicite.[898]

Also regarding the recognition of Montenegro's independence, religious freedom was demanded.[899] Several other requirements were imposed on Montenegro – first, it was not allowed to possess war ships or a battle flag, second, it was compelled to raze its fortresses and forbidden from building new ones, and third, it had reach an agreement with Austria concerning the construction and maintenance of a new railway.[900]

On the 13 July 1878, the States' representatives signed the Treaty of Berlin recognizing the independence of Romania,[901] Serbia,[902] and Montenegro.[903] Attached to the recognition, however, was the requirement of the assurance

---

[896] See at length the Protocols of Congress of the Representatives of Great Britain, Austria-Hungary, France, Germany, Italy, Russia, and Turkey; for the Settlement of Affairs in the East (June, July 1878) LXIX BFSP 862 .

[897] Protocole No 8 (28 June 1878) LXIX BFSP 946 , 959.

[898] 'Serbia, which seeks to enter the European family on the same footing as other States, must first recognize the principles that are the basis of social organization in all States of Europe, and accept them as a necessary condition for the favour it solicits.' (my translation) (ibid, 960).

[899] Protocole No 10 (1 July 1878) LXIX BFSP 978 , 988-89.

[900] ibid, 992.

[901] Act of the Congress of Berlin (signed 13 July 1878) 153 CTS 172, art 43.

[902] ibid, art 34.

[903] ibid, art 15.

of religious freedom in their respective territory. Romania had, in addition, to make restitution of Bessarabia[904] that was detached of Russia by the Paris Peace Treaty.[905] In return, Dobruja was added to the Romanian territory.[906]

After Romania had changed Article 7 of its constitution according to the requirements in Article 44 of the Treaty of Berlin and, hence, assured equality and freedom of religion for all citizens, in particular regarding Jews,[907] other States individually began to recognize Romania: Italy awarded recognition in December 1879,[908] Greece and the Netherlands in January 1880,[909] and France, Germany and Great Britain, in an identical note on 20 February 1880.[910] The US recognized Romania's independence already on 15 August 1878 through a letter in which the appointment of the US consul in Romania had been communicated.[911] Serbia declared its independence on 10 August 1878,[912] whereupon on 3 March 1878 a British minister was accredited in Romania.[913] With regard to Montenegro, however, the representatives of Germany, Austria, France, and Russia admitted already in the negotiations before the conclusion of the Berlin Treaty that they had recognized implicitly or explicitly the Montenegrin independence. Great Britain, on the other hand, had still denied to recognize Montenegro by that point.[914] Hence, whether the Treaty of Berlin actually stood for the final recognition of the three principalities as independent States, particularly of Romania - has been long disputed. Some consider the requirement of religious freedom as a modus, and, therefore, the recognition in the treaty

[904] ibid, art 45.
[905] Peace of Paris (1856) (n 51) art 20.
[906] Act of the Congress of Berlin (signed 13 July 1878) 153 CTS 172, art 46.
[907] Correspondence relative to the Recognition of the Independence of Roumania (1879-1880) LXXI BFSP 1136 , 1176-78.
[908] ibid, 1181.
[909] ibid, 1182.
[910] ibid, 1187.
[911] Mr Evarts to Mr Kasson [Writing concerning the US recognition of Roumania], 9 March 1880 [1880] FRUS 51.
[912] Servian Proclamation of Independence (22 August 1878) LXIX BFSP 1109 .
[913] 4 Hertslet 2785, Fn 4.
[914] Protocole No 10 (1 July 1878) LXIX BFSP 978 (n 899) 988-89.

as final.[915] Others, in contrast, perceived the recognition in the treaty only as conditional in a suspensive manner.[916] Thus, only when Romania had satisfactorily changed its constitution, were other States actually willing to recognize Romania's independence.

8.6 Interim conclusion: The recognitional fitness of the international society of civilized States

After the dawn of the 19th century, the international society grew not only geographically, but also regarding the number of its members. Closely connected to this growth was the gradual change of the recognitional fitness. While effectiveness and independence from the mother country were still essentially necessary, the precedent recognition by the mother country was no longer universally deemed required. The recognitional fitness encompassed additional requirements that were subject to transformation along with the values of the international society. Until that point only Christian States were members of the international society. This changed, however, with the recognition of the Ottoman Empire in the middle of the century. Accordingly, as the main criterion of the contemporary recognitional fitness, Christianity, was successively replaced by the new concept of 'civilization' corresponding to the new canon of values determined by the member States. Thus, in line with abolitionism prevailing in Europe, Brazil was required to abolish slave trade, while the newly independent States on the Balkan had to ensure the protection of religious minorities in order to be recognized.

However, the elements considered necessary to provide evidence of attained civilization were not only kept vague but also very adaptable. This was due to the fact that during the era of the society of civilized States, political and economic calculus played a major part in the recognizant States' con-

[915] For example Chen (n 4) 226; Lauterpacht, *States* (n 3) 362-63; Rivier, *Principes du droit des gens* (n 69) 60; Liszt (n 111) 46-47.

[916] For example Fedor Fedorovič Martens, *Traité de droit international* (Paris, 1883-1887) vol 1, 361; Heinrich Triepel, *Völkerrecht und Landesrecht* (Verlag von CL Hirschfeld 1899) 292, Fn 1; Hillgruber (n 9) 66.

sideration of the required recognitional fitness of an entity seeking to be recognized. Ultimately, it cannot be ignored that the concept of civilization served as a powerful tool that allowed the member States to maintain their power and dominance well into the 20th century. By having absolute definatory power over 'civilization', the member States were able to keep the concept vague and malleable to achieve their goals and serve their purposes. Non-members could then be perpetually deemed uncivilized, regardless of changing circumstances, and thus had little to no chance to enter the international society of civilized states. For member States, then, the motivations to maintain this concept were high, ie retaining their power, while the impetus to phase it out was very low. Therefore it was only after World War II when the concept of civilization eventually lost its meaning.

9 Admission to the global international society

9.1 The global international society

The replacement of the former society of civilized States by the global society of States commenced after World War I. Three main stages can be distinguished in this process. The first phase took place during the interwar period. It was a phase of transition during which the new society came into being while the previous society still existed. The second phase was the phase of the expansion of the new society towards a global level. It evolved after World War II and lasted until the end of the Cold War in the late 1980's. The third phase that was marked by the eventually consolidating globality of the society of States began in the last decade of the 20th century.[917] Despite the fact that the original majority of European members gradually began to decrease, the international society remained largely influenced by European concepts.

The first phase of the development of the new global society originated after World War I. The war was the result of an unabated urge for territorial expansion by the major powers of the international society of civilized States, leading eventually to the collapse of the system established after the Vienna Congress. After this catastrophe of previously unknown dimensions, numerous war-torn States, determined to prevent a similar tragedy, intended to institutionalize a security system. This institution, however, was not to have the form of a world government, but rather that of an association of States both willing and able prevent war by resorting to peaceful means to resolve their conflicts. Hence, the foundation of the League of Nations was an attempt to organize the international society of factual unequal but legally equal States by restructuring their mutual relations. The Covenant of the League of Nations laid down the rules and processes of this new institution whose purpose was 'to promote international co-operation and to achieve international peace and security'.[918] Yet many of these rules and

[917] This third phase, ie the time after the Cold War, is discussed above in the context of State recognition in ch 3 ('Cases of State recognition since the end of the Cold War').

[918] Covenant of the League of Nations (signed 28 April 1919, entered into force 10 January 1920) 13 AJIL Supp 128, Preamble.

concepts still resembled traditional views and practices of the society of civilized States. Thus, while concepts such as sovereignty and judicial equality among independent States were retained, so too were institutions such as capitulations and other imperial instruments of the powerful members of the civilized society. This is why remnants of this mindset are still found in the Statute of the newly established Permanent Court of International Justice, as well as in the Covenant of the League of Nations.[919] Also, in the Inter-American Anti-War Treaty the 'adherence to the effort of all civilized nations' is stressed.[920] Nevertheless, despite the strong pervasiveness of the concepts of civilized States, signs of a transformation to a global conception of the society of States began to emerge. In the Briand-Kellogg Pact, there was still talk about the 'civilized nations of the world' but, at the same time, the hope is expressed that 'all the other nations of the world will join in this humane endeavor' of renouncing war as a political instrument.[921] Similarly, in the Additional Protocol relative to Non-Intervention the signatory governments assure the 'benefits of peace' not only 'in their mutual relations' but also 'in their relations with all the nations of the earth.'[922] Nonetheless, the newly established security system was too weak to enforce its rules on the powerful members of the international society and failed to fulfil the purpose of its creation, ie the prevention of the outbreak of World War II. After World War II, the concept of civilized States was increasingly abandoned,[923] and the old society was replaced by a newly developing society of States expanding to a global level due to the advent of decolonization. This

[919] Statute of the Permanent Court of International Justice (n 730) art 38, para 3; Statute of the International Court of Justice (signed 26 June 1945, entered into force 24 October 1945) 33 UNTS 993, art 22. See on this also s 7.1 ('The international society of civilized States').

[920] Anti-War Treaty (Non-Aggression and Conciliation) ['Saavedra Lamas Treaty'] (signed 10 October 1933, entered into force 13 November 1935) 163 LNTS 405, Preamble.

[921] Briand-Kellogg Pact (n 184) Preamble.

[922] Additional Protocol relative to Non-Intervention, Adopted by the Inter-American Conference for the Maintenance of Peace (signed 23 December 1936) 188 LNTS 32, Preamble.

[923] In spite of its sporadic reoccurrence, for example in Statute of the International Court of Justice (signed 26 June 1945, entered into force 24 October 1945) 33 UNTS 993, art 38 para c.

society, however, was divided by the two superpowers - the USSR and the US. Nonetheless, the 'European tradition of an organized international society' had endured. It is therefore that after the war the two superpowers and their allies agreed to recreate an 'overarching international institution'.[924] But like its predecessor, the League of Nations, it was not to be a world government, but rather a permanent international forum.[925] Access to this new institution, the UN, was open to all 'peace-loving States'.[926] But despite that the term 'peace-loving nation' had already been used in Woodrow Wilson's Fourteen Points,[927] and the UN General Assembly had judged certain applicant States as being 'peace-loving' in a number of cases,[928] the attribute as such had never been defined.[929] Still, the UN Security Council regularly had – and continues to – assess the peace-loving character of applicant States. Among the considered topics are references to the history of the State, the conduct of the applicant during the Second World War, the continued existence of a technical state of war between the applicant and a Member State, the continued possession of territories acquired through aggression in the Second World War, the compliance with the recommendations of the United Nation, the instigation of border incidents, the interference with peaceful foreign shipping in the applicant's territorial waters, and the willingness to employ pacific methods in the settlement of boundary disputes.[930] Nonetheless, regardless of its definitional deficiency,

---

[924] Watson, *Evolution* (n 536) 289.

[925] ibid, 289-90.

[926] UN Charter (n 52) art 4 para 1.

[927] Woodrow Wilson, 'Wilson's Address to Congress, Stating the War Aims and Peace Terms of the United States, 8 January 1918 ['Fourteen Conditions of Peace']' in *President Wilson's State Papers and Addresses* (The Review of Reviews Company 1918) 467, 471.

[928] For example Admission of New Members, UNGA Res 113 (II) C-G (17 November 1947) UN Docs A/RES/113(II) C-G; Admission of New Members, UNGA Res 197 (III) C-G (8 December 1948) UN Docs A/RES/197(III) C-G; Admission of New Members, UNGA Res 296 (IV) A-I (22 November 1949) UN Docs A/RES/296(IV) A-I.

[929] United Nations, *A Repertory of Practice of United Nations Organs: Articles 1-22 of the Charter* (United Nations 1955) 179.

[930] United Nations, *A Repertoire of the Practice of the Security Council, Chapter VII* (vol 1, United Nations 1946-1951) 273.

the concept of 'peace-loving States' constituted a core feature of the new international society and signified an affirmation of the sought-after establishment of peace linked with the permanent renunciation of war as a means of international relations. For the attainment of these endeavours, the members of the international society committed themselves to numerous norms and principles, like open and just relations with each other, the observance of international law, the adherence to treaty obligations, respect for human rights, and the equality of States, laid down first in the Covenant of the League of Nations and later in the Charter of the United Nations.

Yet, particularly in the second phase of development of the global society of States after World War II the question arose whether these norms and principles would really constitute a unified global society of States. Particularly casting doubt on this possibility was the dominance of the two superpowers that divided the world in two systems with different interpretations of these norms and principles and how to comply with them.[931] Certain doubts seemed plausible in light of the fact that, for instance, the veto power[932] of the five permanent members of the UN Security Council undermined to a certain extent, right from the start, the aspired concept of equality of all States.[933] This inequality was further reinforced by the Treaty on the Non-Proliferation of Nuclear Weapons forbidding non-nuclear-weapons States from obtaining such weaponry, while recognizing and tolerating their possession by the five permanent UN Security Council members.[934] Thus whereas some doubted the existence of a global society unified by common norms and principles, others held that despite the separation of the two systems, 'the world remained formally one international

[931] eg Alfred Verdross, 'Die Wertgrundlagen des Völkerrechts' (1953) 4 AVR 129, 30ff; even earlier Georg Schwarzenberger, 'The Rule of Law and the Disintegration of the International Society' (1939) 33 AJIL 56.

[932] UN Charter (n 52) art 27.

[933] ibid, art 2 para 1 actually only refers to the equality of the UN members. But in fact the prerogative of the veto elevates the five powers to superior positions vis-à-vis States not being members of the UN. Thus, in practice the veto power renders the veto-states more powerful than the UN-members as well as non-members.

[934] Treaty on the Non-Proliferation of Nuclear Weapons (signed 1 July 1968, entered into force 5 March 1970) 729 UNTS 168.

society, with a common structure of international law, diplomatic representation and other rules and institutions...'[935] In any case, two of these principles can be identified as being at the core of the expansion of this new global society.

The first principle is the endeavoured renunciation of war in international relations. After World War I, the States, desperate to maintain peace, included certain measures into the Covenant of the League of Nations to prevent another war. These measures concerned disarmament,[936] international security,[937] and conflict solving through arbitration.[938] However, the Covenant still lacked a comprehensive ban on war. Instead, the contracting States only consented to 'the acceptance of obligations not to resort to war.'[939] In 1924 the first attempt to outlaw war was placed in the Geneva Protocol, declaring a war of aggression 'a violation of this solidarity [of the members of the international community] and an international crime.'[940] Additionally, the signatory States agreed 'in no case' to resort to war.[941] Yet, the Geneva Protocol never became effective due to Great Britain's refusal to ratify it. The idea, however, to solve conflicts without recourse to war, but rather through arbitration or judicial settlement endured and lived on in the Locarno Treaties (1925).[942] With the Briand-Kellogg-Pact

[935] Watson, *Evolution* (n 536) 293.

[936] Covenant of the League of Nations (signed 28 April 1919, entered into force 10 January 1920) 13 AJIL Supp 128, arts 8-9.

[937] ibid, arts 10, 16.

[938] ibid, arts 11-15.

[939] ibid, Preamble.

[940] Protocol for the Pacific Settlement of International Disputes ['Geneva Protocol'] (signed 2 October 1924) 19 AJIL Spec Supp 9, Preamble.

[941] ibid, art 2.

[942] Treaty of Mutual Guarantee between Germany, Belgium, France, Great Britain and Italy (signed 16 October 1925, entered into force 14 September 1926) 54 LNTS 289; Arbitration Convention between Germany and Belgium (signed 16 October 1925, entered into force 14 September 1926) 54 LNTS 303; Arbitration Convention between Germany and France (signed 16 October 1925, entered into force 14 September 1926) 54 LNTS 315; Arbitration Treaty between Germany and Poland (signed 16 October 1925, entered into force 14 September 1926) 54 LNTS 327; Arbitration Treaty between Germany and

(1928),[943] the States ultimately banned war 'as an instrument of national policy' not only legally, but also morally.[944] Similarly, in 1933 the signatories of the Saavedra Lamas Treaty,[945] while still referring to 'the efforts made by all civilized nations to promote the spirit of universal harmony', committed themselves to 'condemn wars of aggression in their mutual relations or in those with other states'. Moreover, the desire to eradicate war found further expression, most famously, in the Stimson Doctrine,[946] as the policy not to recognize territorial changes brought about by an act of war. But it was only after World War II, which all these undertakings were eventually futile to prevent, that the UN Charter eventually prohibited not only war as such, but the mere 'use of force against the territorial integrity or political independence of any state'.[947] In 1970 the UN confirmed again explicitly the concept of non-recognition of territorial changes brought about by the use of force.[948]

The second core principle of the newly developing global society of States is the self-determination of people. The origin of this concept can be traced back to the time of the American and French revolution. It was in the time leading up to World War I, however, when it rose to prominence as a central issue of international politics, although based on quite different agendas. In the context of the October Revolution in 1817, Vladimir I Lenin developed his idea of a socialist right of self-determination, which he saw as an instrument for the eventual success of global Socialism.[949] According to the socialist conception, self-determination should not only be granted to eth-

Czechoslovakia (signed 16 October 1925, entered into force 14 September 1926) 54 LNTS 341.

943 Briand-Kellogg Pact (n 184).

944 Patrycja Grzebyk, *Criminal Responsibility for the Crime of Aggression* (Routledge 2013) 22.

945 Saavedra Lamas Treaty (n 920) art 2.

946 See on this s 2.4.3 ('Non-recognition'). This strive is also found as part of the Saavedra Lamas Treaty of 1933.

947 UN Charter (n 52) art 2 para 4.

948 Definition of Aggression (n 187) Annex, art 5 para 3.

949 Vladimir I Lenin, 'The Socialist Revolution and the Right of Nations to Self-Determination' in *Collected Works* (Progress Publisher 1977) vol 26; Vladimir I Lenin, 'Decree on Peace' in *Collected Works* (Progress Publisher 1977) vol 26; Vladimir I Lenin,

nic and national groups as well as to the people of an occupied territory, but also provide for the liberation of people under colonial rule.[950] US president Woodrow Wilson, too, campaigned for self-determination of people albeit with a different vision of the concept. For him it was essential that people be 'governed by their own consent.'[951] For the settlement of colonial claims, the interest of the local people should be given equal weight with the demands of the powers involved.[952] Thus, he marked self-determination as 'an imperative principle of action, which statesmen will henceforth ignore at their peril.'[953] Essentially, he believed self-determination of people to be the key to unlock democracy around the world.[954] After World War I, the self-determination of people was still rather a theoretical concept than an actual right. Self-determination of people was not included either in the Versailles Treaties or in the Covenant of the League of Nations. Moreover, during the territorial reorganization of post-war Europe, the interests of the people concerned in the territories remained largely unconsidered despite referenda in certain territories.[955] Accordingly, the International Committee of Jurists, entrusted by the Council of the League of Nations to provide an advisory opinion on the Aaland Question, concluded that despite the fact that the principle of self-determination had recently gained more political

'Outline Programme for Peace Negotiations' in *Collected Works* (Progress Publisher 1977) vol 26.

[950] See also for greater detail Antonio Cassese, *Self-Determination of Peoples: A Legal Reappraisal* (CUP 1995) 16.

[951] Woodrow Wilson, 'President Wilson's Address to Congress Analyzing German and Austrian Peace Utterance, 11 February 1918' in *President Wilson's State Papers and Addresses* (The Review of Reviews Company 1918) 475.

[952] Wilson, 'Fourteen Conditions of Peace' (n 927).

[953] Wilson, 'Peace Utterance' (n 951) 476.

[954] On this also Denise Brühl-Moser, *Die Entwicklung des Selbstbestimmungsrechts der Völker unter besonderer Berücksichtigung seines innerstaatlich-demokratischen Aspekts und seiner Bedeutung für den Minderheitenschutz* (Helbing 1994) 23.

[955] See on territorial referenda after World War I, Anne Peters, *Das Gebietsreferendum im Völkerrecht: Seine Bedeutung im Licht der Staatenpraxis nach 1989* (Nomos Verlagsgesellschaft 1995) 51-57.

significance, 'it cannot be considered as sufficient to put it upon the same footing as a positive rule of the Law of Nations.'[956]

Only sometime after World War II did the concept transform into a right. Already during the War, British Premier Minister Churchill and US President Roosevelt signed the Atlantic Charter, in which they enunciated their hope for a better future for the world. Essential for this, they considered, amongst other things, the self-determination of people when it comes to territorial changes and the form of government.[957] Even though, they were rather less successful with their aspirations after the war, the basic idea of self-determination was incorporated into the Charter of the newly founded UN.[958] However, while self-determination was included in the new Charter, it was still a principle and not a right. Furthermore, it was not an end to be achieved, but rather listed as a means to 'to strengthen universal peace.' This changed with the conclusion of the two human rights covenants of 1966 which both stated in an identical manner a 'right of self-determination' of all peoples. [959] Beyond this, various references to the self-determination of people is found in other treaties[960] and resolutions of the UN[961] and of regional organizations.[962] Moreover, the ICJ repeatedly confirmed the customary law character of the self-determination of people.[963]

---

[956] *Aaland Question* (n 50) 5.

[957] Declaration of Principles, known as the Atlantic Charter (12 August 1941, made public 14 August 1941) CXLIV BSFP 683 .

[958] UN Charter (n 52) art 1 para 2 and art 55.

[959] 'By virtue of that right they freely determine their political status and freely pursue their economic, social and cultural development.' (International Covenant on Civil and Political Rights [signed 16 December 1966, entered into force 23 March 1976] 999 UNTS 171; International Covenant on Economic, Social and Cultural Rights [signed 16 December 1966, entered into force 3 January 1976] 993 UNTS 3).

[960] eg Universal Declaration of Human Rights, UNGA Res 217 (III) A (10 December 1948) UN Doc A/RES/217(III) A, art 21 para 3.

[961] eg Friendly Relations Declaration (n 189) Principle V.

[962] eg , Final Act ['Helsinki Final Act'], 'ILM' (1 August 1975) Principle VII.

[963] eg *Legal Consequences for States of the Continued Presence of South Africa in Namibia (South West Africa) notwithstanding Security Council Resolution 276 (1970)* (n 241) 31; *Western Sahara* (n 43); in *Case concerning East Timor* (*Portugal v Australia*) (Judge-

9.2 The recognition of States in the course of the decolonization process

The evolution of State recognition in the global international society was not characterized by certain exemplary cases like in the precedent societies of States, but rather by the process of decolonization. After World War II, a new concept of self-determination of people arose: the colonial self-determination of people.[964] This again provided the foundation for decolonization. As a result, the global international society expanded quickly, its growth can be observed in the corresponding growth of the newly founded UN. In 1946, there were 51 States founding the organization, the number of members more than doubled by 1970, and reached more than three times of original membership in 1977.[965] Yet, this process of liberation unfolded very inconsistently in the numerous territories. Whereas certain countries gained their independence relatively swiftly and peacefully, ie the former British colonies,[966] the decolonization in territories of other colonial powers, ie Belgium, France, Portugal, Spain, and the Netherlands, was accompanied by prolonged military violence and ethnic conflicts.[967]

---

ment) [1995] ICJ Rep 90, 90, 102, the ICJ confirmed the erga omnes-character of the principle of self-determination.

[964] eg Daniel Thürer, 'Das Selbstbestimmungsrecht der Völker' (1984) 22 AVR 113, 117ff.

[965] See Growth in United Nations Membership, 1945-present (n 330).

[966] Laurie Fransman, 'Commonwealth, Subjects and Nationality Rules' in Ruediger Wolfrum (ed), *The Max Planck Encyclopedia of Public International Law* (OUP 2012) vol II, 450; also Werner Morvay, 'Decolonization: British Territories' in Rudolf Bernhardt (ed), *Encyclopedia of Public International Law* (North-Holland 1992) vol 1.

[967] For a detailed account, see Freya Baetens, 'Decolonization: Belgian Territories' in Ruediger Wolfrum (ed), *The Max Planck Encyclopedia of Public International Law* (OUP 2012) vol II, on Belgian colonies; Makane Moise Mbengue, 'Decolonization: French Territories' in Ruediger Wolfrum (ed), *The Max Planck Encyclopedia of Public International Law* (OUP 2012) vol II, on French colonies; Matthias Fischer and Saskia Klatte, 'Decolonization: Portuguese Territories' in Ruediger Wolfrum (ed), *The Max Planck Encyclopedia of Public International Law* (OUP 2012) vol II, on Portuguese colonies; Paula Maria Vernet, 'Decolonization: Spanish Territories' in Ruediger Wolfrum (ed), *The Max Planck Encyclopedia of Public International Law* (OUP 2012) vol II, on Spanish colonies; JGC van Aggelen, 'Decolonization: Dutch Territories' in Ruediger

The first signs of a commencing transition became apparent after World War I when the dependent territories of the Ottoman Empire and Germany were transferred into the mandate system of the League of Nations instead of being annexed by the victorious powers. The well-being and the development of the people in these territories was seen as a 'sacred trust of civilization.'[968] The territories were subdivided into three categories according to their respective 'stage of development'. The territories formerly under Ottoman sovereignty were allocated into the first category, as they had 'reached a stage of development where their existence as independent nations can be provisionally recognized...'[969] These territories only gained their independence at the end of World War II. The territories of the second and third category that had been under German rule, however, remained under the administration of a Mandatory after World War II.[970] After World War II, the fate of so-called non-self-governing territories became a subject of the UN Charter. The UN Charter used the term 'non-self-governing territory' for all colonial and other dependent territories, with the exception of the territories under the trusteeship system. With this concept the United Nations continued the League's mandate system under a new name. One of the main purposes of the trusteeship system was to 'to promote the political, economic, social, and educational advancement of the inhabitants of the trust territories, and their progressive development towards self-government or independence...'[971] The trusteeship system was not only intended for previously mandated territories, but also for territories detached after World War II from enemy states, ie mainly territories under German and Japanese administration. Furthermore it was envisioned that States would voluntary place territories in their responsibility under this system.[972] But because no Mandatory ever placed its mandated territories

Wolfrum (ed), *The Max Planck Encyclopedia of Public International Law* (OUP 2012) vol II, on Dutch colonies.

[968]Covenant of the League of Nations (signed 28 April 1919, entered into force 10 January 1920) 13 AJIL Supp 128, art 22.

[969]ibid.

[970]ibid.

[971]UN Charter (n 52) art 76 para b.

[972]ibid, art 77.

voluntarily under this system,[973] States of the third category never existed. According to its purpose, all the territories under the trusteeship system eventually attained their independence.[974]
The majority of the non-self-governing territories, however, were colonies. Hence, the UN imposed the 'sacred trust' on their members that held colonies, 'to develop self-government, to take due account of the political aspirations of the peoples, and to assist them in the progressive development of their free political institutions, according to the particular circumstances of each territory and its peoples and their varying stages of advancement.'[975] Already at the United Nations Conference on International Organization (1944) the opinion had been expressed that the eventual independence of these territories was aspired.

> There is implicitly affirmed – in providing rules of general application for the transition from a colony to a mandate and from a mandate to a sovereign State – the principle that the goal which should be sought is that of obtaining the universal application of the principle of self-determination.[976]

The definitive breakthrough for decolonization, however, was the Decolonization Resolution (1960) that declared that the subjection and exploitation of people by foreign powers not only violates human rights and the UN Charter, but also goes against the promotion of world peace and security.[977] Therefore the territories not yet independent were to be released into inde-

---

[973] See on the Trusteeship System also Andriy Y Melnyk, 'United Nations Trusteeship System' in Ruediger Wolfrum (ed), *The Max Planck Encyclopedia of Public International Law* (OUP 2012) vol X.

[974] The last territory acquiring its freedom was Palau in 1994, see Trust Territories that Have Achieved Self-determination ⟨http://www.un.org/en/decolonization/selfdet.shtml⟩ accessed 1 February 2015.

[975] UN Charter (n 52) art 73 para b.

[976] United Nations Conference on International Organization, Doc 2 G/7 (c) (31 October 1944), vol 3, 52 , 146.

[977] Declaration on the Granting of Independence to Colonial Countries and Peoples ['Decolonization Declaration'], UNGA Res 1514 (XV) (14 December 1960) UN Doc A/RES/1514 (XV), para 1.

pendence, 'without any conditions and reservations.'[978] Furthermore, this declaration revealed a shift of opinion regarding the initial approach towards the independence of colonies. Whereas initially the UN Charter required the colonial powers to ensure the dependent countries' development in order to gain independence, the declaration stated that '[i]nadequacy of political, economic, social or educational preparedness should never serve as a pretext for delaying independence.'[979]

Notwithstanding, five years later the UN members noted that little progress had been achieved in this matter. Thus, they declared that the continuance of colonialism together with apartheid and other forms of racial discrimination is deemed a threat for international peace and security and constituted a crime against humanity.[980] Therefore, the struggle of people under colonial rule was considered legitimate, and all States were asked to supply moral and material assistance to them.[981]

The UN resolved the oppositeness between the explicit support of the struggles of the colonial peoples, on one hand, and the endeavour to curb armed conflicts by stating that struggles 'against colonial and alien domination and racist regimes are to be regarded as international armed conflicts.' In so declaring this, it was implied that struggles for independence were cases of self-defence.[982] Accordingly, the UN members affirmed in the Friendly Relations Declaration (1970) the right of self-determination of peoples and

[978] Decolonization Declaration (n 977) para 5.

[979] ibid, para 3.

[980] Implementation of the Declaration on the Granting of Independence to Colonial Countries and Peoples, UNGA Res 2105 (XX) (20 December 1965) UN Doc A/RES/2105 (XX), Preamble.

[981] Res 2105 (XX) (n 980) art 10; similarly Programme of Action for the Full Implementation of the Declaration on the Granting of Independence to Colonial Countries and Peoples, UNGA Res 2621 (XXV) (12 October 1970) UN Doc A/RES/2621 (XXV); Declaration on de Occasion of the Twenty-fifth Anniversary of the United Nations, UNGA Res 2627 (XXV) (24 October 1970) UN Doc A/RES/2627 (XXV); Implementation of the Declaration on the Granting of Independence to Colonial Countries and Peoples, UNGA Res 2708 (XXV) (14 December 1970) UN Doc A/RES/2708 (XXV).

[982] Res 2708 (XXV) (n 981); also David W Glazier, 'Wars of National Liberation' in Ruediger Wolfrum (ed), *The Max Planck Encyclopedia of Public International Law* (OUP 2012) vol X, 782.

that the 'establishment of a sovereign and independent State, the free association or integration with an independent State or the emergence into any other political status' constituted a mode of implementation of that right.[983] Hence, every State was obliged to refrain from forcible measures that would deprive people of the ability to exercise this right.[984] Besides, it was stated that those formerly living under colonial rule were entitled to 'seek and receive support.'[985] In line with this, the struggle for independence of colonial people had been explicitly excluded from the definition of an act of aggression,[986] and put on equal footing with international armed conflict.[987] Even though the continuance of colonialism was deemed illegal and the unconditional release of all non-self-governing territories imperative, there were, however, certain restrictions regarding process by which this would take place. First, only non-self-governing territories that were 'geographically separate' from the colonial power would be entitled to independence.[988] This requirement, which became known as the 'salt water test' or 'salt water theory', was aimed at preventing separatist movements from within the frontiers of the metropolitan State to declare that their cause falls within the scope of decolonization. The other limitation, particularly regarding colonies on the African continent, was the *uti possidetis* principle.[989] According to this principle, the international borders of the newly independent States were to be the ones formerly drawn by the colo-

[983]Friendly Relations Declaration (n 189).

[984]ibid.

[985]This held true with the limitation that because armed support of the colonial struggles was opposed as illegal, it was not included in the Friendly Relations Declaration (Daniel Thürer and Thomas Burri, 'Self-Determination' in Ruediger Wolfrum [ed], *The Max Planck Encyclopedia of Public International Law* (OUP 2012) vol IX, 117).

[986]Definition of Aggression (n 187) Annex, art 7.

[987]Protocol Additional to the Geneva Conventions of 12 August 1949, and relating to the Protection of Victims of International Armed Conflicts (Protocol I) (signed 8 June 1977, entered into force 7 December 1978) 1125 UNTS 3, art 1 para 4.

[988]Principles Which Should Guide Members in Determining Whether or not an Obligation Exists to Transmit the Information Called for under Article 73 e of the Charter, UNGA Res 1541 (XV) (15 December 1960) A/RES/1541(XV), Annex, Principle IV.

[989]See on this principle also s 3.2 ('The former republics of the Socialist Federal Republic of Yugoslavia').

nial power.[990] The purpose was 'to prevent the independence and stability of new States being endangered by fratricidal struggles provoked by the challenging of frontiers following the withdrawal of the administering power.'[991] Yet, the strict application of this principle ignored the heterogeneity of the ethnic composition of the population within the drawn-up borders, as all those living inside a particular border were treated as one people, entitled to the right of self-determination. This, however, caused numerous conflicts in some of the newly independent States.[992]

9.3 Interim conclusion: The recognitional fitness of the global international society

After World War I, the global international society gradually took the place of the society of civilized States. In this development, three phases are distinguishable. To begin with despite that during the first phase – the transitional phase – in the interwar period, the features of the society of the civilized States were still very present, the first indications of the next society appeared. Instead of being exclusively for civilized States, the rising society was based on an all-encompassing notion. During this time the concept prevailed that an entity should be recognized solely on the effective existence of the three classic State criteria without any further requirements.[993] At the same time, the principle of self-determination of people gained prominence.

The next phase, occurring after World War II, was the phase of the expansion of the international society. Decolonization served as the catalyst for this phase. The recognition of the former colonies had been without further requirements, restricted only by the *uti possidetis* principle and the 'salt water theory', which soon lost its meaning. Whereas outside the colonial context effectiveness was an essential part of the recognitional fitness, this

[990] On this also Giuseppe Nesi, 'Uti possidetis Doctrine' in Ruediger Wolfrum (ed), *The Max Planck Encyclopedia of Public International Law* (OUP 2012) vol X.

[991] *Case concerning the Frontier Dispute* (*Burkina Faso / Republic of Mali*) (Judgement) [1986] ICJ Rep 554, para 565.

[992] For example in Nigeria, Congo, Sudan and Rwanda.

[993] See on this also s 2.1 ('Requirements for recognition').

was less relevant regarding the recognition of the former colonies. This is particularly remarkable given that in many cases after the withdrawal of the colonial administration there ceased to be an effective administration in these countries for some time.[994] Besides this, the doctrine of non-recognition of territorial changes brought about by force was already established in the interwar period.

The third phase of development of the international society emerged after the end of the Cold War, the phase of consolidation. By that time, the decolonization was generally completed. The collapse of the USSR and the Balkan wars resulted in another stage of recognitional fitness. Despite that effectiveness was still seen as necessary, it was considered insufficient on its own. In addition to the sustained principles of *uti possidetis* and the territorial integrity of States, the recognition seeking entities had to commit themselves to the observance of human rights and self-determination of people in the form of democratic structures as well as to the adherence of disarmament and peaceful settlement of disputes prior to recognition.

[994] Österud used the term 'postcolonial dualism' in this regard (Österud [n 496] 182).

V Conclusion

10 Conclusion

This study examined the historical development of State recognition in doctrine and practice based on selected cases. Recognition of States as discussed consisted of political as well as of legal elements in that the granting of recognition is political, while the consequences are of legal nature. The theoretical foundation of this study was constructivism and the English school, as well as elements of the debate between the declaratory and the constitutive approach to recognition. It was assumed that States form a society built on shared values, interests, and norms. The relations between the members are based on equality, but this is not the case with contact between members and States outside the society. The admission to the society, an exclusive club granting its members a set of certain privileges, is regulated by certain requirements. Hence, the explanatory model of 'recognitional fitness' was designed in order to study the requirements necessary to be recognized as a State, and consequently, to be admitted to the international society.

For this, a distinction was made between State criteria and recognition criteria. While according to the declaratory approach, effectiveness as criterion for the existence of a State is sufficient, its recognition by the other States demands the fulfilment of further requirements. While the effective existence of a State remains a necessary element of recognitional fitness, it is not sufficient to be recognized by other States as one of them and to gain admission to the international society. Rather, the fulfilment of further requirements, legality and legitimacy, is necessary. However, over time what was considered legal and legitimate has constantly fluctuated.

First Christianity, later 'features of civilization' were the basic requirements to be considered a member of the international society of States. Then, since the interwar period, effectiveness was the main requirement for recognition, albeit only outside the context of decolonization. This changed after the breakdown of the USSR and the Yugoslavian wars. Now the members of the international society demanded additional requirements from the recognition seeking entities. These new requirements included the commitment to human rights, self-determination of people, and protection of mi-

norities, as well as the observance of the principle of the territorial integrity and the inviolability of borders. Hence, at present effectiveness is necessary but insufficient; recognitional fitness additionally demands legality and legitimacy order to be recognized.
Given the mercurial nature of recognitional fitness due to the continuingly changing requirements, the question arises of the future requirements for the obtainment of recognitional fitness. Ultimately it is up to the individual States to grant recognition, nonetheless, it is desirable to define requirements in order to establish a new, generally accepted recognitional fitness that would, again, further the values and goals of the international society. The foundation for this could be the requirements used for the recognition of the former Yugoslavian and Soviet Republics. For the reason that a fair number of States were recognized based on the fulfilment of the same requirements, this practice can be considered a custom of the international society. Now if a recurrent recognition practice based on the same requirements existed, as well as the common belief by the members of the international society of the rightfulness of the requirements as the foundation of the recognition practice, then this might be an indication for the development of a new, generally accepted, and standardized recognitional fitness.[995] Even though the consideration of political and economic interests regarding the recognition decision could surely not be prevented entirely, at least this new standard would contribute to the clarification of the issue of State recognition.

[995] On a full account of international custom see, for example, Alain Pellet, 'Article 38' in Andreas Zimmermann, Christian Tomuschat, and Karin Oellers-Frahm (eds), *The Statute of the International Court of Justice: A Commentary* (Oxford 2006) 749 et passim.

Bibliography

Ackeret M, 'Moskau verschärft die Konfrontation: Medwedew anerkennt Unabhängigkeit Südossetiens und Abchasiens' *NZZ* (Zürich, 27 August 2008) 1.

Adler E, 'Cognitive Evolution: A Dynamic Approach for the Study of International Relations and Their Progress' in Adler E and Crawford B (eds), *Progress in Postwar International Relations* (Columbia University Press 1991).

– *Communitarian International Relations: The Epistemic Foundations of International Relations* (Routledge 2005).

Aggelen Jv, 'Decolonization: Dutch Territories' in Wolfrum R (ed), *The Max Planck Encyclopedia of Public International Law* (OUP 2012) vol II.

Anderson MS, *The Eastern Question, 1774-1923: A Study in International Relations* (Macmillan 1982).

Anghie A, 'Finding the Peripheries: Sovereignty and Colonialism in Nineteenth-Century International Law' (1999) 40 HarvIntlLJ 1.

Anzilotti D, *Corso di diritto internazionale* (3rd edn, Athenaeum 1928).

Apathy P, Klingenberg G, and Stiegler H, *Einführung in das römische Recht* (Böhlau Verlag 1994).

Arblaster P, *A History of the Low Countries* (2nd edn, Palgrave Macmillan 2012).

Ayala B, *Balthazaris Ayalae I. C. et Exercitus Regii apud Belgas Supremi Juridici: De Jure et Officiis Bellicis et Disciplina Militari Libri III* (Westlake J ed, Bate JP tr, first published 1582, Carnegie Institution 1912).

Azarov V and Blum I, 'Bellingerency' in Wolfrum R (ed), *The Max Planck Encyclopedia of Public International Law* (OUP 2012) vol I.

Badem C, *The Ottoman Crimean War* (Brill 2010).

Baetens F, 'Decolonization: Belgian Territories' in Wolfrum R (ed), *The Max Planck Encyclopedia of Public International Law* (OUP 2012) vol II.
Bar C von and Mankowski P, *Internationales Privatrecht* (CH Beck 2003).
Barman RJ, *Brazil: The Forging of a Nation, 1798-1852* (Stanford University Press 1988).
Barnett M, 'Social Constructivism' in Baylis J, Smith S, and Owens P (eds), *The Globalization of World Politics: An Introduction to International Relations* (6th edn, OUP 2014).
– 'The New United Nations Politics of Peace: From Juridical Sovereignty to Empirical Sovereignty' (1995) 1 GlobGov 79.
Baty T, 'So-called "De-Facto" Recognition' (1921-1922) 31 YaleLJ 469.
Baumgart W, 'Der Krimkrieg 1863-1856: Ein Überblick' in Maag G, Pyta W, and Windisch M (eds), *Der Krimkrieg als erster europäischer Medienkrieg* (LIT Verlag 2010).
Bell C, 'Capitulations' in Wolfrum R (ed), *The Max Planck Encyclopedia of Public International Law* (OUP 2012) vol I.
Bethlehem D and Weller M, 'The Conflict in Yugoslavia – A Chronology' in Bethlehem D and Weller M (eds), *The 'Yugoslav' Crisis in International Law: General Issues* (CUP 1997).
Binavince ES, 'Canadian Practice in Matters of Recognition' in MacDonald RSJ, Morris GL, and Johnston DM (eds), *Canadian Perspectives on International Law and Organization* (University of Toronto Press 1974).
Bindschedler RL, 'Die Anerkennung im Völkerrecht' in *Verhandlungen der 7. Tagung der Deutschen Gesellschaft für Völkerrecht in Frankfurt/Main am 13. und 14. April 1961* (CF Müller 1961) vol 4.
Biondich M, *The Balkans: Revolution, War, and Political Violence since 1878* (OUP 2011).
Black J, *European International Relations 1648-1815* (Palgrave 2002).
Bluntschli JC, *Das moderne Völkerrecht der civilisirten Staten: als Rechtsbuch dargestellt* (Beck'sche Buchhandlung 1868).
Bobbitt P, *The Shield of Achilles: War, Peace, and the Course of History* (Knopf 2002).
Boczek BA, *International Law: A Dictionary* (The Scarecrow Press 2005).

Bodin J, *Les six livres de la République* (first published 1576, Librairie générale française 1983).

Bolovan I, 'Romanians in the Period of Reforms and Democratic revolutions (1820-1859)' in Pop I.-A and Bolovan I (eds), *History of Romania: Compendium* (Romanian Cultural Institute 2006).

Bonjour E, 'Die Loslösung der Eidgnossenschaft vom Reich und J.R. Wettstein' (1948) 8 SM 481.

Borozan Đ, 'Montenegro vom 16. Jahrhundert bis 1918' in Lukan W, Trgovčević L, and Vukčević D (eds), *Serbien und Montenegro* (LIT Verlag 2005).

Bothe M, 'The Law of Neutrality' in Fleck D (ed), *The Handbook of Humanitarian Law in Armed Conflicts* (2nd edn, OUP 2008).

Brierly JL, *The Law of Nations: An Introduction to the International Law of Peace* (6th edn, Clarendon Press 1963).

Brood P, 'The Twelve Years Truce: Textual Explanations' in Lesaffer R (ed), *The Twelve Years Truce (1609): Peace, Truce, War and the Law in the Low Countries at the Turn of the 17th Century* (Brill 2014).

Brown C, 'The Modern Requirement? Reflections on Normative International Theory in a Post-Western World' (1988) 17 Millenium - JIntSt 339.

Brownlie I, *Principles of Public International Law* (7th edn, Clarendon Press 2008).

– 'Recognition in Theory and Practice', in MacDonald RSJ and Johnston DM (eds), *The Structure and Process of International Law: Essays in Legal Philosophy, Doctrine and Theory* (Martinus Nijhoff 1983).

Brühl-Moser D, *Die Entwicklung des Selbstbestimmungsrechts der Völker unter besonderer Berücksichtigung seines innerstaatlich-demokratischen Aspekts und seiner Bedeutung für den Minderheitenschutz* (Helbing 1994).

Buchanan A, *Justice, Legitimacy, and Self-Determination: Moral Foundations for International Law* (OUP 2004).

Buchanan A and Keohane R, 'The Legitimacy of Global Governance Institutions' in *Legitimacy in International Law* (Springer 2008).

Bukovansky M, *Legitimacy and Power Politics: The American and French Revolutions in International Political Culture* (Princeton University Press 2002).

Bull H, *The Anarchical Society: A Study of Order in World Politics* (3rd edn, Palgrave Macmillan 2002).

– 'The Importance of Grotius in the Study of International Relations', in Bull H, Kingsbury B, and Roberts A (eds), *Hugo Grotius and International Relations* (Clarendon Press 1990).

Bull H and Watson A (eds), *The Expansion of International Society* (OUP 1984).

Buzan B, *From International to World Society? The English School Theory and the Social Structure of Globalisation* (CUP 2004).

Calvo C, 'Civilisation' in *Dictionnaire de droit international public et privé* (G Pedone-Lauriel 1885) vol 1.

Cannon A, 'Consequences of Nonrecognition in UK Law' in Wilde R, Cannon A, and Wilmshurst E (eds), *Recognition of States: The Consequences of Recognition or Non-Recognition in UK and International Law* (Chatham House 2010).

Carr EH, *The Twenty Years' Crisis, 1919-1939: An Introduction to the Study of International Relations* (Macmillan 1939).

Cassese A, *International Law* (2nd edn, OUP 2005).

– *Self-Determination of Peoples: A Legal Reappraisal* (CUP 1995).

Chen T.-C, *The International Law of Recognition: With Special Reference to Practice in Great Britain and the United States* (Praeger 1951).

Christ B, 'Die Loslösung der Alten Eidgenossenschaft vom Heiligen Römischen Reich Deutscher Nationen' in Historisches Museum Basel (ed), *Wettstein – Die Schweiz und Europa 1648* (Christoph Merian Verlag 1998).

Clark I, *Legitimacy in International Society* (OUP 2005).

– 'Legitmacy in a Global Order' (2003) 29 RevIntlStud 75.

Claude Jr IL, 'Collective Legitimization as a Political Function of the United Nations' (1966) 20 IO 367.

Combs JA, *The History of American Foreign Policy from 1895* (4th edn, ME Sharpe, Inc 2012).

Crawford E, 'Insurgency' in Wolfrum R (ed), *The Max Planck Encyclopedia of Public International Law* (OUP 2012) vol V.

Crawford J, *Brownlie's Principles of Public International Law* (8th edn, OUP 2012).

– *The Creation of New States in International Law* (2nd edn, OUP 2006).

Croxton D, 'The Peace of Westphalia of 1648 and the Origins of Sovereignty' (1999) 21 Int Hist Rev 569.

Dahm G, *Völkerrecht* (2nd edn, Walter de Gruyter 1989).

Dahms HG, *Grundzüge der Geschichte der Vereinigten Staaten* (4th edn, Wissenschaftliche Buchgesellschaft 1997).

Depkat V, *Geschichte Nordamerikas: Eine Einführung* (Böhlau Verlag 2008).

Despagnet F, *Cours de droit international public* (2nd edn, Librairie de la Société du Recueil Sirey 1899).

Doehring K, 'Effectiveness' in Bernhardt R (ed), *Encyclopedia of Public International Law* (North-Holland 1984) vol 7.

Dominguez JI, *Insurrection or Loyalty:The Breakdown of the Spanish American Empire* (Harvard University Press 1980).

dpa, 'Das Resultat der Abstimmung in Montenegro bestätigt' *NZZ* (Zürich, 22 May 2006) 2.

Drescher S and Finkelman P, 'Slavery' in Fassbender B and Peters A (eds), *The Oxford Handbook of the History of International Law* (OUP 2012).

Driessen C, *Geschichte der Niederlande: Von der Seemacht zum Trendland* (Verlag Friedrich Pustet 2009).

Dunne T, 'New Thinking in International Society' (2001) 3 BJPIR 223.

– 'The English School', in Reus-Smit C and Snidal D (eds), *The Oxford Handbook of International Relations* (OUP 2008).

Egger F, 'Johann Rudolf Wettstein and the International Recognition of Switzerland as a European Nation' in Bussmann K and Schilling H (eds), *1648: War and Peace in Europe* (Westfälisches Landesmuseum für Kunst und Kulturgeschichte 1998) vol 1: Politics, Religion, Law and Society.

Erasmus G, 'The Non-recognition of South Africa's Homelands: The Effect of National Policies' in *Festschrift für Wolfgang Zeidler* (de Gruyter 1987) vol 2.

Fabry M, *Recognizing States: International Society and the Establishment of New States Since 1776* (OUP 2010).

Falk R, 'The Interplay of Westphalia and Charter Conception of International Legal Order' in Falk RA and Black CE (eds), *The Future of the International Order: Trends and Patterns* (Princeton University Press 1969) vol I.

Fassbender B, 'Die verfassung- und völkerrechtliche Bedeutung des Westfälischen Friedens von 1648' in Erberich I and others (eds), *Frieden und Recht* (Boorberg 1998).

– 'Peace of Westphalia (1648)', in Wolfrum R (ed), *The Max Planck Encyclopedia of Public International Law* (OUP 2012) vol X.

Fassbender B and Bleckmann A, 'Article 2(1)' in Simma B (ed), *The Charter of the United Nations: A Commentary* (CH Beck 2002) vol 1.

Fauchille P, *Traité de droit international public* (8th edn, Paris, 1921-1926).

Fisch J, *Die europäische Expansion und das Völkerrecht: Die Auseinandersetzungen um den Status der überseeischen Gebiete vom 15. Jahrhundert bis zur Gegenwart* (Franz Steiner 1984).

– 'Zivilisation, Kultur', in Brunner O, Conze W, and Koselleck R (eds), *Geschichtliche Grundbegriffe: Historisches Lexikon zur politisch-sozialen Sprache in Deutschland* (Klett-Cotta 1997) vol 7.

Fischer Williams J, 'La doctrine de la reconnaissance en droit international et ses développements récents' (1933-II) 44 RdC 199.

Fischer M and Klatte S, 'Decolonization: Portuguese Territories' in Wolfrum R (ed), *The Max Planck Encyclopedia of Public International Law* (OUP 2012) vol II.

Fransman L, 'Commonwealth, Subjects and Nationality Rules' in Wolfrum R (ed), *The Max Planck Encyclopedia of Public International Law* (OUP 2012) vol II.

Freeman AV, 'The First Meeting of the Inter-American Council of Jurists' (1950) 44 AJIL 374.

Frowein JA, 'Anerkennung' in Seidl-Hohenveldern I (ed), *Lexikon des Rechts: Völkerrecht* (Luchterhand 2001).

– *Das de facto-Regime im Völkerrecht: Eine Untersuchung zur Rechtsstellung 'nichtanerkannter Staaten' und ähnlicher Gebilde* (Carl Heymanns Verlag 1968).
– 'De Facto Regime', in Wolfrum R (ed), *The Max Planck Encyclopedia of Public International Law* (Oxford 2012) vol II.
– 'Die Entwicklung der Anerkennung von Staaten und Regierungen im Völkerrecht' (1972) 11 STAAT 145.
– 'Non-Recognition', in Wolfrum R (ed), *The Max Planck Encyclopedia of Public International Law* (OUP 2012) vol VII.
– 'Recognition', in Wolfrum R (ed), *The Max Planck Encyclopedia of Public International Law* (OUP 2012) vol VIII.
Gallati F, 'Die formelle Exemtion der Schweiz vom Deutschen Reich im Westälischen Frieden 1648' (1948) 28 ZSG 453.
Gauss J, 'Die westfälische Mission Wettsteins im Widerstreit zwischen Reichstradition und Souveränitätsidee' (1948) 28 ZSG 177.
Gelderen M van, *The Political Thought of the Dutch Revolt, 1555-1590* (CUP 1992).
Glazier DW, 'Wars of National Liberation' in Wolfrum R (ed), *The Max Planck Encyclopedia of Public International Law* (OUP 2012) vol X.
Glenny M, *The Balkans 1804-2012: Nationalism, War and the Great Powers* (Granta 2012).
Goebel J, *The Recognition Policy of the United States* (Longman, Green 1915).
Gong GW, *The Standard of Civilization in International Society* (Clarendon Press 1984).
Gozzi G, 'History of International Law and Western Civilization' (2007) 9 ICLR 353.
Grant JP and Barker J, *Parry & Grant Encyclopaedic Dictionary of International Law* (3rd edn, OUP 2009).
Grant TD, 'Current Developments: Afghanistan Recognizes Chechnya' (2000) 15 AmUILRev 869.
Grant TD, 'Doctrines (Monroe, Hallstein, Brezhnev, Stimson)' in Wolfrum R (ed), *The Max Planck Encyclopedia of Public International Law* (OUP 2012) vol III.

Grant TD, 'East Timor, the U.N. System, and Enforcing Non-Recognition in International Law' (2000) 33 Vanderbilt Journal of Transnational Law 273.
– *The Recognition of States: Law and Practice in Debate and Evolution* (Praeger 1999).
Grewe WG (ed), *Fontes Historiae Iuris Gentium* (Berlin and New York, 1988-1995).
Grewe WG, *The Epochs of International Law* (Walter de Gruyter 2000).
Gross L, 'The Peace of Westphalia, 1648-1948' (1948) 42 AJIL 20.
Grote R, 'Westphalian System' in Wolfrum R (ed), *The Max Planck Encyclopedia of Public International Law* (OUP 2012) vol X.
Grotius H, *De Jure Belli ac Pacis Libri Tres* (Kelsey FW ed, first published 1625, Clarendon Press 1925).
Grzebyk P, *Criminal Responsibility for the Crime of Aggression* (Routledge 2013).
Guggenheim P, *Traité de Droit international public: Avec mention de la pratique internationale et suisse* (Georg 1953).
Habermas J, 'Legitimation Problems in the Modern State' in *Communication and the Evolution of Society* (Beacon Press 1979).
Haggenmacher P, 'Hugo Grotius (1583-1645)' in Fassbender B and Peters A (eds), *The Oxford Handbook of the History of international Law* (OUP 2012).
Hailbronner K and Kau M, 'Der Staat und der Einzelne als Völkerrechtssubjekte' in Vitzthum WG (ed), *Völkerrecht* (de Gruyter 2010).
Hall WE, *A Treatise of International Law* (2nd edn, Clarendon Press 1884).
Hanioğlu M, *A Brief History of the Late Ottoman Empire* (Princeton University Press 2008).
Harris D, *Cases and Materials on International Law* (7th edn, Sweet & Maxwell 2010).
Heffter AW, *Das europäische Völkerrecht der Gegenwart: Auf den bisherigen Grundlagen* (4th edn, Schroeder 1861).
Herdegen M, *Völkerrecht* (13th edn, CH Beck 2014).

Hillgruber C, *Die Aufnahme neuer Staaten in die Völkerrechtsgemeinschaft: Das völkerrechtliche Institut der Anerkennung von Neustaaten in der Praxis des 19. und 20. Jahrhunderts* (Peter Lang 1998).

Hipold P, 'Die Anerkennung der Neustaaten auf dem Balkan' (1993) 31 AVR 487.

Hitchins K, *Rumania 1866-1947* (Clarendon Press 1994).

Hobbes T, *De Cive: The English Version* (Clarendon Press 1983).

Hobe S, *Einführung in das Völkerrecht* (9th edn, A Francke Verlag 2008).

Hofmann R, 'Annexation' in Wolfrum R (ed), *The Max Planck Encyclopedia of Public International Law* (OUP 2012) vol I.

Holsti KJ, *Peace and War: Armed Conflicts and International Order 1648-1989* (CUP 1991).

Holtzendorff Fv, *Handbuch des Völkerrechts: Auf Grundlage Europäischer Staatspraxis - Bd. 2 Die völkerrechtliche Verfassung und Grundordnung der auswärtigen Staatsbeziehungen* (Verlag von JF Richter 1887).

Honsell H, *Römisches Recht* (7th edn, Springer 2010).

Hornung J, 'Cilivisés et barbares' (1885) XVII RDILC 5, 447, 539.

Hunter WA, *A Systematic and Historical Exposition of Roman Law in the Order of a Code* (4th edn, Sweet & Maxwell 1903).

Hurd J, 'Constructivism' in Reus-Smit C and Snidal D (eds), *The Oxford Handbook of International Relations* (OUP 2008).

Iacob G, 'Romanians during the Emergence of Nation-States (1859-1918)' in Pop I.-A and Bolovan I (eds), *History of Romania: Compendium* (Romanian Cultural Institute 2006).

Ijalaye DA, 'Was "Biafra" at Any Time a State in International Law?' (1971) 65 AJIL 551.

Independent International Commission on Kosovo, *The Kosovo Report: Conflict, International Response, Lessons Learned* (OUP 2000).

Ipsen K, *Völkerrecht* (6th edn, CH Beck 2014).

Israel J, *The Dutch Republic: Its Rise, Greatness, and Fall, 1477-1806* (Clarendon Press 1995).

– 'The Dutch-Spanish War and the Holy Roman Empire', in Bussmann K and Schilling H (eds), *1648: War and Peace in Europe* (Westfälisches

Landesmuseum für Kunst und Kulturgeschichte 1998) vol 1: Politics, Religion, Law and Society.
Jackson R, *The Global Covenant: Human Conduct in a World of States* (OUP 2000).
Jackson R and Sørensen G, *Introduction to International Relations: Theories and Approaches* (2nd edn, OUP 2003).
Jan LFv (ed), *Staatsrechtliches Verhältnis der Schweiz zu dem deutschen Reiche von dem Ursprung der Eidgenossenschaft bis zum Ende des achtzehnten Jahrhunderts* (Monath und Kussler 1801-1803).
Jellinek G, *Allgemeine Staatslehre* (2nd edn, O Häring 1905).
– *Allgemeine Staatslehre* (3rd edn, O Häring 1914).
Johnston D, *Roman Law in Context* (CUP 1999).
Jorio M 'Westfälischer Frieden', *Historisches Lexikon der Schweiz* (2013) ⟨http://www.hls-dhs-dss.ch/textes/d/D8908.php⟩.
Kaser M, *Römisches Privatrecht: Ein Studienbuch* (20th edn, CH Beck 2014).
Kaufmann WW, *British Policy and the Independence of Latin America, 1804-1828* (Yale University Press 1951).
Kegel G and Schurig K, *Internationales Privatrecht: Ein Studienbuch* (9th edn, CH Beck 2004).
Kelsen H, 'Recognition in International Law: Theoretical Observations' (1941) 35(4) AJIL 605.
Keohane RO, *After Hegemony: Cooperation and Discord in the World Political Economy* (Princeton University Press 1984).
Keohane RO and Nye JS, *Power and Interdependence: World Politics in Transition* (Little Brown & Co 1977).
Khan D.-E, 'Territory and Boundaries' in Fassbender B and Peters A (eds), *The Oxford Handbook of the History of International Law* (OUP 2012).
Kintzinger M, 'From the Late Middle Ages to the Peace of Westphalia' in Fassbender B and Peters A (eds), *The Oxford Handbook of the History of international Law* (OUP 2012).
Klemenčič M, 'The International Community and the FRY/Belligerents, 1989-1997' in Ingrao C and Emmert TA (eds), *Confronting the Yugoslav Controversies: A Scholars' Initiative* (Purdue University Press 2009).

Klüber JL, *Europäisches Völkerrecht* (Cotta 1821).
Kohen MG (ed), *Secession: International Law Perspectives* (CUP 2006).
Koskenniemi M, *The Gentle Civilizer of Nations: The Rise and Fall of International Law 1870-1960* (CUP 2002).
Kramer H and Reinowski M, *Die Türkei und Europa: Eine wechselhafte Beziehungsgeschichte* (Kohlhammer 2008).
Krasner SD, *Sovereignty: Organized Hypocrisy* (Princeton University Press 1999).
– 'Westphalia and All That', in Goldstein J and Keohane RO (eds), *Ideas and Foreign Policy: Beliefs, institutions, and Political Change* (Cornell University Press 1993).
Kreiser K, *Der osmanische Staat* (2nd edn, Oldenbourg 2008).
Kropholler J, *Internationales Privatrecht: Einschliesslich der Grundbegriffe des internationalen Zivilverfahrensrecht* (6th edn, Mohr Siebeck 2006).
Kunz JL, *Die Anerkennung von Staaten und Regierungen im Völkerrecht* (W Kohlhammer 1928).
Lauterpacht H, *Recognition in International Law* (CUP 1947).
– 'Recognition of States in International Law' (1944) 53 YaleLJ 385.
Lawrence TJ, *The Principles of International Law* (6th edn, DC Heath & Co, Publishers 1895).
Le Normand R, *La reconnaissance internationale et ses diverses applications: États, governments, belligerants, principes du droit international* (Camis 1899).
Lenin VI, 'Decree on Peace' in *Collected Works* (Progress Publisher 1977) vol 26.
– 'Outline Programme for Peace Negotiations', in *Collected Works* (Progress Publisher 1977) vol 26.
– 'The Socialist Revolution and the Right of Nations to Self-Determination', in *Collected Works* (Progress Publisher 1977) vol 26.
Levi L, *International Law* (D Appleton and Company 1888).
Levine RM, *The History of Brazil* (Greenwood Press 1999).
Liebs D, *Lateinische Rechtsregeln und Rechtssprichwörter* (CH Beck 2007).
Linklater A, 'The English School' in Burchill S and others (eds), *Theories of International Relations* (5th edn, Palgrave Macmillan 2014).

Liszt Fv, *Das Völkerrecht systematisch dargestellt* (Haering 1898).
Lorca AB, 'Universal International Law: Nineteenth-Century Histories of Imposition and Appropriation' (2010) 51 HarvIntlLJ 476.
Lorimer J, 'La doctrine de la reconnaissance: Fondement du droit international' (1884) 16 RDILC 334.
Lynch J, *The Spanish American Revolutions 1808-1826* (2nd edn, WW Norton & Company 1986).
Macfie AL, *The Eastern Question: 1774-1923* (Rev edn, Pearson 2004).
Mackintosh J, *The Miscellaneous Works of the Right Honourable Sir James Mackintosh* (Longman, Brown, Green, and Longmans 1846).
Maissen T, *Die Geburt der Republic: Staatsverständnis und Repräsentation in der frühneuzeitlichen Eidgenossenschaft* (2nd edn, Vandenhoeck & Ruprecht 2008).
Makarov AN and Schmitz E (eds), *Digest of the Diplomatic Correspondence of the European States, 1871-1878* (Carl Heymann 1937).
Malanczuk P, *Akehurst's Modern Introduction to International Law* (7th edn, Routledge 1997).
Mälksoo L, *Illegal Annexation and State Continuity – The Case of the Incorporation of the Baltic States by the UDSSR: A Study of the Tension between Normativity and Power in International Law* (Martinus Nijhoff 2003).
Maltby WS, *The Rise and Fall of the Spanish Empire* (Palgrave MacMillan 2009).
Manchester AK, 'The Recognition of Brazilian Independence' (1951) 31 HAHR 80.
March JG and Olsen JP, 'Institutional Perspectives on Political Institutions' (1996) 93 Governance 147.
– 'The Institutional Dynamics of International Political Orders' (1998) 52 IO 943.
Martens FF, *Traité de droit international* (Paris, 1883-1887).
Martens GFv, *A Compendium of the Law of Nations: Founded on the Treaties and Customs of the Modern Nations of Europe* (Cobbett and Morgan 1802).

– *Einleitung in das positive Europäische Völkerrecht auf Verträge und Herkommen gegründet* (bey Johann Christian Lieterich 1796).

Martens Kd, 'Déclaration remise par le marquis de Noailles, ambassadeur de France près la cour de Londres, à lord Weymouth, secrétaire d'État de S. M. Britannique; du 15 mars 1778' in *Nouvelles causes célèbres du droit des gens* (Brockhaus & Avenarius 1843) vol I.

– 'Exposé des motifs de la conduite du roi de France relativement à l'Angleterre, en 1779', in *Nouvelles causes célèbres du droit des gens* (Brockhaus & Avenarius 1843) vol I.

– 'Mémoire justificatif publié par la cour de Londres, en réponse à l'exposé des motifs de la conduite de la France', in *Nouvelles causes célèbres du droit des gens* (Brockhaus & Avenarius 1843) vol I.

– 'Observations de la cour de Versailles, sur le mémoire justificatif de la cour de Londres', in *Nouvelles causes célèbres du droit des gens* (Brockhaus & Avenarius 1843) vol I.

Martitz Fv, 'Das Internationale System zur Unterdrückung des Afrikanischen Sklavenhandels in seinem heutigen Bestande' (1886) I AöR 3.

Mbengue MM, 'Decolonization: French Territories' in Wolfrum R (ed), *The Max Planck Encyclopedia of Public International Law* (OUP 2012) vol II.

Mearsheimer JJ, *The Tragedy of Great Power Politics* (WW Norton & Company 2001).

Melnyk AY, 'United Nations Trusteeship System' in Wolfrum R (ed), *The Max Planck Encyclopedia of Public International Law* (OUP 2012) vol X.

Mill JS, 'A Few Words on Intervention' in *Dissertations and Discussions: Political, Philosophical and Historical* (William V Spencer 1864) vol 3.

Milton J, *The Tenure of Kings and Magistrates* (Printed by Matthew Simmons 1649).

Mitteis L, *Römisches Privatrecht bis auf die Zeit Diokletians: Grundbegriffe und Lehre von den juristischen Personen* (Verlag von Duncker und Humblot 1908).

Mommsen K, *Auf dem Wege zur Staatssouveränität: Staatliche Grundbegriffe im Basler juristischen Doktordisputationen des 17. und 18. Jahrhunderts* (Francke 1970).

Mommsen K, 'Bodins Souveränitätslehre und die Exemption der Eidgenossenschaft' in *Discordia Concors: Festgabe für Edgar bonjour zu seinem siebzigsten Geburtstag am 21. August 1968* (Helbing 1968) vol 2.

Morgenthau HJ, *Politics Among Nations: The Struggle for Power and Peace* (Alfred Knopf 1948).

Morrison K, *Montenegro: A Modern History* (IB Tauris 2009).

Morvay W, 'Decolonization: British Territories' in Bernhardt R (ed), *Encyclopedia of Public International Law* (North-Holland 1992) vol 1.

Moser JJ, *Grund-Sätze des jetzt üblichen Europäischen Völcker-Rechts in Friedens-Zeiten* (2nd edn, bey Johann August Raspe 1763).

Moser JJ, *Die gerettete völlige Souverainete der löblichen Schweitzerischen Eydgenossenschafft, oder, Gründlicher Beweis, dass in dem Westphälischen Frieden von dem H. Römischen Reich der löbl. Eydgenossenschafft nicht nur die Exemtion... eingeraumt und zugestanden worden seye...: mit Beylegung deren nöthigen Actorum publicorum* (Tubingen, gedruckt bey Joh Heinrich Philipp Schramm 1731).

Müller JP and Wildhaber L, *Praxis des Völkerrechts* (2nd edn, Stämpfli 1982).

Müller K, 'Die Exemtion der Eidgenossen 1648: Ein Beitrag zur Erklärung des Exemtionsartikels im Westfälischen Frieden' (1946) 4 SBAG 216.

Münch I, *Völkerrecht: Ohne Internationale Organisationen und Kriegsvölkerrecht* (de Gruyter 1971).

Muñoz Hernández F, *Legitimität und Legalität im Völkerrecht: Die völkerrechtstheoretische Debatte um die Legitimität Governance-Strukturen* (PhD thesis, University of Thübingen 2011).

Naff T, 'The Ottoman Empire and the European States System' in Bull H and Watson A (eds), *The Expansion of International Society* (Clarendon Press 1984).

'Nahost: Schweiz stimmt für Palästina als UNO-Beobachterstaat' *Swiss Press Agency (SDA) Dispatch* (Zürich, 30 November 2012).

Nesi G, 'Uti possidetis Doctrine' in Wolfrum R (ed), *The Max Planck Encyclopedia of Public International Law* (OUP 2012) vol X.

North M, *Geschichte der Niederlande* (4th edn, CH Beck 2013).

Obregón L, 'The Civilized and the Uncivilized' in Fassbender B and Peters A (eds), *The Oxford Handbook of the History of International Law* (OUP 2012).

O'Brien J, *International Law* (Cavendish 2001).

Oeter S, 'Selbstbestimmungsrecht im Wandel: Überlegungen zur Debatte um Selbstbestimmung, Sezessionsrecht und "vorzeitige" Anerkennung' (1992) 52 ZaöRV 741.

Oppenheim H, *System des Völkerrechts* (Krøner 1866).

Oppenheim LFL, *International Law: A Treatise* (Longman, Green 1905).

– *International Law: A Treatise* (Lauterpacht H ed, 7th edn, Longman, Green 1948).

Orakhelashvili A, 'International Law, International Politics and Ideology' in Orakhelashvili A (ed), *Research Handbook on the Theory and History of International Law* (Edward Elgar 2011).

Osiander A, 'Sovereignty, International Relations, and the Westphalian Myth' (2001) 55 IO 251.

– *The States System of Europe, 1640-1990: Peacemaking and the Conditions of International Stability* (Clarendon Press 1994).

Österud Öyvind, 'The Narrow Gate: Entry to the Club of Sovereign States' (1997) 23 RevIntlStud 167.

Özsu U, 'Ottoman Empire' in Fassbender B and Peters A (eds), *The Oxford Handbook of the History of International Law* (OUP 2012).

Paech N and Stuby G, *Völkerrecht und Machtpolitik in den internationalen Beziehungen: Aktualisierte Ausgabe* (VSA-Verlag 2013).

Pagden A and Lawrance J, 'Introduction' in Pagden A and Lawrance J (eds), *Francisco De Vitoria: Political Writings* (CUP 1991).

Pahud de Mortanges R, *Schweizerische Rechtsgeschichte: Ein Grundriss* (Dike 2007).

Paine T, *Common Sense: Addressed to the Inhabitants of America* (Philadelphia, 1776).

Pavlowitch SK, *A History of the Balkans: 1804-1945* (Longman 1999).

Pellet A, 'Article 38' in Zimmermann A, Tomuschat C, and Oellers-Frahm K (eds), *The Statute of the International Court of Justice: A Commentary* (Oxford 2006).

Perels K, 'Okkupation' in Schnee H (ed), *Deutsches Koloniallexikon* (Verlag von Quelle & Meyer 1920) vol II.

Perillo JM, *Calamari and Perillo on Contracts* (6th edn, Thomson/West 2009).

Peters A, *Das Gebietsreferendum im Völkerrecht: Seine Bedeutung im Licht der Staatenpraxis nach 1989* (Nomos Verlagsgesellschaft 1995).

– 'Die Anerkennung Kosovos als Ermessensfrage' *NZZ* (Zürich, 1 February 2008) 7.

– 'Statehood after 1989: "Effectivités" between Legality and Virtuality', in Crawford J and Nouwen S (eds), *Select Proceedings of the European Society of International Law* (Hart 2012) vol 3.

– 'Unequal Treaties', in Wolfrum R (ed), *The Max Planck Encyclopedia of Public International Law* (OUP 2012) vol X.

– *Völkerrecht: Allgemeiner Teil* (3rd edn, Schulthess 2012).

Phillimore R, *Commentaries upon International Law* (Butterworths 1854-1861).

Philpott D, *Revolutions in Sovereignty: How Ideas Shaped Modern International Relations* (Princeton University Press 2001).

Poggi G, *The Development of the Modern State: A Sociological Introduction* (Hutchinson 1978).

Prescott V and Triggs GD, *International Frontiers and Boundaries: Law, Politics and Geography* (Martinus Nijhoff 2008).

Pütter JS, *Historische Entwickelung der heutigen Staatsverfassung des Teutschen Reichs* (Vandenhoeck 1786).

Quaye C, *Liberation Struggles in International Law* (Temple University Press 1991).

Raič D, *Statehood and the Law of Self-determination* (Kluwer Law International 2002).

Randle RF, *Issues in the History of International Relations: The Role of Issues in the Evolution of the State System* (Praeger 1987).

Rauschning D, 'Gedanken zur Anerkennungserklärung' in Götz V, Selmer P, and Wolfrum R (eds), *Liber amicorum Günther Jaenicke: Zum 85. Geburtstag* (Springer 1998).

Reinhardt V, *Die Geschichte der Schweiz: Von den Anfängen bis heute* (CH Beck 2011).
Reis JJ and Klein HS, 'Slavery in Brazil' in *The Oxford Handbook of Latin American History* (OUP 2011).
Reus-Smit C, 'Constructivism' in Burchill S and others (eds), *Theories of International Relations* (5th edn, Palgrave Macmillan 2013).
Rich R, 'Recognition of States: The Collapse of Yugoslavia and the Soviet Union' (1993) 4 EJIL 36.
Rivier A, *Lehrbuch des Völkerrechts* (2nd edn, Enke 1899).
Rivier A, *Principes du droit des gens* (Rousseau 1896).
Robarts A, 'Crimean War' in Ágoston G and Masters B (eds), *Encyclopedia of the Ottoman Empire* (Facts on File 2009).
Roberts E, *Realm of the Black Mountain: A History of Montenegro* (Cornell University Press 2007).
Roberts PH and Tull JN, 'Moroccan Sultan Sidi Muhammad Ibn Abdallah's Diplomatic Initiatives toward the United States, 1777-1786' (1999) 143 PAPhS 233.
Röling BVA, *International Law in an Expanded World* (Djambatan 1960).
Rousseau C, *Droit international public* (Sirey 1953).
Rowan SW, 'The Common Penny (1495-99) as a Source of German Social and Demographic History' (1977) 10 CEH 148.
Sauveplanne JG, 'Recognition and Acts of State in the Conflict of Laws' (1960) 7 NILR 17.
Savigny FCv, *System des heutigen römischen Rechts* (Veit 1840-1863).
Scelle G, *Précis de droit des gens: Principes et systématique* (Sirey 1932-1934).
Scheuner U, 'Die grossen Friedensschlüsse als Grundlage der Europäischen Staatsordnung zwischen 1648 und 1815' in Repgen K and Skalweit S (eds), *Spiegel der Geschichte: Festgabe für Max Braubach zum 10. April 1964* (Verlag Aschendorff 1964).
Schieder T, 'Paris Peace Treaty (1856)' in Wolfrum R (ed), *The Max Planck Encyclopedia of Public International Law* (OUP 2012) vol VIII.

Schiemann G, 'Modus' in *Brill's New Pauly* (Brill Online 2014) ⟨http://www.paulyonline.brill.nl/entries/brill-s-new-pauly/modus-e808050⟩ accessed 31 January 2015.
Schiller F, *History of the Thirty Years War* (Morrission A tr, first published 1788, Harper Brothers 1846).
Schmalenbach K, 'International Organizations or Institutions, General Aspects' in Wolfrum R (ed), *The Max Planck Encyclopedia of Public International Law* (OUP 2012) vol V.
Schnyder AK and Liatowitsch M, *Internationales Privat- und Zivilverfahrensrecht* (Schulthess 2011).
Schürmann G, 'Art 482' in *Praxiskommentar Erbrecht* (Helbing 2011).
Schwander I, *Einführung in das internationale Privatrecht – Erster Band: Allgemeiner Teil* (Dike 2000).
Schwarzenberger G, 'The Rule of Law and the Disintegration of the International Society' (1939) 33 AJIL 56.
– 'The Standard of Civilisation in International Law' (1955) 8 CLP 212.
Schweitzer M, *Staatsrecht, Völkerrecht, Europarecht* (10th edn, CF Müller 2010).
Seidl-Hohenveldern I, *Völkerrecht* (Carl Heymanns Verlag 2000).
Sharp RH, 'Duties of Non-Recognition in Practice: 1775-1934' (1934) 5 Geneva Special Studies 1.
– *Nonrecognition as a Legal Duty* (Thone 1934).
Shaw MN, *International Law* (6th edn, CUP 2008).
Simons W, *The Evolution of International Public Law in Europe since Grotius* (Yale University Press 1931).
Skidmore TE, *Brazil: Five Centuries of Change* (2nd edn, OUP 2010).
Sloan J, 'Civilized Nations' in Wolfrum R (ed), *The Max Planck Encyclopedia of Public International Law* (OUP 2012) vol II.
Smith HA, *Great Britain and the Law of Nations: A Selection of Documents Illustrating the Views of the Government in the United Kingdom upon Matters of International Law* (London, 1932-1935).
Smith J and Vinhosa F, *History of Brazil, 1500-2000: Politics, Economy, Society, Diplomacy* (Longman 2002).

Sonnenberger HJ, 'Einführungsgesetz zum Bürgerlichen Gesetzbuche (Art. 1-46), Internationales Privatrecht' in *Münchener Kommentar zum Bürgerlichen Gesetzbuch* (4th edn, CH Beck 2006) vol 10.

Stapleton EJ (ed), *Some Official Correspondence of George Canning* (Longmans 1887).

Starke JG, *Introduction to International Law* (Butterworths 1989).

Steck JCWv, *Versuche über verschiedene Materien politischer und rechtlicher Kenntnisse* (Berlin und Stralsund, 1783).

Steiger H, 'Concrete Peace and General Order: The Legal Meaning of the Treaties of 24 October 1648' in Bussmann K and Schilling H (eds), *1648: War and Peace in Europe* (Westfälisches Landesmuseum für Kunst und Kulturgeschichte 1998) vol 1: Politics, Religion, Law and Society.

– 'From the International Law of Christianity to the International Law of the World Citizen – Reflections on the Formation of the Epochs of the History of International Law' (2001) 3 JHistIntLaw 180.

Stier-Somlo F, 'Völkerrechtsgemeinschaft' in Strupp K (ed), *Wörterbuch des Völkerrechts und der Diplomatie Wörterbuch des Völkerrechts und der Diplomatie* (Walter de Gruyter 1929).

Sturm F and Sturm G, 'J. von Staudingers Kommentar zum Bürgerlichen Gesetzbuch: Mit Einführungsgesetz und Nebengesetzen' in Staudinger Jv (ed) (Sellier-de Gruyter 2003).

Suárez F, 'De Legibus, ac Deo Legislatore' in Scott JB (ed), *Selections from Three Works of Francisco Suárez, S.J.* (First published 1612, Clarendon Press; H Milford 1944) vol 1 (Photogaphic reproduction from the original Editions).

– 'De Triplici Virtute Theologica, Fide, Spe, et Charitate', in Scott JB (ed), *Selections from Three Works of Francisco Suárez, S.J.* (First published 1621, Clarendon Press; H Milford 1944) vol 1 (Photogaphic reproduction from the original Editions).

– 'Defensio Fidei Catholicae, et Apostologicae Adversus Anglicanae Sectae Errores', in Scott JB (ed), *Selections from Three Works of Francisco Suárez, S.J.* (First published 1612, Clarendon Press; H Milford 1944) vol 2.

Taki H, 'Effectiveness' in Wolfrum R (ed), *Max Planck Encyclopedia of Public International Law* (OUP 2012) vol III.

Talmon S, *Recognition of Governments in International Law: With Particular Reference to Governments in Exile* (Clarendon Press 1998).

– 'The Constitutive versus the Declaratory Theory of Recognition: *Tertium Non Datur?*' (2004) 75 BYIL 101.

Temperley H, *The Foreign Policy of Canning, 1822-1827: England, the Neo-holy Alliance and the New World* (G Bell and Sons 1925).

Teschke B, *The Myth of 1648: Class, Geopolitics, and the Making of Modern International Relations* (Verso 2003).

Thürer D, 'Das Selbstbestimmungsrecht der Völker' (1984) 22 AVR 113.

Thürer D and Burri T, 'Secession' in Wolfrum R (ed), *Max Planck Encyclopedia of Public International Law* (OUP 2012) vol IX.

– 'Self-Determination', in Wolfrum R (ed), *The Max Planck Encyclopedia of Public International Law* (OUP 2012) vol IX.

Treitel GH, 'The Agreement' in *Chitty on Contracts* (31st edn, Sweet & Maxwell 2012) vol 1.

Triepel H, *Völkerrecht und Landesrecht* (Verlag von CL Hirschfeld 1899).

Trilsch M, 'Protectorates and Protected States' in Wolfrum R (ed), *The Max Planck Encyclopedia of Public International Law* (OUP 2012) vol VIII.

Twiss T, *The Law of Nations Considered as Independent Political Communities: On the Rights and Duties of Nations in Time of Peace* (Clarendon Press & Longman 1861).

Vattel Ed, *Le droit des gens ou principes de la loi naturelle appliqués à la conduite et aux affaires des nations et des souverain* (first published 1758, Carnegie Institution 1916).

Verdross A, *Die Verfassung der Völkerrechtsgemeinschaft* (Springer 1926).

– 'Die Wertgrundlagen des Völkerrechts' (1953) 4 AVR 129.

– *Völkerrecht* (4th edn, Springer 1959).

Vernet PM, 'Decolonization: Spanish Territories' in Wolfrum R (ed), *The Max Planck Encyclopedia of Public International Law* (OUP 2012) vol II.

Verosta S, 'History of International Law, 1648-1815' in Wolfrum R (ed), *The Max Planck Encyclopedia of Public International Law* (OUP 2012) vol IV.

Villiger ME, *Commentary on the 1969 Vienna Convention on the Law of Treaties* (Martinus Nijhoff 2009).
Vitoria FD, 'On Civil Power' in Pagden A and Lawrance J (eds), *Francisco De Vitoria: Political Writings* (first published 1528, CUP 1991).
– 'On Law: Lectures on Summa Theologica I-II. 90-105', in Pagden A and Lawrance J (eds), *Francisco De Vitoria: Political Writings* (CUP 1991).
Vogler G, *Europas Aufbruch in die Neuzeit, 1500-1650* (Eugen Ulmer 2003).
Vogt NP, 'Art. 246' in Honsell H, Vogt NP, and Wiegand W (eds), *Basler Kommentar: Obligationenrecht I* (5th edn, Helbing 2012).
Vyver JD van der, 'Statehood in International Law' (1991) 5 EmoryIntlL-Rev 9.
Wallace R and Martin-Ortega O, *International Law* (Sweet & Maxwell 2009).
Walt SM, *The Origins of Alliances* (Cornell University Press 1987).
Waltz KN, *Theory of International Politics* (Random House 1979).
Watson A, 'European International Society and Its Expansion' in Bull H and Watson A (eds), *The Expansion of International Society* (OUP 1984).
– 'Hedley Bull, States System and International Society' (1987) 13 RevIntl-Stud 147.
– *The Evolution of International Society: A Comparative Historical Analysis* (Routledge 1992).
Webster CK (ed), *Britain and the Independence of Latin America 1812-1830: Select Documents from the Foreign Office Archives* (OUP 1938).
Wendt A, 'Anarchy Is What the States Make of It: The Social Construction of Power Politics' (1992) 46 IO 391.
– 'Collective Identity Formation and the International State' (1994) 88 AmPolSciRev 384.
– 'Constructing International Politics' (1995) 20 IS 71.
– *Social Theory of International Politics* (CUP 1999).
Westlake J, *Chapters on the Principles of International Law* (CUP 1894).
– *International Law* (CUP 1904).
Wettstein JR, *Acta und Handlungen betreffend gemeiner Eydgnosschafft Exemption, und was deren, durch die Cammer zu Speyr, darwider vorgenommenen Turbationen halb so wol bey den Westphälischen Fridens-*

Tracktaten als am Kayserl: Hoof und anderswo negocirt und verrichtet worden (J J Genath 1651).
Wheaton H, *Elements of International Law* (6th edn, Little Brown & Co 1855).
– *History of the Law of Nations in Europe and America: From the the Earliest Times to the Treaty of Washington, 1842* (Gould Banks & Co 1845).
Whitaker AP, *The United States and the Independence of Latin America, 1800-1830* (The Johns Hopkins Press 1941).
Wight M, *International Theory: The Three Traditions* (Leicester University Press 1991).
– *Systems of States* (Leicester University Press 1977).
Wilde R, 'Recognition in International Law' in Wilde R, Cannon A, and Wilmshurst E (eds), *Recognition of States: The Consequences of Recognition or Non-Recognition in UK and International Law* (Chatham House 2010).
Wilson RJ, *The Pursuit of Liberty: A History of the American People* (Alfred A Knopf 1984).
Wilson RR, 'Recognition of Insurgency and Belligerency' (1937) 31 ASILPROC 136.
Witkin MF, 'Transkei: An Analysis of the Practice of Recognition – Political or Legal?' (1977) 18 HarvIntlLJ 605.
Woker M, 'Belgrad beschliesst einen Neuanfang Ja zur Verfassung von "Serbien und Montenegro"' *NZZ* (Zürich, 29 February 2003) 1.
– 'Montenegro erklärt die Unabhängigkeit: Formelle Proklamation des Parlaments in Podgorica' *NZZ* (Zürich, 6 June 2006) 1.
Wood HM, 'The Treaty of Paris and Turkey's Status in International Law' (1943) 37(2) AJIL 262.
Wright Q, 'The Goa Incident' (1962) 56 AJIL 617.
Ziegler KH, *Völkerrechtsgeschichte: Ein Studienbuch* (2nd edn, CH Beck 2007).
Ziemele I, 'Extinction of States' in Wolfrum R (ed), *The Max Planck Encyclopedia of Public International Law* (OUP 2012) vol IX.
Zimmermann R, *The Law of Obligations: Roman Foundations of the Civilian Tradition* (Juta & Co / CH Beck 1992).